MASTERS OF THE GAMES

MASTERS OF THE GAMES

Essays and Stories on Sport

JOSEPH EPSTEIN

ROWMAN & LITTLEFIELD
Lanham • Boulder • New York • London

Published by Rowman & Littlefield
A wholly owned subsidiary of The Rowman & Littlefield Publishing Group, Inc.
4501 Forbes Boulevard, Suite 200, Lanham, Maryland 20706
www.rowman.com

Unit A, Whitacre Mews, 26-34 Stannary Street, London SE11 4AB,
United Kingdom

Distributed by NATIONAL BOOK NETWORK

British Library Cataloguing in Publication Information Available

Library of Congress Cataloging-in-Publication Data
Epstein, Joseph, 1937–
  Masters of the games : essays and stories on sport / Joseph Epstein.
     pages cm
  ISBN 978-1-4422-3653-0 (cloth : alk. paper) — ISBN 978-1-4422-3654-7
(electronic)
  1. Sports. I. Title.
  GV707.E57 2015
  796—dc23
                                                          2014034411

Printed in the United States of America

CONTENTS

INTRODUCTION

Obsessed with Sport

I cannot remember when I was not surrounded by sports, when talk of sports was not in the air, when I did not care passionately about sports. As a boy in Chicago in the late forties, I lived in the same building as the sister and brother-in-law of Barney Ross, the welterweight champion. Half a block away, down near the lake, the Sullivan High School football team worked out in the spring and autumn. Summers the same field was given over to baseball and men's softball on Sundays. A few blocks to the north was the Touhy Avenue Fieldhouse, where basketball was played, and lifeguards trained, and behind which, in a softball field frozen over in winter, crack-the-whip, hockey, and speed skating took over. To the west, a block or so up Morse Avenue, was the Morse Avenue "L" Recreations, a combined pool hall and bowling alley. Life, in short, was games.

My father had no interest in sports. He had grown up, one of ten children of Russian Jewish immigrant parents, on tough Notre Dame Street in Montreal, where the major sports were craps, poker, and petty larceny. He left Montreal at seventeen to come to Chicago, where he worked hard and successfully so that his sons might play. Two of his boyhood friends from Notre Dame Street, who had the comic-book names of Sammy and Danny Spunt, had also come to Chicago, where they bought the Ringside Gym on Dearborn Street in the Loop. Many of the big names worked out at Ringside for their Chicago fights: Willie Pep, Tony Zale, Johnny Bratton. At eight or nine I would take the El downtown to the Ringside, be introduced around by Danny Spunt ("Tony Zale, I'd like you to meet the son of an old friend of mine. Kid,

1

I'd like you to meet the middleweight champion of the world"), and return home with an envelope filled with autographed 8-by-10 glossies of Gus Lesnevich, Tammy Mauriello, Kid Gavilan, and the wondrous Sugar Ray Robinson.

I lived on, off, and in sports. *Sport* magazine had recently begun publication, and I gobbled up its issues cover to cover, soon becoming knowledgeable not only about the major sports—baseball, football, and basketball—but about golf, hockey, tennis, and horse racing, so that I scored reputably on the Sport Quiz, a regular department at the front of the magazine. Another regular department was the Sport Classic, which featured longish profiles of the legendary figures in the history of sports: Ty Cobb, Jim Thorpe, Bobby Jones, Big Bill Tilden, Red Grange, Man o' War. I next moved on to the sports novels of John R. Tunis—*All-American, The Iron Duke, The Kid from Tomkinsville, The Kid Comes Back, World Series*, the lot—which I read with as much excitement as any books I have read since.

The time was, as is now apparent, a splendid era in sports. Ted Williams, Joe DiMaggio, and Stan Musial were afield; first Jack Kramer, then Pancho Gonzales, dominated tennis; George Mikan led the Minneapolis Lakers, and the Harlem Globetrotters could still be taken seriously; Doc Blanchard and Glen Davis, Mr. Inside and Mr. Outside, were playing for Army, Johnny Lujack was at Notre Dame; in the pros Sammy Baugh, Bob Waterfield, and Sid Luckman were the major T-formation quarterbacks; Joe Louis and Sugar Ray Robinson fought frequently; the two Willies, Mosconi and Hoppe, put in regular appearances at Bensinger's in the Loop; Eddie Arcaro seemed to ride three, four winners a day. Giants, it truly seemed, walked the earth.

All learning of craft—which sport, like writing, most assuredly is—involves imitation, especially in the early stages; and I was an excellent mimic. By the time I was ten years old I had mastery over all the big-time moves: the spit in the mitt, the fluid infield chatter, the knocking of dirt from the spikes; the rhythmic barking out of signals, hands high under the center's crotch to take the ball; the three bounces and deep breath before shooting the free throw (on this last, I regretted not being a Catholic, so that I might be able to make the sign of the cross before shooting, as was then the fashion among Catholic high-school and college players). I went in for athletic haberdashery in a big way, often going beyond mimicry to the point of flat-out phoniness—wearing, for example, a knee pad while playing basketball, though my knees were always, exasperatingly, intact.

I always looked good, which was important, because form is intrinsic to sports; but in my case it was doubly important, because the truth is that I wasn't really very good. Or at any rate not good enough. Two factors accounted for this. The first was that, without being shy about body contact, I lacked a certain indispensable aggressiveness; the second, connected closely to the first, was that, when it came right down to it, I did not care enough about winning. I would rather lose a point attempting a slashing cross-court backhand than play for an easier winner down the side; the long jump shot always had more allure for me than the safer drive to the basket. Given a choice between the two vanities of winning and looking good, I almost always preferred looking good.

I shall never forget the afternoon, sometime along about my thirteenth year, when, shooting baskets alone, I came upon the technique for shooting the hook. Although today it has nowhere near the consequence of the jump shot—an innovation that has been to basketball what the jet has been to air travel—the hook is still the single most beautiful shot in the game. The rhythm and grace of it, the sway of the body off the pivot, the release of the ball behind the head and off the fingertips, the touch and instinct involved in its execution, make the hook altogether a balletic thing, and to achieve it is to feel one of the most delectable sensations in sports. That afternoon, on a deserted side street, shooting on a rickety wooden backboard and a black rim without a net, I felt it and grew nearly drunk on the feeling. Rain came down, dirt washed in the gutters, flecks of it spattering my clothes and arms and face, but, soaked and cold though I was, I do not think I would have left that basket on that afternoon for anything. I threw up hook after hook, from every angle, from farther and farther out, off the board, without the board, and hook after hook went in. Only pitch darkness drove me home.

I do not say that not to have shot the hook is never to have lived, but only that, once having done so, the pleasure it gives is not so easily forgotten. Every sport offers similar pleasures, the pleasures taken differing by temperament: the canter into the end zone to meet a floating touchdown pass, or the clean, crisp feel of a perfect block or tackle; the long straight drive or the precisely played approach shot to the green; the solid overhead; the pickup on the tricky short hop or the long ball down one of the power alleys. Different sports, different pleasures. But so keen are these pleasures—pleasures of execution, of craft completed—that, along with being unforgettable, they are also worth recapturing in any available way, and the most available way, when reflexes have slowed, when muscle no longer responds so readily to brain, is from the grandstand or, perhaps more often nowadays, from the chair before the television.

PLEASURES OF THE SPECTATOR

I have put in days on the bench, but years in my chair before the television set. Recently it has occurred to me that over the years I have heard more hours of talk from the announcer Al Michaels than from my own father, who was not a reticent man. I have been thoroughly Schenkeled, Mussbergered, Summeralled, Coselled, DeRogotissed, Garagiolaed, Costassed, and McCarvered. How many hundreds—thousands?—of hours have I spent watching sports of all sorts, either at parks or stadiums or on television? I am glad I shall never have a precise answer. Yet neither apparently can I get enough. What is the fascination? Why is it that, with the prospect of a game to watch in the evening or on the weekend, the day seems lighter and brighter? What do I get out of it?

What I get out of it, according to one fairly prominent view, is an outlet for my violent emotions. Knee-wrenching, rib-cracking, head-busting, this view has it, is what sports are really about, with sports fans being essentially sadists, and cowardly sadists at that, for they take their violence not firsthand but at second remove. Enthusiasm for sports among Americans is little more than a reflection of the national penchant for violence. Military men talk about game plans; the long touchdown pass is called the bomb. The average pro-football fan, seeing a quarterback writhing on the ground at midfield as a result of the ministrations of Joe Greene, Carl Eller, or Brian Urlacher, shivers with glee, finds his ultimate reward, and declares a little holiday in the blackest corner of his heart.

But this is a criticism that comes at sports by way of politics. To believe it one has to believe that the history of the United States is chiefly one of rape, expropriation, and aggressive imperialism. To dismiss it, however, one need only know something about sports. Violence is indubitably a part of some sports; in some—hockey is an example—it sometimes comes close to being featured. But in no sport—not even boxing, that most rudimentary of sports—is it the main item, and in many other sports it plays no part at all. A distinction worth insisting on is that between violence and roughness. Roughness, a willingness to mix it up, to take if need be an elbow in the jaw, is part of rebounding in basketball, yet violence is not. Even in pro football, the most maligned of modern American sports, more of roughness than of violence is involved. Roughness raises the stakes, provides the pressure, behind execution. A splendid because true phrase has come about in pro football to cover the situation in which a pass receiver, certain that he will be tackled upon the instant he makes his reception, drops a ball he should otherwise have caught easily—the phrase, best delivered in a Southern accent such as Don Meredith's, is "He heard footsteps on that one, Howard." Although a part of the attraction, it is not so much those footsteps that fill the stands and the den chairs on Sunday afternoons as it is those men who elude them: the Lynn Swanns, Jerry Rices, the Fran Tarkentons, the Walter Paytons. The American love of violence theory really will not wash. Dick Butkus did not get us into Vietnam.

Many who would not argue that sports reflect American violence nevertheless claim that they imbue one with the competitive spirit. In some who are already amply endowed with it, sports doubtless do tend to refine (or possibly brutalize) the desire to win. Yet sports also teach a serious respect for craft. Competition, though it flourishes as always, is in bad odor nowadays; but craft, officially respected, does not flourish greatly outside the boutique.

If the love of violence or the competitive urge does not put me in my chair for the countless games I watch, is it, then, nostalgia, a yearning to regain the more glowing moments of adolescence? Many argue that this is precisely so, that American men exist in a state of perpetual immaturity, suspended between boy- and manhood. "The difference between men and boys," said Liberace, "is the price of their toys." Such unending enthusiasm for games may have something to do with adolescence, but little, I suspect, with regaining anything whatever. Instead, it has more to do with watching men do regularly and surpassingly what, as an adolescent, one did often bumblingly though with an occasional flash of genius. To have played these games oneself as a boy or a young man helps immeasurably the appreciation that in watching a sport played at professional caliber one is witnessing the extraordinary made to look ordinary. That a game may have no consequence outside itself—no effect on history, on one's own life, on anything really—does not make it trivial but only makes the enjoyment of it all the purer. Art for art's sake does not apply only to actual art.

The notion that men watch sports to regain their adolescence pictures them sitting in the stands or at home watching a game and, within their psyches, muttering, "There, but for the lack of grace of God, go I." And it is true that a number of contemporary authors who are taken seriously have indeed written about sports with a strong overlay of yearning. In the men's softball games described in the fiction of Philip Roth, center field is a place akin to Arcady. Arcadian, too, is the outfield in Willie Morris's memoir of growing up in the South, *North Toward Home*. In the first half of *Rabbit Run* John Updike takes up the life of a man whose days are downhill all the way after hitting his peak as a high-school basketball star—and in the writing Updike himself evinces a nice soft touch of undisguised longing. In *A Fan's Notes*, a book combining yearning and self-disgust in roughly equal measure, Frederick Exley makes plain that he would much prefer to have been born into the skin of Frank Gifford rather than into his own.

But most men who are enraptured by sports do not think any such thing. I should like to have Kareem Abdul-Jabbar's sky hook, but not, especially for civilian life, the excessive height that is necessary to its execution. I should like to have Rafael Nadal's ground strokes, but no part of his mind. These are men born with certain gifts, gifts honed by practice and determination, that I, and millions along with me, enjoy seeing on display. But the reality principle is too deeply ingrained, at least in a man of my years, for me to even imagine exchanging places with them. One might as well imagine oneself in the winner's circle at Churchill Downs as the horse.

Fantasy is an element in sports when they are played in adolescence—an alley basket becomes the glass backboard at Madison Square Garden, a concrete park district tennis court with grass creeping out of the service line becomes center court at Wimbledon—but fantasy of this kind is hard to come by in later years. Part of this has to do with age; but as large a part has to do with the age in which we live. Sport has always been a business but never more so than currently, and nothing lends itself less to fantasy than business. Reading the sports section has become rather like reading the business section—mergers, trades, salary negotiations, contract disputes, options, caps, and strikes fill the columns. Along with the details of business, those of the psychological and social problems of athletes have come to the fore. The old *Sport* magazine concentrated on play on the field, with only an occasional digressive reference to personal life. But the now more popular *Sports Illustrated* expends much space on the private lives of athletes—their divorces, hang-ups, race relations, need for approval, concern for security, potted philosophies—with the result that the grand is made to seem rather small.

On the other side of the ledger, there is a view that finds a shimmering significance in everything having to do with sports. Literary men in general are notoriously to be distrusted on the subject. They dig around everywhere, and can be depended upon to find much treasure where none is buried. Norman Mailer mining metaphysical ore in every jab of Muhammad Ali's, an existential nugget in each of his various and profuse utterances, is a particularly horrendous example. Even the sensible William Carlos Williams was not above this sort of temptation. In a poem entitled "The Crowd at the Ball Game," we find the lines, "It is the Inquisition, the / Revolution." Dr. Williams could not have been much fun at the ball park.

THE REAL THING

If enthusiasm for sports has little to do with providing an outlet for violent emotions, regaining adolescence, discovering metaphysical truths, the Inquisition or the Revolution, then what, I ask myself, am I doing past midnight, when I have to be up at 5:30 the next morning, watching on television what will turn out to be a seventeen-inning game between the New York Mets and the St. Louis Cardinals? The conversation coming out of my television set is of a very low grade, even for sports announcing. But the dreary talk cannot put me off—the rehash of statistics, the advice to youngsters to keep their gloves low when in the field, the thin jokes. The only possible effect that this game can have on my life is to make me dog-tired the next day. Yet I cannot pull myself away. I want to know how it is going to end. True, the score will be available online in the morning. But that is not the same thing. What is going on here?

One thing that is going on is the practice of craft of a very high order, which is intrinsically interesting. But something as important is involved, something rarer in contemporary life, the spectacle of which gives enormous satisfaction. To define this satisfaction negatively, it is the absence of fraudulence and fakery. No small item, this, when one stops to think that in nearly every realm of contemporary life fraud and fakery have an established—some would say a preponderant—place. Advertising, politics, business, and journalism are only the most obvious examples. Fraud seems similarly pervasive in modern art: in painters whose reputations rest on press agentry; in writers who write one way and live quite another; in composers who are taken seriously but whose work cannot be seriously listened to. At a time when *image* is one of the most frequently used words in American speech and writing, one does not too often come upon the real thing.

Sport may be the toy department of life, but one of its abiding compensations is that, at least on the field, it is the real thing. Much has been done in recent years in the attempt to ruin sport—the ruthlessness of owners, the greed of players, the general exploitation of fans. But even all this cannot destroy it. On the court, down on the field, sport is fraud-free and fakeproof. With a full count, two men on, his team down by one run in the last of the eighth, a batter (as well as a pitcher) is beyond the aid of public relations. At match point at Wimbledon a player's press clippings are of no help. Last year's earnings will not sink a twelve-foot putt on the eighteenth at Augusta. A linebacker galloping up along a quarterback's blind side figures to be neglectful of that quarterback's image as a swinger. In all these situations, and hundreds of others, a man either comes through or he doesn't. He is alone out there, naked but for his ability, which counts for everything. Something there is that is elemental about this, and something greatly satisfying to watch.

Another part of the satisfaction to be got from sports—from playing them, but also from watching them being played—derives from their special clarity. Sports offer clarity of a kind sufficient to engage the most serious minds. That the Cambridge mathematician G. H. Hardy closely followed cricket and avidly read cricket scores is not altogether surprising. Numbers in sports are ubiquitous. Scores, standings, averages, times, records—comfort is found in such numbers. ERA, RBIs, FGP, OBP, pass completions, turnovers, category upon category of statistics are kept for nearly every aspect of athletic activity. (Why, I recently heard someone ask, are records not kept for catchers throwing out runners attempting to steal? Because, the answer is, often runners steal on pitchers, and so it would be unfair to charge these stolen bases against catchers.) As perhaps in no other sphere, numbers in sports tell one where things stand. No loopholes here, where figures, for once, do not lie. Nowhere else is such specificity of result available.

Clarity about character is also available in sports. "You Americans hold to the proposition that it is self-evident that all men are created equal," I not long ago heard an Englishman say, adding, "it had better be self-evident, for no other evidence for it exists." Sport coldly demonstrates physical inequalities—there are the larger, the faster, the stronger, the more graceful athletes—but it also throws up human types who have devised ways to redress these inequalities. One such type is the hustler. In every realm but that of sports the word *hustle* is pejorative, whereas in sports it is approbative. Two of the hustler breed, Dustin Pedroia of the Boston Red Sox and Joachim Noah of the Chicago Bulls, are men who supplement reasonably high levels of ability with unreasonably high levels of courage and desire. Other athletes—Joe Morgan and Oscar Robertson come to mind—brought superior athletic intelligence to bear upon their play. And Bill Russell, late of the Boston Celtics, who if the truth be known was not an inherently superior athlete, blended hustle and intelligence with what abilities he did have and through force of character established supremacy.

Whence do hustle, intelligence, and character in sports derive, especially since they apparently do not necessarily carry over into life? Joe DiMaggio and Sugar Ray Robinson, two of the most instinctively intelligent and physically elegant athletes, brought little of either of these qualities over into their business or personal activities. Some athletes can do all but one important thing well: Wilt Chamberlain at the free-throw line, for those who recall his misery there, leaves a permanent picture of a mental block in action. Other athletes—Connie Hawkins, Ilie Nastase,

Dick Allen—had all the physical gifts in superabundance, yet, because of some insufficiency of character, some searing flaw, never came near to fulfilling their promise. Coaches supply yet another gallery of human types, from the fanatical Vince Lombardi to the comical Casey Stengel to the measured and aptly named John Wooden. The cast of characters in sport, the variety of situations, the complexity of behavior it puts on display, the overall human exhibit it offers—together these supply an enjoyment akin to that once provided by reading interminably long but inexhaustibly rich nineteenth-century novels.

In a wider sense, sport is culture. For many American men it represents a common background, a shared interest. It has a binding power that transcends social class and education. Some years ago I found myself working in the South among men with whom I shared nothing in the way of region, religion, education, politics, or general views; we shared nothing, in fact, but sports, which was enough for us to get along and grow to become friends, along the way showing how superficial all the things that might have kept us apart in fact were. More recently, in Chicago, at a time when race relations were in a particularly jagged state, I recall emerging from an NBA game, in which the Chicago Bulls in overtime beat the Milwaukee Bucks, into a snowy night and an aura of common good feeling that, for a time, submerged the enmity between races; laughing, throwing snowballs, exuberant generally, the crowd leaving the Chicago Stadium that night was not divided by being black and white but unified by being Bulls fans.

In sports as in life, character does not much change. Some years ago I began to play racquetball, and found I would still rather look good than win, which is what I usually did: look good and lose. I beat the rumdums but went down before quality players. I got compliments in defeat. Men who beat me admired the whip of my strokes, my wrist action, my anticipation, the power I got behind the ball. When this occurs I feel like a woman who is complimented for the shape of her bottom when it is her mind she craves admiration for, though of course she will take what praise she can get.

R. H. Tawney, the great historian of religion and capitalism, once remarked that the only progress he could note during the course of his lifetime was in the deportment of dogs. For myself, I would say that the chief progress in the course of my lifetime has been in the quality and variety of athletic gear. Rackets made of metal, aluminum, wood, and fiberglass, balls of different colors, sneakers of all materials and designs, posh warm-up suits, tube socks, sweatbands for the head and wrist in various colors and pipings; only the athletic supporter, the old jockstrap, remains unornamented.

Sports can be impervious to age. My father-in-law, a man of style, seriousness, and great good humor who died in his late sixties, was born in South Bend, Indiana, and in his early manhood left the Catholic Church—two facts that conjoined to give him an intense interest in the fortunes of the teams from Notre Dame. He loved to see them lose. The torch has been passed on. I now love to see Notre Dame lose, and when it does I think of him and remember his smile.

When I was a boy I had a neighbor, a man who, after retirement, had a number of strokes. An old man and a young boy, we had in common a love of sports, which, when we met on the street, was our only topic of conversation. He once inspected a new baseball glove of mine, and instructed me to rub it down with neat's-foot oil, place a ball firmly in the pocket, wrap string tightly around the glove, and leave it like that for the winter. I did, and it worked. After his last stroke but one, he seldom left his house. Afternoons he spent in a chair in his bedroom, a blanket over his lap, listening to Cubs games over the radio. It was while listening to a ball game that he quietly died. Not, really, a bad way to go.

ESSAYS

A BOY'S FAVORITE AUTHOR

Taste in reading, like taste in food, tends to be formed early and changed seldom. Despite all the therapeutically salutary effects that Bruno Bettelheim claims fairy tales have on children, my own recollection is that, when read to me by my father, they bored the Doctor Dentons off me. I do not wish to exaggerate the sapience of my early childhood, but I do not think I lent much credence to stories about witches, spiders, and giants. I considered Hansel and Gretel dopes for letting themselves be so easily taken in; and as for Jack and the Beanstalk, I felt that anyone dumb enough to trade a live cow for a mess of beans had whatever trouble he encountered coming to him. I preferred Robin Hood, with his heroism and battles against injustice. I was also nuts about Bible stories, read to me by my father in a children's version, which featured blood and thunder—like those of Abraham and Isaac, Samson and Delilah, David and Goliath—and in which something serious was at stake. Right out of the chute, then, my tastes in literature ran to realism, and to realism they still chiefly run.

For someone given a rather nice literary start in life by a thoughtful father, I never read much on my own once I was in school, and hence I suppose it could be said that I dropped the ball. More precisely, once in school I picked up the ball, becoming a kid who played almost full time whatever ball game was in season. There were other fine distractions: radio programs, the movies, comic books. Classic Comics, a company that produced comic-book versions of such classic adventure stories as *The Swiss Family Robinson*, *The Count of Monte Cristo*, and *Tom Brown's School Days*, was then flourishing. For minor racketeers such as yours

15

truly, who already had too many strenuous demands on his time to allow for the reading of books, these were extremely useful as fodder for
the classroom exercise known as book reports. Somewhere between the
ages of nine and twelve I believe I read two books, *Hans Brinker and the
Silver Skates* and *The Black Stallion*. I hugely enjoyed both, yet did not
do anything to search out others. My case was similar, I suppose, to that
of Nancy Mitford's father, Lord Redesdale, who claimed to have read
only one book in his life, Jack London's *White Fang*. "It's so frightfully
good," he is reported to have announced, "I didn't see how it could
possibly be topped, so I've never bothered to read another." For my
part, I never bothered to find out if the authors of *Hans Brinker* and *The
Black Stallion* had written other books; and to this day, in fact, I do not
know their names.

Most children, I suspect, are inchoate New Critics, in that they
are mainly interested in stories and poems, the work itself, and not in
the man or woman who wrote it or the conditions of its composition.
I must have heard the names of Dickens and Shakespeare, and possibly
that of Mark Twain, but the first author who had a distinct existence
for me when I was a boy was a man, still very much alive when I began
to read his books in my thirteenth year (1950), named John R. Tunis.
I don't believe anyone recommended a Tunis book to me; mine was
not a crowd in which that sort of thing happened. (If there were any
readers among the boys I ran with, they would have to have been closet
readers.) But I do remember slipping a volume, bright red and trimmed
in black, off one of the lower shelves of the library of the Daniel Boone
Public Elementary School, my attention having been caught by its title,
which was *All-American*. It was, as I had hoped, a story about football,
high-school football; better still, among its characters, though not its
protagonist, was a Jewish halfback named Meyer Goldman. It had lots of
action, prejudice and snobbery, drawings by an illustrator named Hans
Walleen, a fit moral—and the whole thing was brought in at under two
hundred and fifty pages. I lapped it up in a single sitting.

Over the next year or so I scrambled to locate every book by John
R. Tunis that I could find. He had written a few nonfiction books, I
discovered, though I took a pass on those and read only his novels and
then only those novels in which sports played a central role. I read him
on football, I read him on basketball, I read him on baseball (more on

baseball than on any other sport), I read him on track, and I read him on tennis, a sport I had myself just begun to take up in a fairly serious way. I lived a good deal of the time between my thirteenth and fourteenth year in a world of John R. Tunis's imagining—that is, I imagined myself a character in one or another of Tunis's novels. "'Pock' went the big serve, and Joe Epstein strode to the net."

John R. Tunis's novels were about a good deal besides sports—he was, as I have discovered on rereading a number of them, almost relentlessly preaching, a true and full-time message man—but it was the subject of sports that snared me. In his autobiography Sidney Hook reports that, during his early years as an elementary-school teacher, he was able to teach a class of mentally delinquent boys the rudiments of arithmetic and geography by demonstrating the use of arithmetic in compiling baseball batting averages and the use of geography in determining the location of big-league teams. My own mental delinquency was not quite so considerable as that, but the truth is that sports was all I cared to read about. The sports section was the only portion of the newspaper that interested me. Apart from thumbing through the pages of each week's *Life*, the only magazine I read was a monthly called *Sport*, and this I read with the intensity of a full-court press, cover to cover, the letters from readers, up and down the masthead, the whole thing. Among the editors were men with such names as Al Silverman and Ed Fitzgerald (please note the locker-room familiarity of Al and Ed, no Allans or Edwards permitted). The magazine contained profiles of contemporary athletes. "Yogi likes plenty of pizza in the off-season," a characteristic line from *Sport* might run, "and can usually be found hanging out at his friend Phil Rizzuto's bowling alley." The magazine also carried splendid historical pieces, under the rubric of "The Sport Classic," about such legendary figures as Jim Thorpe (The Carlisle Indian), Ty Cobb (The Georgia Peach), Jack Dempsey (The Manassa Mauler), and Bill Tilden (Big Bill, who, it was later to be revealed, liked plenty of boys in the off-season). There was also a Sport Quiz, which tested your knowledge of all sports, past and present. It was the only test on which I ever cared passionately about doing well.

In me John R. Tunis had an ideal reader—but not, I hasten to add, in me alone, for thousands of boys similarly hooked on sports read him with something like the same ardor. Tunis published his first novel for boys in 1938, when he was forty-nine years old, and from the outset generations have read him and, apparently, still do. It is to Tunis I owe my first knowledge that reading can be as intense a pleasure as any that life has to offer. This dawned on me when, to my own youthful astonishment, I stayed home one sunny summer afternoon with a Tunis novel, preferring, in this amazing instance, to read about baseball when I could have been out playing it.

An audience of youngsters is a tough audience to crack. Tunis knew this very well. In his autobiography, *A Measure of Independence* (1964), written when he was seventy-five, he addressed the question directly:

> A book written for my audience doesn't have to be merely as good as a book for adults; it must—or should be—better. Not only does youth deserve the best, but also no youths read a book because it is on the best-seller list. There is no best-seller list. Nor do they read it because it has a huge advertising budget, or is well reviewed; they read it for one reason alone, they want to. They find it says something to them in an area they know and understand. These readers are important, perhaps the most important in the country today.

What, I wonder, did John R. Tunis's novels say to me when I first read them at thirteen? What did I think when, early in the novel *All-American*, I read the following sentence: "After all, it was something to have a father who had played football, who understood these things"? The man in question, Robert Perry, who is the father of the young hero of the novel, played, moreover, at Yale, has a high position in a bank, and sends his son to pick up his resoled golf shoes. My own father left school in Montreal to come to Chicago at seventeen, worked in the costume jewelry business with men with such names as Sidney Ginsberg, Abe Levine, and Manny Dubinsky, and owned business shoes only. "Two different worlds," the old song runs, "we come from two different worlds."

The world John R. Tunis wrote about—small-town, Gentile, very American—was one about which I had the kind of intense curiosity available only to those who felt themselves ultimately excluded from it. What I did not know at the time, having no interest in authors apart from their ability to deliver an interesting story, was that so, in a way, was Tunis excluded from the kind of life he wrote about. Tunis was not a Jew, nor the son of immigrants, but he did grow up without a father and in highly unusual circumstances. His father's was a wealthy New York family, of Dutch descent, who had done extremely well in various kinds of speculation around the time of the Civil War. In the view of his family, Tunis's father made two crucial mistakes: the first was to leave the Episcopalian Church to become a (Harvard-trained) Unitarian minister; the second was to marry a woman, three or so years older than he, whose father was a waiter. Tunis's father was disowned for this latter act; no Tunis appeared at his wedding in New York. Even though he later returned to Episcopalianism, when he died of Bright's disease— John was then seven, his brother five—no member of the Tunis family appeared at the funeral.

In no John R. Tunis novel I have read—and, now, reread—does a mother figure as more than a sweet but mild pain in the neck. A mother in these books is generally someone who reminds a boy to take along his jacket or not to forget his galoshes. But in a case of art refusing to imitate life, John R. Tunis's own mother was a completely formidable woman, the chief influence in her two sons' lives, John's guide and critic and inspiration. After her young husband's death, she alone, quite without outside help, held her family together, kept up standards, and provided a model for her sons, both of whom loved her without qualification.

Caroline Roberts Tunis had gone to Normal College in New York (later Hunter College). When her husband died, she took a job first at the Brearley School for girls on the East Side of Manhattan. But before long she moved with her boys and her retired father—whom she never referred to as a waiter but always as a "steward"—to Cambridge, Massachusetts, principally, Tunis reports in his autobiography, because she wanted her sons to be near Harvard. "My mother had two articles of faith; first, that we should be brought up in the church of our father (Episcopalian), and second, attend Harvard, his college." Through her deceased husband's churchly connections, she arranged, with the help of Reverend Endicott Peabody, rector of Groton, to open an eating house for former students of Groton now at Harvard. This went quite well until 1904, when a student named Franklin Delano Roosevelt turned his fellow Grotonians against the idea of walking all the way to Mrs. Tunis's establishment in cold weather. Tunis's mother then turned to substitute teaching along with teaching immigrants the English language at night, and continued to teach until her retirement.

She was a Teddy Roosevelt Republican—her son John's one serious dissent from his mother was to become a liberal Democrat—a woman who believed in hard work, self-improvement, and the importance of culture. She read only serious books, usually with a critical eye; had reams of poetry stored in her memory; was often off to a concert or the opera; and read and argued with the editorials in the Boston *Evening Transcript*. In later life, she offered a running critical commentary on her son's books and articles—and later life lasted a good while, since she died at ninety-two. (Tunis himself died in 1975, at eighty-six.) "At ninety," she wrote to her son, "one does not get around as easily as at eighty-five. I find myself inclined to give in these days, instead of urging myself on as I once did." Perhaps the main reason John R. Tunis never included a mother figure like his own in any of his novels is that he did not have to, for his mother's spirit and idealism reign in everything he wrote.

Although Tunis grew up fatherless, without the security of money, written off by his father's wealthy family (who did later provide funds for him and his brother to attend college), he maintains in his autobiography that, despite all this, "never did we feel sorry for ourselves, for there was nothing to feel sorry about." One is ready to believe that, especially with so gallant a woman as his mother around, yet it must have been difficult watching her returning exhausted from cooking for other boys or from a double load of teaching. A boy growing up without a father, no matter how strong his mother, remains half an orphan; and this, too, could not have been easy. In many of Tunis's novels, the father is the moral center of the book, the figure whom a young man can turn to for balanced thought, perspective, good guidance. Where the father fails—as he does, notably, in *Yea! Wildcats!*, one of Tunis's Indiana high-school basketball novels—the coach steps in to play this role. But during many an adolescent crisis—physical courage, sportsmanship, masculine honor—a boy can only turn to a man for help.

It would be pushing things to say that Tunis grew up like Stephen Crane's Maggie, a child of the streets, but it is true to say that, had his father not been disowned by his family, Tunis and his brother would have gone to a school like Groton rather than had their mother cook for the boys who went there. Still, there were much worse streets to grow up on than those in Cambridge around the turn of the century. Once when he and his brother were out playing, their ball hit a carriage containing the baby of Professor Irving Babbitt, who complained to the police. Babbitt lived across the street, and the Cambridge Public Library, which was a big item in Tunis's life, was not far away. A few blocks distant were the thirty clay tennis courts of Jarvis Field, used by Harvard students but also available to the Tunis boys, who hung around hoping to be asked to fill in for someone else's missing doubles partner.

Sport was Tunis's passion as a boy, and he would later, of course, make a living out of writing about it. His grandfather taught him to read—to study is perhaps more precise—the sports pages in the daily newspaper. It was this same grandfather, his mother's father, who took him and his brother to their first major-league baseball game, which happened to be played in a National League park and thus left him a National League fan for life. (American or National League is one of those choices a sports-minded boy makes early in life and from which he rarely departs.) His mother was puzzled by her son's passion for games, but did nothing to interfere with it. Tunis, ever the moralist, maintains that as an adolescent he may never have learned the disciplines of working and saving, but he did acquire the disciplines of sport, which meant, among other things, "how to accept defeat, a lesson most Americans hate to accept, although defeat comes to us all in the end and we had better be ready for it."

Tennis appears to have been Tunis's own best sport. Although he claims his brother was a more natural athlete than he—better co-ordinated, more stylish—he himself must have been a player of high competence. He played tennis for Harvard and, while working as a journalist abroad, he mentions playing in what sound like fairly serious second-line tournaments in Europe. Tennis was in any case the sport that lit him aflame with an excitement that went beyond the sport itself. In *A Measure of Independence* he tells how, in his fourteenth year, in 1903, he and his brother trekked out to the Longwood Cricket Club in Brookline to see the American national champion William A. Larned play a Davis Cup match against Laurie Doherty, representing England, who had won at Wimbledon. The Tunis boys had no money for a ticket of admission, so instead they watched the match sitting atop the huge barrels of a brewery wagon parked just outside the court. Tunis describes what he saw:

> I can still see Larned storming the net behind his powerful service, and Doherty passing him with an elegant backhand down the line, feet apart, his racket high in the air, poised in his follow-through like Mercury himself. Those fluid strokes, the crisp punched volleys of Larned, the classical purity of Doherty's shots off the ground, the attacks and ripostes of the two nervous men gave me, without my knowledge at the time, a feeling for art and beauty that was to be mine forever. This scene of grace and movement at Longwood that afternoon reached into me, touched my inner self, changed me for good. I was a boy no longer.

In this handsome paragraph, Tunis hints at a relationship between sport and art that I have never seen discussed. When he remarks that watching these two tennis players gave him "a feeling for art and beauty that was to be mine forever," he reminds me that sports provided my own first glimpses of mastery over materials, economy of execution, and elegance, which are among the qualities shared by the superior athlete and the artist. The superior artist is of course a figure of greater importance than the superior athlete, for what he creates has a chance to endure, but in the form, power of innovation, and authority of the athlete I, for one (and I suspect there have been thousands like me), had my first blessed inkling of what art can do. That there is an artistic component to the athlete is a point never pushed but always subtly hovering in the background of Tunis's sports novels for boys, though I cannot say that I myself picked up on it at thirteen.

Despite his mother's intellectual earnestness, Tunis was far from being a good student, and claims to have "possessed no intellectual disciplines, being ignorant, lazy, and uninterested." In 1907 this did not prevent him from being admitted to Harvard, at a tuition fee—parents of today will be dismayed to learn—of $90, with the single condition that he take something called English A that sounds suspiciously like a remedial course. By his own reckoning, Tunis did not make very much of the intellectual opportunities at Harvard. He ran cross-country in the autumn, played tennis in the spring, and whenever possible sneaked off to the theater or a concert in Boston.

His closest friend when he entered Harvard was Conrad Aiken, the poet and critic, who, once at Harvard, began to move among such intellectually serious undergraduates as T. S. Eliot and Walter Lippmann. John Hall Wheelock, Van Wyck Brooks, Robert Benchley, and Norman Foerster were undergraduates at Harvard when Tunis was there, but he never saw them. He did become friends with a student whom he describes as "a worse runner than myself" named Frederick Lewis Allen, who later became editor of *Harper's*, for which Tunis wrote articles in the 1930s. (Joseph Kennedy, Sr., who was a year behind Tunis at Harvard, roomed across the hall from him.) The crucial—to hear him tell it, the only—intellectual experience of his Harvard days was hearing William Jennings Bryan speak at Sanders Theater; the Great Commoner's speech that afternoon turned him away from his Republican heritage and into a Democrat of strong populist-liberal strain.

In 1936, in the midst of the Depression, Tunis produced a book entitled *Was College Worth While?* that was timed to mark the twenty-fifth anniversary of his own class of 1911 and which turned out to be a strong attack on the hidebound nature of most Harvard men. Surveying his own class, he noted that "we are practically barren of leaders of public life" and that only "a small minority . . . appear to have done any original thinking in their field"; and he ends by saying that the chief ambition of this same class of men, "if their record tells the truth, is to vote the Republican ticket, to keep out of the bread line, and to break 100 at golf." (In an interview given to Jerome Holtzman when Tunis was eighty-four, this was changed to "break 80 at golf.") He eased the stringency of his criticism of Harvard a few years later, when, in 1938, he published a novel entitled *Iron Duke*, about a boy from Waterloo, Iowa, who comes east to Harvard and feels left out, nearly flunks out, but finally wins out though not on Harvard's rather snobbish terms but on his own: he becomes a track star, he makes the dean's list, and he turns down membership in an exclusive undergraduate club.

This book, written when he was forty-nine, changed John R. Tunis's career. He had written novels before, but this was the first work he produced that was sold, in the trade lingo, as a "juvenile." When he learned that this was how Alfred Harcourt, the founder of Harcourt, Brace, planned to sell his book, Tunis was astounded—"shocked, rocked, deflated," he reports in his autobiography—for he did not write it as a book for young readers. The book sold more than 60,000 copies and twenty-five years after its publication was still bringing in respectable royalties. "I continued writing these so-called boys' books," Tunis told Jerome Holtzman, "but I've never considered them that." Perhaps herein is the secret of the success of Tunis's books for young readers: an absolute absence of condescension in their composition.

Until *Iron Duke*, Tunis was a freelance, turning out as many as two books a year, picking up magazine pieces where he could, covering European tennis tournaments in the summers for American newspapers, knocking out roughly 2,000 words a day six days a week—doing, in short, all the dog work of the sadly misnamed freelance. For a time he wrote sports pieces for Harold Ross at the *New Yorker*, usually for $50 apiece and, as late as the early 1930s, $200 for a longish profile. Of Ross, Tunis wrote: "Curiously Ross knew less about sport than any male American I ever met." (This has a familiar ring; other writers have remarked that Harold Ross was equally ignorant about culture and politics; all he seemed to know, apparently, was how a *New Yorker* piece on any given subject ought to read.) Tunis tells about the time that Ross, being strapped for cash, offered Tunis sixty shares of *New Yorker* stock in lieu of payment he owed him for pieces. He would have taken it, too, had he not met Frank Crowninshield, the editor of *Vanity Fair*, returning from lunch at the Algonquin, who told him that the magazine's future looked shaky and to go for the cash. He took Crowninshield's bad advice, later determining that, with stock splits and dividends, this little disaster on 44th Street cost him somewhere in the neighborhood of a million dollars.

Although Tunis had begun to sell fiction to *Collier's* and to write nonfiction pieces for the *Saturday Evening Post*, his "so-called boys books" eventually took him off the freelancer's financial treadmill; they are also the chief reason for the endurance of such fame as Tunis still has. Of these books, Tunis, toward the end of his life, said, "They can be read by adults." Having just read—in most instances, reread—nine of them, I would say that the remark requires some qualification. Tunis's books can be read by an adult, but then an adult can also eat a bag of gum drops. It is probably a good idea for an adult not to do either too often. Still, I found Tunis's books highly readable and, for personal reasons, very moving.

★ ★ ★

To return to the books one loved in one's youth is to risk disappoint-ment—in both the books and in oneself when young. I should not care ever to return to Willard Motley's *Knock on Any Door*, which at age sixteen I stayed awake through an entire night reading in the Brown Hotel in Des Moines, Iowa, while on the road working with my father. John Dos Passos's *USA*, which thrilled me the first time around at nine-teen, many years later seemed, well, a bit hokey. As for John R. Tunis's books, there is nothing junky, or sickening, or second-rate about them. They do suffer from want of a very high level of complexity, but then I hardly expected Jamesian subtlety. In fact, upon rereading them I am rather proud of my thirteen-year-old self for thinking as well of them as I did. Although my memory of myself is that of a fairly frivolous, genial goof-off, perhaps after all I was rather more serious than I remember.

I say this because, I now realize, the Tunis books are pretty seri-ous, and I was utterly absorbed in them. All the novels I then read—and now have reread—are about sports, but they are only ostensibly about sports. Sports is the subject; other matters make up the theme. And even when sports is being discussed, things peripheral to the game itself loom interestingly large. Soon after *The Kid from Tomkinsville* (1940), which is probably Tunis's best baseball novel, gets going, Tunis invites his readers to consider the situation of the thirty-eight-year-old catcher Dave Leonard, on his way to spring training with the Brooklyn Dodg-ers. At thirty-eight, Leonard's mind is very much on staying with the club and even more on his future. He is making $12,500 (the year is 1940), which is a good salary. But he is a family man. "Twelve-five," he thinks. "They don't pay salaries like that to rookie catchers at any rate. Nor to veterans either, for long." Still, at his age, an age when most businessmen are just getting going, he is coming to the end of the line. "Twelve-five, yep, sounds like a lot of money. But he needed three years before some of his insurance came due and the load lightened."

What did I think of this when I first read it at thirteen? Why should a kid of thirteen give a rat's rump about the financial problems of an old guy of thirty-eight? I cannot recall exactly, but my guess is that I loved such passages in Tunis. For one thing, there was the realism of it (the son of parents who had come through the Depression, I had heard often enough how tough it could be to make a living); for another, it was fine to have such adult—such *real*—problems up for discussion. Material of this kind took you behind the scenes; it treated you, as a reader, like a grownup, which was a genuine compliment, especially since at thirteen, you probably thought of yourself as a grownup anyway.

Tunis's books are studded with such stuff. In *Yea! Wildcats!* (1944) he tells you about the corrupt way that tickets are parceled out for the state high-school basketball tournaments in Indiana. The coach in that novel refuses to get tickets for anyone, an independent stand that, like all such stands in Tunis, comes to cost him dearly. Sometimes the presentation of inside material is conjoined with Tunis's own strong views. Although he had worked as a journalist himself, Tunis did not much care for the general run of the breed: he took them to be paid kibitzers whose self-appointed job was to spread dissension among athletes, increase pressure on everyone, and make trouble generally. In *Rookie of the Year* (1944), another of his baseball books, he sets out the various techniques that sports writers use to sniff out a story, and leaves them with the grandeur of, say, a third-class hotel house dick. "An ounce of curiosity plus a pound of brass coupled with the sensitivity of a rhino and the pertinacity of a tiger," he writes in *Rookie of the Year*, "that's what makes a reporter." I am not certain what I made of that formulation at thirteen, but it now seems to me quite on target.

Of course, how ballplayers feel about night games, the outside pressures on managers and coaches, the conditions of tournament tennis—none of this would have made much impression if John R. Tunis were not extremely good at telling a story. And telling a story, in a sports novel, largely means being able to describe action. This Tunis can do exceedingly well. He has a commanding sense of pace; he knows when to describe a game sketchily and when to go into intricate detail. He has a nice sense of proportion, which prevents him from ever allowing his heroes to become supermen, and hence unbelievable, on the field. He is excellent at describing tennis, good at football, a bit less sure of himself at basketball, and perhaps best of all at baseball. He has the knack of instructing while describing without making a reader feel as if he were being talked down to. Narrating a doubleplay in *Keystone Kids* (1943), for example, Tunis writes:

> The two boys were off together. Both were near the ball, on top of it almost, so fast that either could have stabbed for it. But Bob suddenly realized his brother was the one to make the play, and

as he neared the bag sheered away to clear the path for the throw. Spike picked up the ball a few feet from the base, and in one continuous motion touched the bag and hurled the ball to first in time to nab the fastest runner in baseball. Only an expert could have felt their understanding, their coordination as they made that decision in the fraction of a second when the ball roared toward them. The two men in the box behind the dugout missed nothing. They looked at each other. Base hits, they knew, were a matter of feet. Doubleplays were a matter of inches.

John R. Tunis, as they say about superior infielders, could pick it.

I suppose a boy of thirteen reading Tunis today might miss an item or two of a factual kind. Such a boy, a habitual reader of today's sports pages, might be mildly amused at the relatively small sums ballplayers then earned (there is talk in one of the Tunis novels about a World Series winner's share of $6,000 per player and endorsements earning only $250). There is a real possibility that he might miss references to such then–living figures as Grantland Rice, Al Schacht, and Hank Greenberg. Will he know that the defensive shift used against the character Cecil McDade in the novel *Highpockets* (1948) is based on the shift used on Ted Williams; or that an announcer named Snazzy Beane is based on Dizzy Dean; or that Jack McManus, the owner of the Brooklyn Dodgers in the baseball novels, is loosely based on Larry McPhail? Then there are distinctly time-bound references to the Quiz Kids, the Aldrich family, Fred Allen (not the *Harper's* editor, the radio comic). Such a boy might be puzzled by the period slang—"Thunderation!," one character thinks, and the phrase "That was something like!" occurs repeatedly— or by the corny nicknames Tunis is in the habit of assigning his ballplayers: Spike and Bones and Razzle and Rats and Fat Stuff. A young boy today, rising from his computer, might be put off by any or all of this.

But it would be a pity if he were, for he would miss a great deal. Not least, he would miss Tunis's teaching, which is to say his moral instructions, which is to say his message(s). Recounting his own methods of composition in his books for boys, Tunis writes that the story must be told "simply, quickly, effectively," and that "when you allow a 'message' to take over, you are lost." He also remarks in his autobiography, apropos of the George Alfred Henty *Rollo* books he read in his own youth: "As boys have ever done—and thank God, ever will—we skipped the culture and the moralizing and gulped down the accounts of life in distant lands." Nothing of any of this applies to Tunis's own books, which taken together have more messages than Western Union. True, the messages in Tunis are generally artfully mixed with the action of the stories, but I know that I picked them up when young, and if I had not, so plain are they, I would have to have been declared a moral dyslexic.

Tunis's many messages divide into general and particular categories. In the general category, there are the lessons that sport teaches: the need for discipline, for the willingness to subsume one's own selfish interests in the greater good of the team, for the courage to come back from defeat. In *The Kid from Tomkinsville*, when the Dodgers come from well behind to make a stretch drive for the pennant, even the fans of the rival New York Giants at the Polo Grounds are impressed. "Because," Tunis writes, "sport offers no more inspiring spectacle than the man or the team who comes back, who takes the cracks of fate and pulls them together to rise once more." *Highpockets* is about a great natural athlete who turns from being a selfish loner, out only to compile impressive statistics that will earn him a larger salary, to become a team player. "'That's the trouble with this country nowadays,'" an older player and coach tells him after he comes around, "'everyone out for himself, aiming to hit the long ball over the fence.'"

The sense of a team is the great moment in Tunis novels; it is one of the overarching ideas in all his work. This applied to life as well as to sports. When a child is operated on in *Highpockets*, medicine, too, turns out to be "a sort of team, y'see." And what was this almost mystical entity, a team? "It was everything in sport and in life, yet nothing you touch or see or feel or even explain to someone else. A team was like an individual, a character, fashioned by work and suffering and disappointment and sympathy and understanding, perhaps not least of all by defeat." What Tunis is addressing here is character in its collective sense; in his novels the molding of character is always an individual matter, with a high-school athlete or professional ballplayer put through the test. Character, in Tunis, is won through discipline, through perseverance, through learning from defeat. This is a very old-fashioned notion. John R. Tunis taught me to believe in it when I was a boy. I still believe in it.

On the particular side, Tunis's messages tended to be those of the old-style liberal, the hater of snobbery and prejudice. *All-American*, a novel written in 1942 when the defeat of Hitler was far from certain, turns out to be a book about American democracy. In it a quarterback named Ronald Perry transfers from a prep school called the Academy to a public school called Abraham Lincoln High. Many are this book's messages, a number of them delivered by the public-school principal: "In this school, Ronald, every pupil has to be responsible for himself. That's one of the principles of a democracy, isn't it?" Several are the book's conflicts, the concluding one occurring when Abraham Lincoln High's football team learns that, after winning their conference, Ned LeRoy, their fine Negro end, cannot travel with the team to an intersectional game in Miami because of Southern segregation policy. The team, led by Ronald, decides not to play without Ned and so the trip is canceled, much to the consternation of the town's leading citizens. In Tunis's novels about high-school athletes, adults almost invariably are wrong when they take too keen an interest in high-school sports, interfering in a way that turns out to be detrimental to the boys and to the sport itself. A notable exception is Hooks Barnum, the coach of Ridgewood High, in *Go, Team, Go!* (1954), whose coaching and character have a salubrious effect on the team, "as the character of a good man always does in sport." But in the main the message is that, left to themselves, youngsters have fairly good instincts about fair play, and so they ought, in fact, to be left to themselves.

In *Keystone Kids*, Tunis takes on the subject of anti-Semitism in telling the story of Jocko Klein, the rookie catcher of the Dodgers, who is taunted by his own teammates as well as by opposing teams for being a Jew. Helping Jocko fight off the anti-Semitism of his own teammates is the young Southern manager of the Dodgers, Spike Russell, who himself does not exactly possess an advanced degree in social work from the University of Chicago. Instead he has an instinctual sense of the unfairness of singling out a man in this way, a feeling that anti-Semitism is tearing apart not only the man but the team, and the strong belief that it cannot be allowed to go on. He offers some crude advice to Jocko— "You gotta think of yourself as a catcher, not as a Jew"—and some that turns out to be important to him: "Boy, you gotta take it in this game same as you gotta take it in life. Get me? Understand. . . . Don't quit." And—need I say it?—Jocko does not quit; he eventually faces down his chief tormentor; the team finally unites and returns to the business at hand, which is winning the National League pennant.

Later in the same novel, Tunis runs through the ethnic origins, and offers potted histories, of the ancestors of the various members of the Dodgers, extending his notion of the concept of the team into a metaphor for America itself which not even so unliterary a kid as I could have missed. My guess is that, when I first came across it, I was much moved. It reads strangely today, nearly thirty years after it was written and after the great efflorescence of ethnic pride that has swept this country. Reading it now, I am still moved, even though the dream of America as a team made up of very different people—a dream that was also at the center of Tunis's vision as a writer—seems rather tattered and fading.

"Don't quit," Spike Russell tells Jocko Klein, in what may be John R. Tunis's essential message. It is the message that he apparently took from his own life. Of the difficulties of his own early freelancing days, he writes in his autobiography: "Often I stumbled and fell; but usually got up, bruised and sore, and went on. It wasn't courage but stupidity that kept me going. . . . How many times in life when talent is lacking, sheer persistence pays off." I believe that, too. On rereading him now, I find that there is not much at the heart of John R. Tunis's books for boys that I do not still believe. Whether I originally acquired these beliefs from him, or whether I had first to hack my way through jungles of intellectual obfuscation before returning to them, I do not know. But of the influences that helped form me, I now think of the books of John R. Tunis as a very real one.

"Highpockets had learned something," Tunis writes. "There's no easy way to a boy's heart. Like everything else, you have to work for it." John R. Tunis did, and he still has mine.

THIS SPORTING LIFE

Time, how do I waste thee? Let me count the ways: In lengthy telephone conversations with friends, chatting and laughing, schmoozing away the irreplaceable substance in fifteen-, thirty-, and forty-five-minute chunks. In reading bland and mostly biased accounts of terrible troubles in Ukraine and Damascus, Beirut and Bombay, then watching it served up yet again, this time with audiovisual aids, by creamy-cheeked men and women whom we call anchor-persons, the English call newsreaders, and the French call *speakerines*—the news, which as soon as it is written or said isn't new anymore, much time dropped down the drink here. In dreaming while awake, casting my mind back over its increasingly lengthy past, sliding it forward over its increasingly shortened future, lolling about in time past and time future while effectively obliterating time present. In other innumerable small ways—the little detour into the used bookshop, the false start on yet another intellectual venture, the empty social evening—I have devised no shortage of efficient methods of smothering time. I am someone who knows very well what Wallace Stevens meant when he spoke of the "necessary laziness" of the poet. I only wish a person equally distinguished had come forth to speak on behalf of my condition—the unnecessary laziness of the non-poet.

But I seem to have left out my most impressive achievement in wasting time. Far and away my most serious work as a time-waster is in watching men—sometimes but less often women—in various costumes running or jumping or hitting each other, smacking, kicking, shooting, or stroking balls of different sizes into cylinders, goals, gloves, or nets.

31

With the sole exception of auto racing, there is no game, match, contest, or race I will not watch. "Dear Boy," wrote Lord Chesterfield to his illegitimate son, Philip Stanhope, "There is nothing which I more wish that you should know, and which fewer people do know, than the true use and value of time. It is in everybody's mouth; but in few people's practice." In this same letter, Chesterfield tells the boy, "I knew a gentleman, who was so good a manager of his time, that he would not even lose that small portion of it, which the calls of nature obliged him to pass in the necessary-house; but gradually went through all the Latin poets, in those moments." I tremble to think what, were I Chesterfield's son, his reaction would be to his learning that I, over the past year, have spent time watching men with permanents and blow-dry hair-dos bowling, other men in lavender and yellow trousers hitting golf balls, and stout women arm wrestling. "Dear Boy," I imagine him writing to me, "You seem to be making a necessary-house of your entire life."

From time to time I tell myself that I am going to stop, I am going to knock off watching all these games and useless competitions. Enough is enough, I say, quit now, while you're well behind; go cold turkey, put paid to it, be done, write finis, mutter kaput—enough is too much. The prospect dangling deliciously before me if I were to stop watching so much sports is that of regaining ample hunks of time that I might otherwise, and oh so much more wisely, spend. What might I do with the time not spent watching sports? Ah, what might I not do? Listen to opera, acquire a foreign language, learn to play the flute, go into the commodities market, actually play a sport. The possibilities, while not precisely limitless, are nonetheless very grand. Perhaps I shall one day do it. Wait, as loyal fans in cities with losing teams say, until next year.

If it were actually to come about, if next year I were to free myself of my bondage to watching sports, it would be a year like no other I can recall in my life. From earliest boyhood I have been a games man, passionately interested in playing games and in everything to do with them. In the neighborhoods in which I grew up, being a good athlete was the crowning achievement; not being good at sports was permitted, though not caring at all about sports, for a boy, was a certain road to unpopularity. Ours was strictly a meritocracy, with merit measured in coordination and agility and knowledge about sports.

The best-loved kid in our neighborhood was a boy named Marty Summerfield, whose father had pitched briefly for the Chicago White Sox. Marty was smallish, but he combined very high athletic prowess with absolutely astonishing physical courage. Still in grade school, I can recall him at least twice having to be carried off football fields with a concussion; in baseball, he would chase a foul pop-up off the playground into the street, where he would catch it to the screech of car brakes and the angry honking of horns; in later years I saw him refuse to back away from fights with young men six inches taller and fifty or so pounds heavier than he. There was no brag to him or any meanness. He had a smile that made you happy. He was our Billy Budd, but, thank goodness, there was never any need to hang him.

Although Marty Summerfield was very intelligent—he went off to college on a Westinghouse science scholarship—I do not recall his showing much interest in the statistics, lore, or other of the spectatorial aspects of sports; certainly not as much as I and others of us who were not anywhere near so good at sports as he. I have noted this phenomenon repeat itself in later years. Truly good athletes, men and women who can or once could really do it, seem not all that interested in talking about it. (Please allow for many exceptions here, chief among them the former athletes hired by television networks and stations to do "color" or to report sports news.) Ernest Hemingway's endless talk about sports—about baseball and boxing and hunting—has always made me think that he was merely passable as an athlete. As with sex, so with sports: too much talk about it tends to leave one a bit dubious.

Somehow it seems unlikely that a great writer would also be a very good athlete, almost as if the two forms of grace—verbal and physical—were in their nature necessarily contradictory. William Hazlitt was very earnest about the game called "fives," but how good he was at it I do not know. Orwell played a version of rugby football at Eton, though, unlike Hazlitt, never, as far as I know, wrote about sports. Vladimir Nabokov played soccer at Cambridge and is said to have been a very respectable tennis player, yet his pleasure in any game was greatly exceeded by his pleasure in lepidopterology. F. Scott Fitzgerald claimed that not playing football at Princeton was one of the great disappointments in his life. Evelyn Waugh played field hockey for his college (Hertford) at Oxford, noting of it, rather Waughfully, "There is a pleasant old world violence about the game which appeals to one strongly." This makes Waugh seem the possessor of greater athletic aplomb than he apparently had. A former student of Waugh's during his teaching days in the early 1920s remembers otherwise:

> In the matter of games he was in fact so undistinguished a performer that after a few humorous episodes it was thought better that he should not exercise with the senior boys. He was issued with a whistle and allowed to amble harmlessly around the football field with the ten-year-olds. In the summer term, still wearing his plus fours, he was a reluctant umpire at the cricket games of novices.

It would be a monumental surprise, not to say an outright astonishment, to learn that Henry James was a superior athlete, but the facts hold no such surprise in store. Yet throughout his adult life Henry James, in his ultimately losing battle against corpulence, had recourse to one or another athletic activity as a form of exercise. He rode horses in Rome, took fencing lessons in London, cycled round Sussex after he had moved to Rye; at one point he lifted dumbbells, difficult as it may be to picture Henry James, as we now say, "pumping iron." There is a lovely letter in the fourth volume of the *Henry James Letters*, from James to his godson Guy Hoyer Millar, in which he writes to the boy: "I learned from your mother, by pressing her hard, some time ago that it would be a convenience to you and a great help in your career to possess an Association football—whereupon, in my desire that you should receive the precious object from no hand but mine I cast about me for the proper place to procure it." In the course of the letter, in which James informs the boy that the football is on its way to him in a separate parcel, he allows that "I'm an awful muff, too, at games—except at times I am not a bad cyclist, I think—and I fear I am only rather decent at playing at godfather."

As a boy, I was not an awful muff at games, but neither was I awfully good at them either. I was quick and well coordinated, but insufficiently aggressive and too much concerned with form. I don't believe I was ever deceived, even as a small boy, about my being able to play a sport in college or professionally, although I should have loved to have been good enough to be able to do so. To attempt to take my own athletic measure, I would say that, for a writer, I am a fair athlete, while among serious athletes I am, as an athlete, a fair writer. I think here again of poor Hemingway, of self-deceived Hemingway, always quick with the inapposite sports metaphor, who, in a *New Yorker* profile written by Lillian Ross, talked about his quality as a writer in boxing terms:

> I started out very quiet and I beat Mr. Turgenev. Then I trained hard and I beat Mr. de Maupassant. I've fought two draws with Mr. Stendhal, and I think I had an edge in the last one. But nobody's going to get me in any ring with Mr. Tolstoy unless I'm crazy or I keep getting better.

This rather famous passage makes me want to talk, in something like the same terms, not of my writing but of my athletic abilities. Let me put it this way: I'm ready anytime to play Ping-Pong with Mr. Balzac. And if Mr. Dostoyevsky ever cares to go one-on-one half court with me or to shoot a little game of "Horse," I'm ready to take him on, too. If either Miss Austen or Mrs. Woolf wishes to go head-to-head with me in an arm wrestling match, I think they both know where I can be reached. As for boxing, whenever he's ready to put on the gloves, tell Mr. Proust all he has to do is give me a jingle.

Until such time as any of these writers accepts my challenge, I can almost certainly be found seated on the south end of a couch, in a book-lined room, eight or so feet from a fifty-two-inch Sony color television. There—you can count on it—I shall doubtless be watching exceedingly tall men slamming balls into baskets, or lumpily muscular men in helmets slamming themselves against one another. Then again I might be watching adolescent girls figure skating or doing gymnastics, or extremely wealthy young men and women thwacking fuzzy balls across a net, or slender men and women almost any of whom might easily qualify as the centerfold for Gray's *Anatomy* running distances far greater than the human body was ever intended to run. But if I were a betting man—which, as it happens, I am—I would bet that I would most likely be found watching a baseball game, for this game, which I never played very well as a boy, has become the game I more and more enjoy watching. Coaches speak of "benching" athletes, but I have been "couched." I don't want to know with any exactitude how much time I have spent over the years watching games from my couch, but my guess is that the amount of time would be—this is, as they say, a ballpark figure—roughly twice that which Penelope spent waiting for the return of Odysseus.

Booze and drugs, gambling and tobacco do not begin to exhaust the list of life's potential addictions. Some people cannot get through the day without a newspaper. Others take their fix in chocolate. I have been told that there are people who wig out on pasta. *The Concise Oxford Dictionary* defines *addict* colloquially as "enthusiastic devotee of sport or pastime." That's me—a colloquial addict. I don't require my fix every day, although I somehow feel rather cheerier if I know a game is coming up later in the day or during the evening. And if too many days pass without one, I do tend to get a touch edgy. I had my first serious intimation of this some eight or so years ago while on a two-week holiday in England, where, one evening in Bath, I realized that I hadn't watched a sports event for fully ten days and strongly felt the craving to do so. I turned on the television set in the hotel room to listen to the news. Then, suddenly, the BBC news-reader began to intone—it sounded like music to me—"East Birmingham 6, Brighton 4; Leeds 3, West Manchester 2; Bournemouth 4, Winchester 1." These were scores from soccer matches. I have almost no interest in soccer; I have certainly seen none of these teams. Yet I found the mere recitation of these scores soothing, and for the remainder of the holiday I looked forward to hearing soccer scores each evening. I believe this strange little anecdote establishes my bona fides as an addict—or, in the harsher term, "sports nut."

I have described some of the symptoms and labeled the disease, but you would be gravely mistaken if you are anticipating a cure. I have not found one and do not expect to. Instead of a cure, which is apparently unavailable, I seek a justification. What can be said on behalf of all the time I have put in watching games? Does it come to nothing more than—in the most literal sense of the word—a pastime, or passing time? Have my many hours spent watching games, either before my television or "live" (what a word!), been without any redeeming value? Am I doing nothing more than killing time? Enough questions. Stop stalling. Justify yourself or get off the couch. All right, since I have a few hours on my hands while awaiting a football game from the West Coast, let me try.

Although I scarcely watch sports for this reason, one of the benefits of watching them is that it keeps me in rather close touch with great numbers of my countrymen in a way that, without sports, I might otherwise have no hope to be. If you haven't a clue to what I mean here, please cast your eyes back over my previous sentence. What kind of person uses words such as *scarcely* or *rather* in the way that they are used in that sentence? Allow me to tell you what kind of person does—a bookish person. Without actually setting out to do so, I have become bookish. I am undeniably marked by the possession of general culture. I first noted this a few years ago when, after dining with a friend at an Italian restaurant in a lower-middle-class neighborhood, a woman waiting to be seated asked, "Where do you fellas teach?" "What do you mean 'teach'?" I asked. "My friend is the defensive line coach for the Miami Dolphins and I have a Buick agency in Terre Haute." This earned mild laughter, of the kind that follows enunciation of the phrase "Fat chance." In fact, my friend looked to me very much like a professor, which he is, but I had hoped I wasn't myself so readily identifiable. I guess I was still hopeful of passing for a not very successful lawyer, or perhaps a chemist, someone at any rate a little more in the world.

Not only do I apparently look to be what I am, but I also sound to be what I have become. A year or so ago, in connection with a book I had written, I agreed to do a radio interview. The interview was taped, and four or five weeks later, on a Saturday morning, I listened to it play over the local public radio station. As I did so, I thought, My God, I have somehow acquired one of those FM classical music station voices—a voice better adapted to saying words such as *Köchel*, *thematic*, *Hindemith*, and *motif* than to saying words such as "Yes, a hamburger sounds great to me." I sounded to myself a bit pretentious, not to say a mite snooty. Could it be locutions like "not to say" that did it? Or could I be imagining the entire thing? Any hope that I might be imagining it was ended when, last month, the six-year-old daughter of friends asked my wife about me, "Why does he speak English instead of American?"

The point of all this is that I believe there is a major division in this country between a small group composed of people who care a great deal about language and ideas and art, and another, vastly larger group for whom such concerns are considerably less than central. The problem, in my experience, is that this first group, even when it does not intend to, has a way of putting the second group off, making its members feel uncomfortable, slightly inferior, as if their lives were brutish and their pursuits trivial. It may well be that many members of the first group are truly contemptuous of the second group. Often, though, the contempt works the other way round. It isn't for no reason, after all, that piano players in whorehouses used to be called "professor." Anyone who has belonged to the first group must at one time have felt the sting of the division I have in mind. I recall being about four hours into a poker game with a number of printers, and, when the deal passed to me, I said, "OK gents, ante up for five-card draw." At which point the guy sitting to my left, who was losing about eighty dollars, said, "Whaddya, some kind of goddamn Englishman?" Ah, me, as Turgenev's nihilist Bazarov says, "That's what comes of being educated people."

Not that I am displeased with being what I am—a man, that is, marked by the possession of general culture. I talk as I talk; I think as I think; I am what I am. My mind, such as it is, remains my greatest stay against boredom. Still, I find this division between the two groups sad. As a member of the first of these groups, I know I do not feel any contempt for the members of the second group. (Sorry to have to proclaim my own virtue here, but apparently no one else will come forth to proclaim it for me.) In fact, I tend to feel rather more contempt for members of my own group, the culturati, with whom I am more familiar—contempt, after all, being one of the items familiarity breeds.

Yet one of the things that make it possible to jump the barrier and cut across this division, at least in masculine society, is sports—more specifically, knowledge and talk about sports. (Here I must add that I have met many intellectuals, scholars, novelists, and poets whose addiction to sports is not less than my own. "Closet sports fans" is the way I think of them. Yet how easily they are flushed out of the closet. All one has to do is offer a strong opinion about one or another team or player in their presence and out they come.) For a bookish fellow in a democracy, knowledge about sports seems to me essential. But not for the bookish alone; not even for a fellow alone. A friend tells me about a woman he knows who operates at a fairly high level in the real estate business and who began to study the morning sports pages in the hope of making lunches with male colleagues and clients easier. The hope, as it turned out, was justified, for sports talk is the closest thing we have in this country to a lingua franca, though I wouldn't use that phrase in, say, a bowling alley or pool hall.

Sports talk is easier for me than for the woman in the real estate business, I suspect, for I have grown up with sports, played at them as a kid, know them, and love to talk about them. I also know how inexhaustible sports can be as a subject; it sometimes seems, in fact, that there is more to say about yesterday's baseball game than about *Hamlet*. Nor do I think there is anything the least phony about using sports this way. As a conversational icebreaker, sports is very useful. It can rub away artificial distinctions. While sports may well be the toy department of life, not of towering intrinsic importance in itself, it can lead in and on to other, more intrinsically important subjects. Start with sports and before you know it you are talking economics, sociology, philosophy, personal hopes and fears. Socially, sports talk can be a fine lubricant.

I know I have often pressed sports into service, usually with decent results. I say "usually" and use the modest word "decent" because I think I may sometimes have gone too far. A few decades ago, for example, I found myself working in an urban renewal agency in the South. My fellow workers were mostly country boys. What they made of me I do not know. There was much to divide us: region, religion, politics. Asking them what they thought of the merits of the fiction of Jorge Luis Borges did not strike me as a happy way to glide over our differences. What did was sports. We talked Southwest Conference football, we talked baseball, we talked basketball. We got along.

I may have talked sports a little too well, for after a few weeks I was invited to play on the agency's basketball team in the local YMCA league. I showed up for the first game and learned that there were six members on the team, one of whom was in his early fifties. I was, in other words, a starter. Our opponents were made up of lean eighteen- and nineteen-year-olds of considerable height with, I remember thinking, rather menacing angularity of elbow. I had trained for this game by never smoking fewer than two packs of cigarettes daily for the previous ten years. Five or six times up and down the floor and I recall wondering if my life insurance premiums were paid. Evidently time-outs had not yet been discovered in the South, for during the first ten minutes none was called. I had somehow managed to score three points, on a free throw and a crisp lay-up. At the buzzer marking the end of the quarter, I walked over to the drinking fountain, into which I suavely vomited. Four or five games later, I went up for a rebound and, as good luck would have it, came down on my wrist, which was badly sprained. This excused me from further athletic combat. But the games I did play allowed me permanently to climb the barrier; in the eyes of the men I worked with I was OK and not a carpetbag intellectual.

But I don't want to push too hard the social advantages of knowing about sports. I don't watch them for social advantages. I watch them because most of the time they give pleasure. Nor do I believe that the reasons for my pleasure have much to do with personal psychology; I don't believe, in other words, that in watching sports I am attempting to regain my youth, or finding an outlet for violent emotions, or living vicariously through the physical exploits of others. No, part of the pleasure for me in watching sports is that of witnessing men and women do supremely well what may not be worth doing at all. It is the craft of superior athletes that is so impressive, and that seems all the more impressive at a time when standards of craftsmanship seem badly tattered. Literary awards, academic chairs, political power, journalistic eminence—all frequently seem to be awarded to people whose claims upon them appear so thin, and sometimes even actually fraudulent. But when a sixteen-year-old girl gymnast needs a perfect ten-point performance to win an Olympic gold medal, or a twenty-year-old college basketball player has to sink two free throws to win a game while fifteen thousand people are screaming at him and a few million more are watching him over television, or a golfer has to sink a tricky twelve-foot, slightly uphill putt—none of them, in these moments, can call on public relations, or social connections, or small corruptions, or fast talk. All they can call on is their craft, which they either have or don't have.

Sports also supply the pleasures of craft under pressure. I find I respond extremely well to pressure—to other people under pressure, that is. It excites me; I marvel at it. Much of sports is pressure organized. At any rate, the great moments in sports are those when athletes play through and win out under immense pressure. I am all the more admiring of people who are able to do this because, in the few moments of athletic pressure I felt as a boy, I have known something of its crushing weight. "Clutching," "choking," "the lump" are but a few of the descriptions for people whose athletic craft is reduced as a result of pressure. "Coming through," two of the loveliest words an athlete hopes to hear, is the phrase reserved for those whose craft is not impaired—is sometimes, in fact, heightened—by the presence of pressure. The grand spectacle of people coming through is one of the keenest pleasures of watching sports—and it is a spectacle not usually on display elsewhere with such shining clarity.

The spectacle of athletes not coming through, though not at all grand, is nonetheless much more moving. While we may admire the winners, most of us tend to side with the losers. Sports, it has been said, is about losing. There is a great deal to this, certainly when it comes to team sports. Coaches with preponderantly winning records exist in plenty, yet few are the teams that over the years seem to be able to repeat championship seasons. In professional sports, I can think of only four: the Montreal Canadiens, the New York Yankees, the Boston Celtics, and the Chicago Bulls during the Michael Jordan era. I have never cared enough about hockey to have passionate feelings about it, but I have liberally despised—"hated" is too passive a word—both the Yankees and the Celtics. What I have despised about them is that they won too frequently. I have discovered many people have similar feelings. Unless they happen to be one of your hometown teams, too-frequent winners in sports tend not to be appreciated. "Everybody loves a winner" is a truism that, in sports, doesn't hold up.

Of course, I speak as a fan, and a fan, it is well to remember, is short for a fanatic. Sports in America may well be the opiate of the people, but, as opiates go, it isn't a bad one. Often when watching a game on television, I will note the television camera focus on the crowd, whose members are to be found, index fingers raised aloft, screaming, "We're number one! We're number one!" and think how easily, in another country, similar faces might be screaming, "Perón! Perón!" or "Khomeini! Khomeini!" I have never seen an adequate explanation for the passion of the fan. Roger Angell, who writes about baseball for the *New Yorker*, has written that "belonging and caring" is what being a fan is about. But I have encountered too many instances of behavior on the part of fans that go beyond mere belonging and caring. I have a cousin with ulcers whose doctor advised him, unsuccessfully, to stop listening to Chicago Cubs games. Of fans of the same team, I recently read about a widow who each spring places a Cubs pennant on her husband's grave. A Chicago Cubs fan myself, when that team in 1984 lost its first chance to appear in a World Series in thirty-nine years by dropping its final play-off game to the San Diego Padres, I found I was mired in a slough of glumness that lasted fully a week. Fan-tastic. Such behavior cannot be explained to anyone who is not interested in sports; I cannot quite explain it to myself.

If we tend to idolize our athletes more than our politicians, I do not think that altogether a bad thing. I myself have not idolized an athlete since I was a small boy, but I have enjoyed the hell out of the really superior ones. *Dumb* appears before the word *jock* as frequently as *wily* before the name *Ho Chi Minh* and *untimely* before *death*, but I, for one, don't think athletes are unintelligent. They are unbookish, certainly; inarticulate, frequently; but dumb, scarcely ever, at least not at high levels of play. Instead their intelligence is concentrated upon their craft, and this they know in a way I can only hope I know about my own craft of writing. The only place I have ever seen the intelligence of athletes recognized is in the novel *Guard of Honor*, by James Gould Cozzens, where one of the book's protagonists assigns a military mission of importance to a young officer partly on the basis of his having played Big Ten football and thus being used to exerting his intelligence under real pressure.

While I do not idolize athletes, neither do I envy them. I consider them privileged human beings, men and women who have drawn lucky numbers in life's lottery. They are in the condition of someone born beautiful or to extremely wealthy parents. Lucky indeed. Professional athletes play games they love for salaries that take them effectively out of the financial wars that the rest of us must go on fighting our lives long. For a time the huge salaries that athletes have in recent years begun to earn bothered me. They are, in fact, immensely overpaid. Yet, as the economist Sherwin Rosen has explained, in an essay entitled "The Economics of Superstars," owing to television and now cable television revenues, the money is there, and I myself would just as soon that Julius Erving, or Dave Winfield, or Walter Payton have ample chunks of it than that even more of it go to some real estate or insurance millionaire who owns a sports franchise chiefly to soothe his own itch for publicity. Some say that athletes are too privileged, that they garner too many rewards too soon. I recall once watching an interview with Wayne Gretzky, the great hockey player of the Edmonton Oilers. One of the television broadcasters pointed out to him that he, Gretzky, was then at twenty-three already a millionaire many times over, that he had broken most of the records in his sport, that he would go down in history as one of the greatest hockey players the world has known. "Well, Wayne," the broadcaster said, "what can you possibly have to look forward to?" Gretzky, not a fiercely articulate fellow, paused, then said, "Tonight's game."

Addict and fanatic that I am, I must also confess that few of the supposed "issues" having to do with sports in its contemporary settings greatly trouble me. Amateurism, for one, is an issue upon which much false piety has been expended. In college athletics violations having to do with recruiting athletes do occur, and are punished when discovered. But everyone—excepting perhaps the officials of the National Collegiate Athletic Association—assumes that a great many others go undiscovered. I once heard a radio announcer, a former pro football player covering a Chicago Bears–Detroit Lions game, ask where a tackle on the Lions had gone to college. "Notre Dame," said his companion in the broadcast booth. "He went from Notre Dame to Detroit?" the first announcer responded. "Hmm. He must have taken quite a cut in pay." The next week the announcer himself took quite a cut in pay, for he was fired. Perhaps rightly. Violations in amateur sports are like adultery: everyone knows it goes on; still, it will not do to talk about it too openly.

Tennis has now all but dispensed with amateurism, and nearly all involved in the sport feel better for having done so. Track and field looks as if it might be the next sport to do so. In Eastern European and other Communist countries there is no hypocrisy about amateurism because there isn't any amateurism; in this regard one may say about them what Randall Jarrell said about the college president in his novel *Pictures from an Institution*: "He had not evolved to the stage of moral development at which hypocrisy is possible." Most universities and colleges that have big-time football and basketball programs have arrived at that requisite stage of moral development—and, hence, at hypocrisy, too. With millions and millions of dollars involved in gate receipts and television revenues and millions more for those teams that get to bowl games and postseason tournaments, college athletics aren't what they used to be.

But, then, neither is college. And because it is not, because so much of the prestige of college has been dissipated and the quality of education degraded, it becomes more and more difficult to think of the majority of college athletes at schools with big-time programs as anything other than young men serving out their athletic apprenticeships in the hope of one day becoming professionals. When such basketball players as Magic Johnson and Isaiah Thomas leave school at the end of their second or third year, or when a young man skips college altogether to make a run at a baseball career, one no longer exclaims, sadly, "But their education! What a shame!" Education is good, after all, only if it is really education. What is impressive to me is a young man who plays a major sport at a major school and is still able to find time to devote himself to serious studies, let alone excel in them. My guess is that the number of such young men is not legion.

At this point I believe I am scheduled to deliver a political rant, bemoaning the rise of the power of money and the fall of the prestige of education. But sports fans, when it comes to sports, are curiously apolitical. They tend to take the world of sports pretty much as they find it. Within the realm of sports itself, they tend to be purist conservative— that is, they want the sports world forever to remain as they found it. Innovation is anathema. Apart from improvements in equipment, almost all changes that affect the games themselves are regarded as regrettable. This at any rate is my view. I dislike the advent of Astro Turf in baseball and football; I dislike the new dominance of the slam dunk in basketball; I dislike the designated hitter in baseball; I dislike the tie-breaker in tennis. . . . Some sports seem less sacrosanct than others: gradual changes in the game of pro football are permissible, yet alter baseball and you are fooling with the liturgy. To paraphrase the old and long-dead Chicago alderman Paddy Bauler, "Sports ain't ready for reform."

As much pleasure as sports have given me over the years, I am sure I do not want to have more to do with them than I now do. True, before I hang up my couch, I should like to see, in person, "live," a few World Series games, a Super Bowl, a Kentucky Derby, a Wimbledon final. But I shouldn't want to be a sportswriter or broadcaster. I once wrote an article about an elegant pro basketball player named Bob Love; in preparation for it I went to eight or ten of his team's practice sessions; I interviewed him and his coach and his teammates. Along with the fee for the article, I was given a press pass for a full season's games. It was good fun, superior jock-sniffing. Somehow, though, I felt too much like a camp follower, which is the true relation of the press to the actions they cover. One such article is all I ever care to write. Visiting the toy department is nice, but who wants to live there?

In watching sports, I seek not so much a golden mean or even a silver one but will settle for something akin to a tarnished bronze mean. Achieving anything like real moderation here is now well beyond me. If I never watch another game, I have already seen many more than my share. But I fully intend to watch another game, and another and another and another. My justification is that doing so gives me great delight; my defense is that it causes no known harm, and, on occasion, I learn a thing or two from it. A number of years ago I recall hearing that Eric Sevareid, who was then reading the Sunday evening news on CBS, complained that it was demeaning to as serious a man as he to have to give the day's sports scores on his news show. I hope that this is true, for if it isn't I owe Mr. Sevareid an apology for thinking of him, ever after, as a starter on my All-American Pomposity team, along with William Jennings Bryan, Daniel Ellsberg, Barbara Walters, and the older Orson Welles. I don't know about anyone else, but I would rather have those sports scores than Eric Sevareid's opinions about NATO, the Sino-Soviet dispute, and the balance of payments. Not that I don't think about such things. I do, but I can't say that I look forward to them. What do I look forward to? Among other things, like Wayne Gretzky, to tonight's game.

CONFESSIONS OF A LOW ROLLER

Ours has long been a distinguished publishing family, if you take the adjective "distinguished" in a loose sense and if you allow a definition of "publishing" broad enough to include bookmaking. I don't mean to brag about family lineage, but I had an uncle, dead some years now, who had fully two sobriquets: in some quarters he was known as Lefty and in others as Square Sam. All gamblers, it is often enough said, die broke, but my uncle, whom I scarcely knew, is reported to have left the planet with something on the order of twenty-five Ultrasuede jackets hanging in the closet of his home in Los Angeles. Beginning life as a professional gambler, he soon went into publishing (or bookmaking) and eventually owned a small piece of a large casino-hotel in Las Vegas. To place him for you socially, he was a man at whose granddaughter's wedding a guest was Frank Sinatra. Need I say more?

Although this uncle did not carry my family name, there was a prominent gambler who did. Some years ago I read a lengthy obituary in a Chicago newspaper about a man who carried my exact name, Joseph Epstein, and who was described in the obit headline as "Gentleman Big-Time Bookie, Dies at 75." My namesake—or am I his?—turns out to have run, in the words of the obituarist, "a large betting layoff operation from offices [that covered] wagers that bookies across the nation could not handle." The obituarist continued: "Although his associates were more often coarse, devious, violent men, [he] had the reputation of a bookmaker who kept his word and was mild-mannered in the extreme. He was well-read, fancied himself as a Talmudic scholar and was clearly the intellectual bookie of his time." It gets better. It seems that this Joseph Epstein also served as a Professor Henry Higgins to a gang-land moll named Virginia Hill, who came to Chicago from Alabama at seventeen, whose great and good friend, as *Time* magazine used to put it, he was, though she finally left him for Benjamin (Bugsy) Siegel. "A nonsmoker," the obituary notes, "he remained in robust health almost until his death by taking long, daily walks through the city [of Chicago] from his hotel on Ohio St."

The gentleman big-time bookie bearing my name died in Chicago in 1976, a fact that fills me with double regret, first for his death, for he appears to have been a decent sort, and second because I wish I had had the chance to meet and talk with him. It is not about the Talmud that I wish I could have talked with "the intellectual bookie of his time," but about shop—specifically, about gambling. No photograph appeared with his obituary, but I imagine him to be a smallish man, silver-haired, expensively yet not gaudily dressed, good shoes well shined, nails mani-cured. We might have walked along Michigan Boulevard together on a late, lightly breezy afternoon in May, past Tiffany and Cartier and Saks Fifth Avenue and Neiman Marcus, stopping off for an aperitif in the cool, wood-paneled Coq d'Or bar in the Drake Hotel. Seated at one of the small tables in the dark room where sound tends to be gen-tly muffled, I would have encouraged him to recount anecdotes about noble behavior on the part of crooks, in exchange for which I would have supplied him with anecdotes about what crooks academics can be. We should, I do not doubt, have addressed each other as "Mister," with the charm of adding to it our selfsame last name.

If the mood were right, perhaps our talk might have ascended to philosophy, always within the confines of shop, of course. Why do men gamble? I might have asked him. Is gambling in the end always a ruin-ous diversion? Is there something masochistic about it? Was Malraux right when he called it, in connection with his character Clappique in *Man's Fate*, "suicide without death"? Is gambling not a metaphor but a metaphorical activity, since, as has been noted, life itself goes off at something like 6–5 against, though some think these odds unduly gen-erous? Why does gambling excite, exhilarate, and depress some people while not arousing the least interest in others? What does gambling do for those people who go in for it in a big way? For those who enjoy it only occasionally? And, while I am at it, I might just have lowered the tone of the conversation and inquired if I was a chump to agree to an arrangement whereby I would have to pay 10 percent juice, or vigorish, on a $300 bet on the past year's World Series.

Consider, please, that figure $300, or $330 if I lost. Something rather hopeless about those numbers, if you ask me, something neither here nor there. I had originally intended to bet $1,000 ("a grand," in the grand old term), which is a good deal more than I have ever bet on anything, and then I decided that $500 was sufficient. But when I reached an old friend who has a bookie—I bet much too infrequently to have my own bookie—I heard myself say $300. I don't mean to suggest that $300 is a negligible sum; if one is down and out, it is a most impressive sum. I am sure that someone reading this is ready to inform me, in a properly moral tone, that a family of four could eat for a month on $300. Nowadays, though, there are restaurants in New York where one has to cut corners—go for the California instead of the French wine—to get a full dinner for two for less than $300. I myself consider it immoral to dine in such places. "It is all," as Albert Einstein must at some time have said to Max Planck, "relative."

If all this sounds a little goofy, it is merely because it is. No activity has been more rationalized than gambling—odds figured, probabilities worked out, point spreads meticulously established—and no activity, surely, is finally more irrational. In this essentially irrational activity, the first item that must be fixed, and with some precision, is the stake. Above all, it cannot be too little; it must be enough to stimulate whatever those emotional glands are that gambling calls into action. The punishment must fit the crime; the agony of losing must be roughly equivalent to the ecstasy of winning. In this sense, it becomes clear that no bet can ever be too large; and herein lies the madness inherent in gambling, for the more you have, the more you need to risk.

"Important money" is what professional gamblers used to call big bets, and such fabled gamblers as Pittsburgh Phil (a horseplayer), Nick the Greek (cards and dice), and Ray Ryan (gin rummy) never played for unimportant money. Nick the Greek, whose last name was Dandolos, claimed once to have bet $280,000 on a five coming up before a seven in a crap game. The same Mr. Dandolos is said to have lost $900,000 in a single night in New York on the eve of a holiday trip to Europe, which—Surprise! Surprise!—had to be canceled. Winning a bet, Nick

Dandolos used to say, is man's greatest pleasure; the second greatest pleasure, he held, is losing a bet. In more than fifty years of serious gambling, something on the order of $50 million is supposed to have trafficked in and out of his hands. Yet Nick the Greek was no money snob. The late Jimmy Cannon, the sportswriter, told the story of the Greek's playing twenty-four hours straight at Arnold Rothstein's crap table and, after the crap game broke up, sitting down to play casino for twenty-five cents a hand with one of Rothstein's stickmen. "Action is all he wants," Cannon concluded, "and he has lasted longer than any of them and held on to his dignity."

Some gamblers get a thrill out of the action itself, while others need to be in action at high prices. The greater the stakes, the greater the pressure, the greater the cool (or courage) required. Damon Runyon, a gambler all his life and a student of gamblers, maintained he knew "men who will beat far better card players at gin [rummy] if the stakes are high enough just on simple courage." A gambler is like an airplane in that at a certain altitude—for the gambler, at certain high sums—the controls start to shake. I earlier mentioned certain emotional glands that needed to be stimulated by gambling, but anatomical ones are often also called into play, producing sweaty hands, dry mouth, inconvenient loss of control of the facial muscles. No, nothing quite relaxes a fella like an evening of gambling.

Growing up in Chicago, I had a friend whose father was reputed to have bet $100,000 on a baseball game—and lost. This was during the early 1940s, when $100,000 was extremely important money and not the annual salary of a Marxist professor of English at Duke University. Inconveniently, my friend's father didn't have the money; conveniently, there was a war on. As the story goes, he showed up the next afternoon at the bookie's with a smile and in a set of U.S. Navy bell-bottoms, having enlisted that morning. The uniform, supposedly, saved his life, for no one was about to kill a man in uniform during wartime, and he was able to arrange terms to pay off his debt.

What made him bet such a sum? He was living in Los Angeles at the time—always a hot gambling town, according to Damon Runyon—and must have waked one sunny weekday morning (I always imagine it to be a Tuesday) in an impatient mood. A voice within must have whispered, "Let 'er rip!" He did, and it nearly tore him in two.

Almost all baseball games were played during the day at that time, so he must have known not much later than 3:30 P.M. Los Angeles time that he had made a serious mistake. I am pleased not to have been the one to serve him that evening's dinner, or to have to ask him if the lamb was properly underdone.

He died before I knew him, whether of heart attack, cancer, or stroke I cannot recall, but he couldn't have been more than in his early fifties. His wife and only son lived on after him in what I think of not as shabby gentility but elegant shabbility. They lived in a small one-bedroom apartment in a building with a doorman on a once posh but now fading Chicago street. Wife and son spoke of him with affection and awe, and in one corner of the small apartment were framed glossy signed photographs taken of him in the company of famous Jewish comedians and Italian singers—or was it Italian comedians and Jewish singers? Not a marathon man, he lived life at a sprint, going fast and dying young. Why is it that we look with wonder upon a man who one day bets $100,000 on the outcome of a game and loses yet feel no wonder whatsoever looking upon a man who works a lifetime to stow away a few million?

My own interest in gambling—and now we return to someone never likely to have the mad courage to bet $100,000 or the powers of concentration to earn millions—initially derived from the social atmosphere in which I came of age. By this I certainly don't mean my home. My father had not the least interest in cards, sports, or gambling generally, preferring situations, such as the one he had inserted himself into as the owner of a small business, in which as far as possible he could control his own destiny. Most of the men in the rising middle-class Jewish milieu that I grew up in felt much the same. They were physicians and lawyers and businessmen and worked hard so that their children could have an easier life than they, as the sons of immigrants, had had. Some among them gambled—played a little gin rummy or in a small-stakes poker game, bet $50 on a prizefight—but clearly work was at the center of their lives. They believed in personal industry, in thrift, in saving for the future. Entrepreneurial in spirit, they also believed that only a fool works for someone else.

On the periphery, though, were a small number of men who lived and believed otherwise. Two boys among my school friends and acquaintances had fathers who were bookies, and rather big-time ones, judging by the scale on which they lived. Nothing back-of-the-candy-store or Broadway-cigar stand about them; they were rather like the rest of our fathers, but home more often and with better tans and more telephones in the house. They lived on the edge of the criminal world. So, too, I gather did the father of a girl I knew in high school; he played golf from April until October and from October until April played high-stakes gin rummy at a place atop the Sheraton Hotel called the Town Club; the younger brother of a Capone lieutenant, he was rumored to collect a dollar a month on every jukebox installed in Chicago. The brother of a man I once worked for when I was in high school was said to be a full-time gambler, making his living (he was a bachelor) betting on sports events. In his forties then, he carried the nickname "Acey"; if he is still alive, he would now be in his seventies, which is a bit old to carry around such a nickname. I would often see him at baseball games on weekday afternoons, where, well groomed and well rested, he looked as if his personal motto, an abridged version of my father's and my friends' fathers', might read: "Only a fool works."

When young, I felt a strong attraction to such men. The attraction was to their seemingly effortless access to what I then took to be the higher and finer things in life. Their connection to corruption also excited me. Corruption was endemic to Chicago, a city that prided itself on its gangsters the way that other cities were proud of their artists, and one had to be brought up in a glass bubble—make that an isinglass bubble—not to come in contact with it. Dickens, Dostoyevsky, Dreiser, and many a novelist since knew that corruption is more alluring, and more convincingly described, than goodness. Goodness, on first acquaintance, is a bit boring—and, when young, the only thing duller than goodness is common sense.

I had an acquaintance whose father became a very rich man in a very brief time through selling very ugly aluminum awnings. One Saturday afternoon I went with him to his father's small factory, where, among his father and his father's salesmen, each with a high stack of bills in front of him, a serious poker game was in progress. My own father often used the phrase "place of business" with something of the same reverence that some reserve for the phrase "place of worship," and the idea of a poker game on the site of his business would have appalled him. At the time, it rather thrilled me. But then it would be many years until I came round to my father's view, which was essentially the view set out by Henry James in a youthful letter to his friend Charles Eliot Norton: "I have in my own fashion learned the lesson that life is effort, unremittingly repeated . . . I feel somehow as if the real pity was for those who had been beguiled into the perilous delusion that it isn't."

So beguiled, I spent much of my adolescence in imitation of what I took to be the model of the gambler. During our last year of grammar school, my friends and I met for penny poker games on Saturday afternoons before ballroom-dancing lessons. There we sat, at thirteen years old, neckties loosened, jackets draped over the backs of chairs, cigarettes depending unsteadily from the sides of our mouths, smoke causing our eyes to water and squint, playing seven-card stud, deuces usually wild. Quite a scene. Each of us must have thought himself some variant of George Raft, James Cagney, Humphrey Bogart, or John Garfield, when Leo Gorcey and the Dead End Kids gone middle-class was much more like it. "My pair of jacks see your three cents, Ronald, and I bump you a nickel."

A misspent youth? I suppose it was, though I never thought of it as such. Perhaps this was owing to its being so immensely enjoyable. In high school, gambling went from an occasional to an almost incessant activity. Although we never shot dice, my friends and I played every variation of poker, blackjack, and gin rummy. From city newsstand vendors we acquired and bet football parlay cards. Every so often, on weekend nights, we would travel out of the city to the sulky races, or "the trotters" as we called them, at Maywood Park. Some unrecognized genius among us invented a game called "pot-luck," a combination of blackjack and in-between, which guaranteed that no matter how minimal the stakes to begin with, one would soon be playing for more than one could afford. With its built-in escalation element, pot-luck was a game that produced high excitement, for it was not unusual for someone to walk away from these games a $200 winner. I won my share, but more vividly than any win do I remember one gray wintry afternoon when, between four and six o'clock, I lost $80—this at a time when that figure might pay a month's rent on a two-bedroom apartment in a respectable middle-class neighborhood. If the end of the world had been announced on that evening's news, I, at seventeen, shouldn't in the least have minded. In fact, as I recall, I felt it already had.

Gambling, though scarcely a valuable education in itself, did teach a thing or two about one's own nature. I learned about the limits of my courage with money, for one thing; for another, I learned that in gambling, as in life, you could figure the odds, the probabilities, the little and large likelihoods, and still, when lightning struck in the form of ill luck, logic was no help. I learned I had to put a good, and insofar as possible stylish, face on defeat, even though losing was very far from my idea of a nice time. If you were even mildly attentive, gambling revealed your character to you, showed it in operation under pressure, often taught you the worst about yourself. Some people wanted to win too sorely; they whined and moaned, banged the table and cursed the gods when they lost and seemed smug and self-justified in victory. Others sat grim and humorless over their cards, gloomy in defeat and always ready to settle for a small win. Still others exhibited, even at sixteen or seventeen, a certain largeness of spirit; they were ready to trust their luck; they had a feeling for the game, which I took to be a feeling for life itself, and were delighted to be in action.

"In action" is an old gambler's phrase; and "the action" used to refer to gambling generally. Yet, for all its insistence on action, gambling can be excruciatingly boring. During one stretch in the army, I played poker at Fort Chaffee, in Arkansas, almost nightly for roughly six weeks; I played less for the excitement of gambling than to combat the boredom of army life when one is confined to a post. It turned out to be boredom pitted against boredom. In a rather low-stakes game over this period I emerged roughly a $400 winner. Some of this money I sent to a friend to buy me books in Chicago. The rest I spent on a steak and champagne dinner in the town of Fort Smith, Arkansas, for eight or nine barracks mates. Doing this seemed to me at the time a gesture of magnificence befitting a gambling man.

I remember this especially because it is the only use to which I can ever remember putting any money that I have won gambling. I cannot otherwise recall buying with gambling winnings a sweater, a shirt, a pair of socks, a Q-Tip. Such money has had a way of disappearing from me. Poof: not very easily come, altogether mysteriously gone. Which reminds me that gambling has never, for me, been primarily about money. I was fortunate, of course, in never having to gamble with money intended for rent or food, thereby, as a character in Pushkin's gambling story "Queen of Spades" puts it, risking "the necessary to win the superfluous." When the money wasn't there—when I was a young husband and father with no extra "tease," as the old horseplayers used to call money—I was easily enough able to refrain from gambling, which strengthens me in my cherished belief that as a gambler I am merely a dreamer and a fool and not an addict.

Gambling addicts are not on the whole an elegant sight. The crowds one encounters at a Nevada casino or at a sulky track on a wintry Wednesday night are quite as depressing as those at a national meeting of the Modern Language Association. Many years ago, in an effort to turn up a bit of tease without actually having to gamble for it, I wrote a piece of journalism on an outfit known as Gamblers Anonymous, which operates on the same principles—confession and comradeship in crisis—as Alcoholics Anonymous. At these meetings one hears an *Iliad* of woe, with enough material left over for an *Odyssey* of misery and an *Aeneid* of heartbreak: story after story of disappointed children, weeping wives, broken homes accompanying unpaid debts, busted-up marriages destroyed by busted-out gamblers. On view here is the other side of gambling, the creepy and crummy side, where a man recounts how he broke into his son's silver-dollar piggy bank for action money, then says nothing when his wife accuses his young son's best friend of taking the money; a man . . . but you get the general idea.

A more particular idea that attendance at these Gamblers Anonymous meetings conveys is the power that gambling can exert over those hooked on it. In its thrall, all other appetites tend to diminish. While one is gambling, food is of no interest, nor is alcohol. Gambling can also throw off one's interior clock, and while at it one is capable of prodigious wakefulness, so that, within limits, gambling can be said to triumph over time and fatigue. When serious gambling is going on, sex seems quite beside the point. At the compulsive level, gambling is all-consuming, and while it doesn't, like drugs or alcohol, fog the mind, it generally monopolizes it. When winning at gambling, one is in the country of the blue; when losing, the world seems mean and red and utterly hopeless. Gambling, one is either flying or crawling, elated or degraded. If any gambler was ever able to find the golden mean, he would probably bet it on the six horse in the fourth race at Pimlico.

As an activity that issues only in extreme states, gambling is of course a great Russian subject. Russians have gone in for gambling in a big way, both actually and literarily. Pushkin turned a card or two in his time, and his story "Queen of Spades" gives ample evidence of his knowing at first hand the desolation of a resounding defeat at the tables. The dissipated young Count Leo Tolstoy was passionate about cards, and not very good at them, even though he devised a system that he set down on paper under the title "Rules for Card-Playing"; like many another such system, it plunged its creator into great debt. A 3,000-ruble loss forced Tolstoy to put himself on a 10-ruble-a-month budget. After suffering gambling losses, the young count would proceed to flog himself—in his diary, of course. When his debts grew too great, he could always sell off a meadow or forest or horses from his estate. This is the stuff out of which nineteenth-century Russian novels are made. Tolstoy didn't simply make it all up.

Nor did Dostoyevsky, whose gambling problem ran deeper than Tolstoy's if only because he, not being an aristocrat, had no estate to sell off to clear his debts. Unlike Tolstoy, too, Dostoyevsky's gambling was not a form of dissipation. He gambled for the most commonsensical of reasons: he needed the money. The problem is that gambling—especially roulette, which was Dostoyevsky's game—may be the quickest but is clearly not the most efficient way of obtaining it. According to Joseph Frank, in his splendid biography of Dostoyevsky, the novelist was unfortunate in winning 11,000 francs in his first attempt at gambling. The hook was in. Yet Dostoyevsky, again according to Professor Frank, was not a pathological gambler but a fitful and sporadic one. He suffered the inability that gamblers share with gluttons—that of not knowing when to leave the table. After each of his inevitably disastrous gambling episodes, Joseph Frank reports, "Dostoyevsky always returned to his writing desk with renewed vigor and a strong sense of deliverance." Dostoyevsky's losses, then, turned out to be world literature's gain. Fate sometimes uses a strange accounting system.

A highly superstitious man, ever on the lookout for omens and portents, Dostoyevsky had a theory about how to win at gambling that was utterly opposed to his own nature. Dostoyevsky's theory, or system, or secret called for mastery of the emotions while in action. "This secret," Dostoyevsky writes in a letter, "I really know it; it's terribly stupid and simple and consists in holding oneself in at every moment and not to get excited, no matter what the play. And that's all; it's then absolutely impossible to lose, and one is sure of winning." Tolstoy's system, too, called for control of the emotions and moderation—precisely the two things Tolstoy himself was incapable of achieving. "Those who are indifferent are those who are rewarded," wrote Jack Richardson, formulating this view in a single, short, well-made sentence in *Memoir of a Gambler*, his elegant, amusing, and profound book that itself sadly came up snake-eyes, double-zero, and busto in the casino of American publishing when it first appeared in 1979. Richardson's view, like those of Dostoyevsky and Tolstoy, assumes that the gods who watch over gambling are themselves not indifferent or likely to be fooled by men pretending to a coolness it is not theirs to control. That either assumption is correct is, at best, 9–2 against.

If gambling seems an activity well suited to the Russian temperament with its taste for provoking fate, it is very far from un-American. To have come to America in the first place was to take a serious gamble. To advance with the country's frontier was another gamble. When one says that Americans like to gamble, one is of course really saying that the people who have come to America like to gamble. Whenever I have been in a casino, I have noted what seemed to me a high percentage of Asians, most of them Chinese. Jimmy Cannon recalls the older Irishmen in Greenwich Village, where he grew up, disapproving of gambling unless a man was single. Blacks were big for the numbers game and are now, I observe, heavy players in state lotteries. Jews and Italians grew up in gambling cultures—or at least they did when I was a boy—and some among them cross to the other side of the table, becoming bookies or casino owners, donning the expressionless face and the Ultrasuede jacket, like my deceased uncle, most righteous of Leftys, squarest of Sams. Texans, to touch on what is almost another ethnic group, have been known to be most earnest about poker played for heart-attack stakes. All of these are what are known as risky generalizations, subject to vehement exceptions: a friend who grew up in a Jewish working-class neighborhood, for example, informs me that in his youth a gambler was considered lower even than a Rumanian. Various anti-defamation leagues— Chinese, Black, Jewish, Italian, Irish, Texan, Rumanian—wishing to protest this paragraph may reach me at my office, care of the director, Center for Advanced Ethnic Insensitivity.

Men seem to go in for gambling more than women because, as boys, they often play games and thus early acquire the habits of competition. Games that absorb one's energies in the playing of them do not require gambling for enjoyment. This is true of football, basketball, and baseball—on which men do often bet to get their competitive juices flowing after they are no longer able to play the games themselves—as well as tennis, running, and gymnastics. It isn't true of golf, which needs the stimulus of little side bets to get one round the course, or billiards, every shot of which seems to cry out for a bet. Chess and bridge are games of sufficient intellectual intricacy to be played without gambling, even though I realize many people—Somerset Maugham among them—have played bridge for high stakes. Poker, blackjack, and gin rummy without money riding on the outcome are games suitable only for some knotty-pined recreation room in hell.

In bringing up boyhood with regard to gambling, I am, I fear, playing into the strong hand of the Freudians. This is a dangerous thing to do, for those guys will sandbag you and whipsaw you. They endlessly raise the stakes. If you open by allowing that gambling is connected with youth, they will call and raise you by saying that it is a neurosis. Bid that gambling can give pleasure, they return by saying—I quote Dr. Otto Fenichel in *The Psychoanalytic Theory of Neurosis*—that the passion for gambling "is a displaced expression of conflicts around infantile sexuality, aroused by the fear of losing necessary reassurance regarding anxiety or guilt feelings." Aver that gambling issues in excitement, they—I quote Dr. Fenichel again—will counter by asserting that "the unconscious 'masturbatory fantasies' of gambling often center around patricide." I realize that W. H. Auden once remarked that "the attitude of psychology should always be, 'Have you heard this one?'" but "masturbatory fantasies" and "patricide"? Is this what is truly going on when one gambles? I wouldn't bet on it.

Freud claimed that much of what he knew he learned from the poets, and I, for one, would rather consult the poets than the Freudians on the subject of gambling. Unfortunately, the poets—and writers generally—do not seem to have had all that much to say about it. Pushkin's story "Queen of Spades" is about a young officer who commits murder in the attempt to obtain a secret system for winning at cards, a murder that is revenged when the system betrays him and causes him to live out his days in madness. Pushkin's is a morality tale and is not quite up to the mark either in explaining or depicting the passion for gambling. Dostoyevsky's *The Gambler* is much more like it. The novella's scenes set in the casino are absolutely convincing, not only in detail but in the understanding behind them of the wild roller coaster the gambler travels from exhilaration ("I was only aware of an immense enjoyment—success, victory, power—I don't know how to describe it") to damnable despair expressed in "calm fury" at realizing that one is not "above all these stupid ups and downs of fate" but finally, like everyone else, their victim. *The Gambler* is not among Dostoyevsky's great works; with its characters' propensity for bizarre behavior and the many loose ends that never quite get tied up at the story's conclusion, it is perhaps rather too Dostoyevskian, but it does have the immense authority of a work written by a man who knew his subject from the inside.

For my money, though, the best literary work on the subject of gambling was written by an outsider. That story is "James Pethel" in the collection *Seven Men* by Max Beerbohm, who, so far as I know, had no interest whatsoever in gambling. The James Pethel of Beerbohm's story is known as an active taker of big risks and one who has had tremendous good luck: in stock market speculation, at the baccarat tables at the casino at Dieppe, on wildly venturesome foreign investments. Beerbohm makes plain that the mere sight of habitual gamblers "always filled me with a depression bordering on disgust." Pethel, however, is no ordinary gambler. On the night that he and Beerbohm meet, after Beerbohm warns him that the water isn't safe to drink, Pethel is encouraged to order not one but two glasses of it, the risk of typhoid only making it more enticing. Casino gambling, one learns, is really only Pethel's way of keeping in trim for such ventures as swimming in dangerous water, driving at maniacal speed (with his wife and daughter, whom he dearly loves, and Beerbohm in the car), and stunt flying. Pethel is, in short, a risk freak, the ultimate gambler who can finally be stimulated only by the ultimate gambles—those in which his own life and the lives of those he loves are on the line. The story is made all the more chilling when at the end we learn that Pethel has died of a heart attack after a flying session, with his daughter and her infant son aboard, and that he had been suffering from a bad heart condition for many years. Beerbohm, with consummate artistry, concludes: "Let not our hearts be vexed that his great luck was with him to the end."

Max Beerbohm despises James Pethel; adore Max Beerbohm though I do, I cannot come down so strongly on his creation, even though I recognize him for the monster he is. The reason I cannot is that through my veins run a few stray particles of the virulent virus that has him firmly in its grip. To the vast majority of people it never occurs to gamble—on anything. To others the possibility of gambling is scratched at the painful prospect of losing; Montaigne, interestingly, was among this group, for, though a cardplayer and crapshooter in his youth, he gave up gambling for the reason that "however good a face I put upon my losses, I did not fail to feel stung by them within." A small group of us feel the same sting Montaigne did—with, I suspect, quite the same intensity—but persist. Why?

Why, I ask myself, do I, who am surely among the world's luckiest men in my career and family life (I touch wood as I write out that last clause), need to risk $330 on a series of baseball games, the outcome of which is otherwise of less than negligible interest to me? I think it has to do with the need I from time to time feel for venturing forth, for striking out against what has become the general quietude and orderliness of my life. As a boy, I never expected to live so calmly as I now do, with the risk of sending up my cholesterol count from eating an occasional steak being perhaps the biggest chance I take. I live, by a choice I do not quite recall having made, a quiet life, for the most part contemplating the world's foolishness instead of partaking in it directly. But when the quiet life grows too quiet, when it threatens to lapse into the most dread disease I know, which is fear of living, then I call on the antidote of gambling.

Perhaps there are quicker antidotes than a World Series bet on which the tension can be drawn out over more than a week's time. But this was the medicine nearest to hand, and I availed myself of it. Observing myself in action over the course of what turned out to be an extended gamble provided its own slightly tortured amusement. As the Series unfolded, I went from mild depression to measured hopefulness to dignified optimism to serene confidence. I passed a local jeweler's window and noted that he was running a sale of 40 percent off on

Movado wristwatches. I already own a Movado watch, but I thought I might use my winnings to buy another. Then it occurred to me to begin a small gambling account, out of which I would begin betting more regularly than I do now. Grand plans were abuilding when—*wham!*—the team I had bet on lost the last two games of the World Series, and I was seated at my desk writing out a check for $330.

The gods, it is pleasing to learn, are still watching over me.

BALLS-UP

Three fantasies:

Primo: A Manhattan town house at a quite good address. The women in the room are very smartly dressed; the men are in dinner clothes. My hostess comes up to ask if I will agree to play. I demur, thanking her all the same. "Oh, please do," she says, with an earnestness I cannot find it in my heart to refuse. As I move toward the piano, a well-polished Baldwin grand, I hear a woman say, "He's going to play." Across the room, another woman murmurs, "He's going to play—I was so hoping he would!" I rub my hands together briefly, bend and unbend my fingers, and proceed to toss off a flawless rendering of "Rhapsody in Blue." As I finish, I notice that everyone seems to have gathered round the piano. Ice cubes tinkle; cigarette smoke wafts to the ceiling. I play and sing two Cole Porter songs, then follow up with Noel Coward's "Imagine the Duchess's Feelings," which has everyone in stitches. I move on to play and sing—first in English, then in French—"I Won't Dance." I close, gently and with just a touch of profundity, with "September Song." Applause envelops me. "Now that," says my hostess, handing me a fresh drink, "was simply unforgettable!"

Secondo: A hill overlooking the Loire Valley. I appear over the crest of the hill in white linen trousers, a chambray shirt, a wide-brimmed straw hat of the kind Pope John XXIII used to wear when he would go into the streets of Rome. It is a perfect day: the sun shines, flowers are everywhere in bloom, the river is a serene azure. I set up my easel, my canvas chair, and, before beginning to mix my palette, eat a lunch of what Henry James once called "light cold clever French things." After lunch, working in watercolors, I begin to paint the vista before me in a strong line and with a use of color that falls between that of Degas and Dufy. I achieve a work that is obviously representational yet, such is the force of my character, my sensibility, my vision, is just as obviously a small masterpiece. When I am done, I put away my materials with the confidence of a man who, though he knows he is out of step with the times, knows that his own time will come.

Terzo: A large empty room, good wood floors, clean light flowing in from the windows along its north wall. On the south wall is a mirror reaching from floor to ceiling. I enter, remove my suit coat, loosen my tie. I stretch my arms out to the side, turn my head first clockwise, then counterclockwise. I bend over to pick up three rubber balls, one red, one yellow, one blue. I toss the red ball from my right hand to my left, then back again to my right hand. I feel the heft and balance of each of the balls in my hands. I begin to juggle them, flipping a new ball into the air each time the previous one reaches its peak and begins its descent, all the while softly humming to myself the strains of "Lady of Spain." After three or four minutes of this, I add a fourth ball, a green one, which joins the cascade I create by juggling the balls gingerly from hand to hand. Then I add a fifth ball, orange; later a sixth, purple. Six balls in the air! The cascade has now become a rainbow revolving before me. My control is complete, my pleasure in this control no less. My only regret is that there is not room in my hands for a seventh ball. Perspiring lightly, effortlessly keeping all these balls in the air, I smile as I hum "Over the Rainbow."

Now of these three fantasies, two are not merely improbable but, for me, utterly impossible. Although I spend a goodly amount of time listening to CDs and going to concerts, I can neither read music nor play a musical instrument. Worse, I was one of those children who, in grade school, was asked not to sing but just to mouth the words, lest my naturally off-key voice carry the rest of the class along with me into the thickets of dissonance. My drawing was of roughly the same discouraging caliber. In school periods devoted to art, teachers who walked up and down the aisles checking their students' sketches and paintings never stopped, or even hesitated, to gaze at mine, which were so clearly beyond help or comment. If there were an artistic equivalent to mouthing words—a colorless crayon, say, or disappearing paint—I would, I am certain, have been asked to avail myself of it.

Denied these two gifts, of song and of drawing, I have, in life's rather arbitrary lottery, been allotted a third. I am reasonably well coordinated. Delete that "reasonably": I am extremely well coordinated. ("Don't be so humble," Golda Meir once said, "you're not that great.") I was never big or fast or physically aggressive enough to be a first-class athlete, but, as a boy, I could catch anything, or so I felt. Grounders, liners, fly balls—I gobbled them up. Throw a football anywhere within fifteen yards of me, and I would be there to meet it. In tennis I was most notable for flipping and catching my racquet in various snappy routines. In my teens I mastered most of the ball-handling tricks of the Harlem Globetrotters: spinning a basketball on my index finger, rolling it down my arm and catching it behind my back, dribbling while prone. Quite simply, I had quick and confident hands. Perhaps I should be more humble about these playground skills, for I make myself sound pretty great.

Great and humble though I apparently am, juggling is something I have never been able, yet have long yearned, to do. It is one of those fantasies possible of fulfillment, like going to Greece. Besides, juggling seemed a harmless enough fantasy, involving neither the disruption of the ecosystem nor the corruption of children. And then one day not long ago, in the produce section of the grocery store where I shop, I saw the owner's wife, an Irishwoman of great high spirits, juggling three navel oranges. So filled with envy was I that I determined then and there to learn to juggle.

When an intellectual wants to learn something he goes to the library. He reads up. But it turned out that at my library there was not much to read on the subject of juggling. The library's two books on juggling had been taken out. The library also had a novel entitled *The Juggler* by Michael Blankfort, but it, too, was gone from the shelves. Doubtless this novel is not about juggling at all but instead uses the word metaphorically, as does the final entry in the library's catalogue on the subject, *Juggling: The Art of Balancing Marriage, Motherhood, and Career.* No help there. It was beginning to look, as the English say, like a bit of a balls-up.

I remembered that Hazlitt wrote an essay entitled "The Indian Jugglers," which I reread. It starts magnificently: "Coming forward and seating himself on the ground in his white dress and tightened turban, the chief of the Indian Jugglers begins with tossing up two brass balls, which is what any of us could do, and concludes with keeping up four at the same time, which is what none of us could do to save our lives, nor if we were to take our whole lives to do it in." Hazlitt proceeds to describe the Indian juggler's act, noting that the juggler astonishes while giving pleasure in astonishment. "There is something in all this," he writes, "which he who does not admire may be quite sure he never admired really anything in the whole course of his life." Reading this I felt one of the keenest delights that reading offers: the discovery that someone more intelligent than you feels about a given subject exactly as you do.

Hazlitt then moves on to compare the juggler's skill with brass balls to his own skill with words—and finds the latter paltry in comparison. Nothing in his own work is so near perfection as that which the Indian juggler can do. "I can write a book: so can many others who have not even learned to spell," Hazlitt writes. His own essays—some of the greatest written in English—he calls "abortions." "What errors, what ill-pieced transitions, what crooked reasons, what lame conclusions. How little is made out, and that little how ill!" The juggler can keep four balls in the air, but for Hazlitt "it is as much as I can manage to keep the thread of one discourse clear and unentangled." The juggler, through patient practice, has brought his skill to perfection, something which Hazlitt feels unable to come anywhere near doing with his. "I have also time on my hands to correct my opinions and polish my periods: but the one I cannot, and the other I will not do."

Anyone who does intellectual work will instantly recognize the cogency of Hazlitt's comments. So little does such work allow for a true sense of completion, or a satisfying feeling of perfection. Every artist has felt this, and the better the artist the more achingly has he felt it. "A poem is never finished," said Valéry, "but only abandoned." If Hazlitt and Valéry, two workers in diamonds, felt this way about their works, imagine how those of us who labor with zircons feel about ours! As an old costume jeweler, I must say, I appreciate the possibility that juggling holds out for perfection—for doing the small thing extremely well.

For me, though, more is involved. Within very serious limits I am a self-improvement buff, if only a failed one. Of myself in this connection I can say, every day in every way I stay pretty much the same. A few years ago, for example, I set out to learn classical Greek. Aglow with the luster of self-betterment, I enrolled myself in a course in Greek at the university where I teach—and lasted a cool and inglorious two weeks. Walking into the room on the first day of class, I was taken for the teacher, a natural enough confusion since I was more than twenty years older than anyone else in the course (except for the actual teacher, who turned out to be roughly twenty years older than I). Being the old boy, I felt a certain obligation not to appear stupid. The option taken by a likable fellow named Fred McNally, who many years ago sat next to me in an undergraduate French class, and who whenever called upon answered through an entire semester, "Beats me, sir," did not seem an option open to me. Given my natural ineptitude with foreign languages and my fear of having to avail myself of the McNally ploy, I found myself studying Greek two hours a night. Add to this another hour for class and yet another hour for getting there and back, and nearly one fourth of my waking life was given over to this little self-improvement project. The result was the general disimprovement of everything else in my life. In the end I decided that learning Greek would have to be on that long list of items I must put off until the afterlife.

Juggling balls is surely less time-consuming than juggling Greek paradigms, but is it really self-improving? Having thought a bit about this, I have concluded that it is not a whit self-improving. Juggling is in fact the recreational equivalent of art for art's sake. It is not good exercise; you do not do it in the sunshine; it is not an excuse for gambling; it does not simulate the conditions of life; it teaches no morality (you can't even cheat at it, a prospect which lends so many games, from golf to solitaire, a piquant touch). Unlike, say, playing in the outfield, you cannot even think of anything else while doing it. Juggling is all-absorbing and an end in itself: *le jeu pour le jeu*.

Juggling is play, almost with a vengeance. "We may call everything play," writes Santayana, "which is useless activity, exercise that springs from the physiological impulse to discharge energy which the exigencies of life have not called out." Juggling also satisfies some of the criteria Huizinga lays down for play in *Homo Ludens*. It does, as Huizinga puts it, "create order, is order. Into an imperfect world and into the confusions of life it brings a temporary, a limited perfection." And juggling is certainly, to quote Huizinga again, "invested with the noblest qualities we are capable of perceiving in things: rhythm and harmony." Excluding people who use it to make a living by entertaining others, however, juggling is neither a fine nor a useful art, but rather a delicate, slightly perverse activity. No self-improvement, no end other than itself, sheer play, exquisitely useless—these are among the qualities that endear juggling to me.

Some people can do entirely without play, but I am not one of them. Neither is Georges Simenon, who, I was surprised to learn while recently reading his journal, *When I Was Old*, is of all things a golfer. Nor was Hazlitt, who was a dedicated player of fives, an English version of handball. Matthew Arnold was an ice skater. Ezra Pound enthusiastically—as, unfortunately, he did everything—played tennis. Edmund Wilson was a passionate amateur magician. Other artists and intellectuals, if not themselves players, were devoted followers of games: G. H. Hardy, the Cambridge mathematician, of cricket, and Marianne Moore of baseball. While I am unable to report that T. S. Eliot had a bowling average of 192 or that Einstein was a pool shark, my guess is that among the most serious mental workers there is many a hidden player.

My own small problem is that sources of play have been drying up on me. For many years now I have been unable to take any interest in mental games: crossword puzzles, chess, bridge, Scrabble. Even poker, a game I once loved, no longer retains much interest for me, unless the stakes are high enough to frighten me. Basketball, another former love, is now too vigorous a game for me, and I can today walk under a glass backboard without even wistfully looking up. As a boy, I was a quite decent tennis player, but I find I have no appetite for being a mediocre player in a game I used to play well. I did play the game called racquetball, and played it fairly well, but long ago gave it up.

The reason I no longer take any interest in mental games, I have concluded, is that I do mental work, and consequently seem to have little in the way of mental energy left for mental play. I have noticed, by the way, that many people who have a great deal of zest for such games, and who are very good at them, are often people of real intelligence whose work does not require them to make strenuous demands on their mental powers. For myself, I would rather be thinking of phrases or formulations to be used in essays than of how best to get off a blitz or of a four-letter word that means payment in arrears.

As for my loss of interest in physical games, here the problem, I think, is that I have lost the power to fantasize while playing. When playing tennis or basketball, for example, I find I can no longer imagine myself at center court at Wimbledon or in the final game of the NCAA at Pauley Pavilion, the sort of thing I invariably did as a boy. Nor am I sufficiently competitive to enjoy winning for its own sake, even though on the whole it is rather better than losing. The friend with whom I played racquetball and who is a much better athlete than I—as a boy he was an all-state football player and later a Big Ten wrestling champion—was even less competitive than I. Sometimes I wondered how either one of us ever managed to win the games we played against each other, and it usually turned out that not the better man but the least tired man won.

Nor have I ever had the discipline or concentration to play solitary games. Running, still much in vogue, is out of the question for me. I have never been able to take calisthenics of any sort seriously. I own a bicycle, which I ride occasionally and which gives me pleasure, but this is scarcely a game. In fact, it has become most useful to me as part of a riposte. Lately, when people suggest I must be making a lot of money as a fairly productive writer, I reply, "If I am doing so well, how come I'm still riding a reconditioned three-speed Huffy?"

All this makes it the more interesting to me that I am so keen about juggling—a form of play that is both solitary and requires real discipline. Despite such drawbacks, juggling thrills me. In the phrase of the bobby-soxers of the late 1940s, it really sends me. Another drawback is that juggling, unlike other games and sports—if juggling is indeed a game or a sport—does not have an established lore, a pantheon of heroes. It is, of course, a very old form of play: court jesters, I believe, had juggling in their repertoires. But if there was a Babe Ruth, a Jim Thorpe, or a Joe Louis of juggling, I have not heard of him.

True, many of the silent-movie stars, who came out of vaudeville, juggled. Charlie Chaplin did and so did Buster Keaton. I recall a hilarious Buster Keaton movie—which of his movies isn't hilarious?—in which Buster is a contestant on a radio amateur hour whose talent turns out to be juggling. Juggling, mind you, over the radio. In the movie Keaton, deadpan as always, is blithely tossing balls in the air while in their homes the members of the listening audience are banging away on the sides of their Philco consoles, certain that the silence is attributable to a loose tube. A splendid bit.

W. C. Fields broke into show business as a juggler, a skill at which he is said to have been consummate. In Robert Lewis Taylor's biography, *W. C. Fields: His Follies and Fortunes*, Fields is said to have begun juggling at the age of nine, inspired by the vaudeville performance of a group calling itself the Byrne Brothers. Fields's father hawked fruit and vegetables in Philadelphia, and Fields practiced on his father's wares. "By the time I could keep two objects going," he said, "I'd ruined forty dollars worth of fruit." He later worked with cigar boxes, croquet balls, Indian clubs, and odd utensils. In his early adolescence he was obsessed with juggling. He worked hours and hours at it, teaching himself to keep five tennis balls in the air, catching canes with his feet, and performing any other kind of trick he could dream up.

Field's specialty as a juggler was to appear to fumble, then recover from what had all the marks of a disastrous error. He never lost his relish for this artful bumbling. Later in life, while serving his guests at large dinner parties, Fields would fill a plate, preferably for a comparative stranger, and, as he would begin to hand it down the line, drop it, "provoking," as his biographer tells it, "a loud concerted gasp. With consummate nonchalance he would catch it just off the floor, without interrupting whatever outrageous anecdote he was relating at the moment." But the best juggling story Robert Lewis Taylor tells is about the night Fields was working on some new trick in a hotel room in Pittsburgh, when his continual dropping of a heavy object disturbed the tenant in the room below, a bruiser who came up to complain. The complainant recognized Fields as the juggler he had seen earlier that evening at a local theater. To calm the man down Fields taught him a simple trick calling for juggling two paring knives. "I hope he worked at it," Fields said in recounting the story, "because if he did, he was almost certain to cut himself very painfully." Fieldsian, absolutely Fieldsian.

Juggling today appears to be undergoing a small renaissance. Street jugglers appear in profusion along Fisherman's Wharf in San Francisco. In Manhattan they mingle among the multitudes of street vendors.

Although I myself have not seen the act, there is at work nowadays a group known as the Brothers Karamazov that is said to give great satisfaction. Along with other odd-shaped objects, the Brothers K juggle running buzz saws and, most astonishing of all, live cats. A few juggling books have recently been published: *Juggling for the Complete Klutz* is the title of one and *The Juggling Book* that of another. Have we the makings here of a wildly popular fad?

My guess is that we do not. For one thing, juggling is just too damned difficult to catch on—if you will pardon the expression—with great numbers of people. For another, it lacks manufacturing possibilities. Balls can still be bought at dime stores (if not quite, lamentably, for dimes). So far as I know, Adidas, Nike, Puma, and other sports equipment manufacturers have yet to produce juggling shoes, juggling shorts, or juggling watches. Certainly there is no need for them. I myself, when juggling, wear the simplest costume: buskins turned up at the toes, gold pantaloons, a leathern jerkin, and a cap with bells.

But the time, surely, has come to get some balls in the air. How good a juggler am I? In two words, not bad. In trying to explain my quality as a novice juggler I feel rather as Buster Keaton must have felt while juggling over the radio. I can keep three balls in the air for roughly two minutes. I do the conventional beginner's pattern known as "the cascade," in which the balls appear to be flowing over a perpetual waterfall. While juggling I can go from a standing to a kneeling position; I can juggle sitting down. I can vary the cascade pattern with the pattern known as "the half-shower," in which. . . . But I hear you banging on your Philco. Let me conclude then by saying that, as a juggler, I am far from ready for Vegas, television, or even small family parties.★

Yet such limited prowess as I have I owe to my mentor, a man who calls himself, on the title page of *The Juggling Book*, Carlo. His real name is Charles Lewis. Mr. Lewis has done a bit of this and a bit of that, from teaching math and science in public schools to leading encounter groups to founding a spiritualist newspaper to organizing a small circus troupe.

★ Here I cannot resist bragging. Since writing this essay, I have learned all the fundamental tricks of juggling with three balls. I can also do a number of four-ball tricks, and have only recently begun to learn to juggle with plastic clubs. I am, therefore, ready for small family parties, but only useful, I fear, to end especially dull ones, as someone once suggested that two long-play records of the late Ludwig Earhart explaining the German economic miracle was, similarly, good for ending dull parties.

From the photograph of him on the back of the book—long dark hair, a gray beard, corduroy jeans, loose-sleeved East Indian shirt—he looks rather guruish, and guruish he turns out to be. The Carlo Method, as Mr. Lewis styles his teaching, is not without a large measure of current psychobabble. Given half a chance—and as the author of his own book, he has more than half a chance—Carlo will babble on about "levels of awareness," "great possibilities for creativity," "control and direction of body forces," "inner states," "healing effects on your psyche," and, natch, that old rotting botanical metaphor, "growing." Juggling, Carlo advises, will help me "continue to grow." Thank you, Carlo, but I was growing before I read your book: growing older, growing feebler, growing closer to death—growth enough, I should think.

When Carlo knocks off the psycho-spiritual palaver, which I find so *antipatico*, he is an excellent teacher. He writes clearly, and he takes the novice through each step slowly. He had me worried at first, though, when he said that juggling, like riding a bicycle or whistling, is something everyone can learn to do, since I, after repeated attempts to learn, can whistle only pitiably. Juggling turns out to be one of those activities (tennis is another) in which one benefits greatly from professional instruction at the outset. Fundamentals—how to position your body, how to hold the balls, how to toss them—are decisive. Unlike almost any other ball game, for example, you do not use your fingertips in juggling but instead toss the balls from your palms. In all these matters Carlo is very helpful. Sometimes, too, he will strike off a delicately humorous sentence, as when he advises not to reach up to catch the balls but rather to let them fall into your hands. "The balls will come down," he writes, "which I can guarantee from long experience." Sometimes he will hit exactly the right lyrical note, as when he writes: "Somehow there is a ball up there that's never going to come down. You realize suddenly that you never have to stop; you can juggle forever." He is right about that, and when it occurs, it is a golden moment. On the day it finally happened to me, after more than a week of practice, I felt sheer exhilaration and wanted to shout, "Look, Ma, both hands!"

Earlier I said that juggling does not provide much in the way of exercise. Let me amend that by saying that at the beginning you do get quite a bit of exercise—chasing the balls you drop. To cut down the chasing I began practicing in my wife's and my bedroom, juggling over the bed and thereby, as a friend remarked, turning a conjugal into a conjuggle bed. Not long afterward, by turning on our clock-radio, I added music to my practice sessions and discovered that the piano rags of Scott Joplin are particularly nice as juggling music. As my juggling began to improve, so did the music. Stan Getz's saxophone makes for fine juggling accompaniment and so do Haydn's piano trios and Telemann's wind concertos. Juggling to Strauss waltzes and Glenn Miller swing is also lovely. Opera is no good at all.

Part of the delight of juggling is the rhythmical pleasure created by the clear and steady beat of the balls slapping against the palms. This gives a satisfaction roughly analogous to that which a beginning pianist must feel when running through rudimentary practice exercises. Tossing the balls first high, then low, then in wide, then in narrow arcs, I can also create pleasing if altogether ephemeral designs of a kind I could never achieve with a crayon or paintbrush. In these small ways, then, juggling has compensated me for two common pleasures—those of rhythm and design—that my natural inaptitudes have hitherto prevented me from enjoying.

To drift slightly into metaphor, juggling has supplied the possibility, however small, of chaos in my life. Since beginning to juggle I now realize how exceedingly well ordered my life has become. I read, I write, I live among family and friends whom I love. Nor would I have it otherwise. At the same time I have always marveled at, without necessarily admiring, those people who seem to have so high a threshold for chaos in their lives: people who can simultaneously carry on love affairs while behind in their alimony payments, have government liens on their businesses, and undergo chemotherapy—people who, to use a juggling metaphor, somehow manage to keep a lot of balls in the air. One such chaos merchant of my acquaintance, a man in his early fifties, recently married a woman of twenty-three while concurrently acquiring a mistress in her late forties, a brilliant reversal of the norm that had his friends surmising that he married for sex and kept a mistress for conversation. Whatever the case, the man is obviously a juggler.

At the same time, juggling is an exercise in subduing chaos. Keeping the balls in the air, making of them a fluid pattern, one achieves a pleasing kind of order. As with much art, the trick in juggling is to make the difficult look effortless. As Samuel Butler once put it,

> As lookers-on feel most delight,
> That least perceive a juggler's sleight,
> And still the less they understand,
> The more th' admire his sleight of hand.

Yet in juggling many are the moments—when a ball slips loose, when two balls collide in midair—when chaos wins and panic, for an instant, clutches the heart. At such moments one hears the knock of the house detective, feels the unopened IRS letter in the hand, sees the X ray being slid dramatically from its envelope.

While the balls are in the air, describing their arcs, slapping gently against my hands, with everything under control, I am happy. Perhaps this happiness comes from my complete preoccupation with what I am doing. Perhaps it comes from the thrill of beginning to master a skill, however small and insignificant. It is a thoughtless happiness, an almost animal happiness, but no less real for all that. With the balls flying about me, I am happy but not, I must confess, altogether content. Even in my happiness I wonder if it is not time to move on and learn new tricks. Ought I to begin to master juggling four balls? What about rings and then Indian clubs? My man Carlo says that juggling on your back while on a trapeze is just about as far as one can go with this sort of thing. "Man thou art a wonderful animal," says Hazlitt, "and thy ways past finding out." William, I say, you don't know the half of it.

EP, THE BULLS
ARE SIX-POINT DOGS

For the 50th year reunion of the Senn High School class of 1955 each of us was asked to submit a few words about his life since graduation. Here are some of mine: "I've written a few books. For 30 years I taught in the English Department at Northwestern University, and remain attached to the football coaching staff there, working exclusively with Jewish wide-receivers, which leaves me lots of free time for my writing."

I'm not sure everyone got the joke, but joke of course it is, since in the history of football there has probably never been a Jewish wide receiver. Wide receivers, especially in professional football, tend to be tall, slender, wiry black men. When catching passes either at the sidelines or especially in the middle of the field, they take a terrific beating. Jewish wide receivers are as rare as Jewish coal miners or, to return to football to complete my simile, as Jews in the front four.

Was I playing into the stereotype about Jews being more thoughtful than physical? I suppose I was. Do I in fact believe in the stereotype? Here I am less sure. About Jewish bravery in the clutch, or crunch, there can be no doubt. Exhibit A: the Israeli Army. The question is, are Jews willing to risk crippling themselves for mere sport? The answer, unsatisfactory as a generalization, is some are, some aren't.

As a boy athlete, I discovered I was one of those who wasn't. I grew up in a neighborhood where for boys there were two possibilities, and two only: be a decent athlete or be witty. Having an aptitude for science, playing piano or violin, performing well in the classroom—

none of this cut it, not in the least. Talent, valor, excellence was displayed on the playground, and nowhere else.

In my athletic career, I seem to have peaked in grade school. In those days I was a T-formation quarterback, a shortstop, and a point guard. Small but well-coordinated, I had a mimetic gift that allowed me to imitate the moves of professional athletes. In high school I only made it as far as the frosh-soph basketball team and played on the tennis team.

As an athlete, I lacked the essential quality of physical aggression. I knew I lacked it because Marty Summerfield, a Jewish kid no larger than I with whom I went to grammar school, had it *in excelsis*. Marty was without fear. He would never run away from a fight, even with boys fifty pounds heavier than he; race into nearby street traffic after a foul ball; incur concussions while playing halfback without a helmet. Marty didn't go on to athletic glory, but became interested in science, and in high school won a Westinghouse scholarship to Swarthmore for work on enzymes.

Every Jewish neighborhood had its great athlete. Philip Roth caught this nicely in creating his character Swede Levov in *American Pastoral*. One of our Swede Levovs was a boy named Joel Farber who started for the University of Wisconsin basketball team, as did a boy who lived down the block from me named John Stack. Another contemporary, Howie (Hershie, to those of us who played with him) Carl, was a 5'8" point guard with an astonishingly fluid jump shot. Hershie held the record for total points scored at DePaul University, which was only broken by Mark Aguirre, who later played for the Detroit Pistons. A boy two years younger than I named Ronnie Rubenstein played basketball for Louisville, then as now a college basketball power. He was also, at one point, the second-ranked racquetball player in the country. Running into the Rube at the old Chicago Stadium after a twenty-five or so year hiatus, his first words to me were: "Ep, can you believe it, the Bulls are six-point dogs?"

Jews fared less well in football. The sons of the steel workers on the far southside of the city went to Chicago Vocational High School (alma mater of Dick Butkus) and Mount Carmel (alma mater of a number of Notre Dame quarterbacks), whence they dominated. When I was a little boy, along the lakefront behind our apartment on Sheridan Road, I used to watch Sullivan High School's predominantly Jewish football team practice. The team's coach, a barrel-chested, deep-throated man named Ralph Margolis, would blow his whistle at players who screwed up and scream "*Schtunk.*"

My boyhood—the middle–late 1940s and early '50s—was a grand era in sports. These were great years for boxing, and no sports event in those days attracted greater attention than a heavyweight title fight. Many athletes now considered legendary were then active. When I was eight years old, a man for whom my father worked named Johnny Bieler, knowing my interest in sports, one Sunday asked me if I preferred to join him in watching either Bob Feller pitch against the White Sox at Comiskey Park or the Bears play the (as they then were) Cleveland Rams with their star quarterback Bob Waterfield (husband of the movie actress Jane Russell) at Wrigley Field. I chose the Bears game, largely because of Sid Luckman, who was the first quarterback to master the T-formation and was tough, smart, and (best of all) Jewish.

Across town, Marshall Goldberg, who graduated from Pitt and was on the same 1939 College All-Star team with Luckman, played in the backfield for the Chicago Cardinals. One night at the Standard Club in Chicago I met Goldberg, then in his early eighties. Compact and still fit but of middling size, he was a reminder that in an earlier day to succeed in football one didn't have to be a monster: a 300-plus-pound lineman, a 250-plus pound running back, a 6'5" and above quarterback. Goldberg was less than enthusiastic about contemporary players. He was of the era when most professional players went both ways, which didn't mean that they were bisexual, but stayed in the game for both offense and defense, playing the full sixty minutes. He was also well along in the sad stage in an athlete's life of vastly diminished fame. He was genuinely pleased, I sensed, that I remembered who he was.

Sid Luckman's fame has been of longer endurance. Today, if one wishes to speak of the three great Jewish athletes, that triumvirate often includes Luckman, the Detroit Tigers' Hank Greenberg, and the Los Angeles Dodgers' Sandy Koufax, with the swimmer Mark Spitz sometimes tossed in as a fourth. There have been other great Jewish athletes—Benny Leonard, Barney Ross, Dolph Schayes, Al Rosen, et al.—but their numbers have not been myriad, and probably never figure to be. Applying strict standards, the Jewish Athletes Hall of Fame could probably be accommodated in a second-floor single at your local Holiday Inn.

Tennis, the game upon which my own athletic passions were almost exclusively lavished in my last years in high school, had a few great Jewish players. A few years ago, I published an article on tennis in the *Wall Street Journal*, and had a call in response to it from Dick Savitt, who in 1951 won both the Australian Open and Wimbledon and was ranked second in the world that year. I mentioned in my article that Savitt and Vic Sexias were two Jewish tennis players who had come to prominence in an era when tennis in America was a country club sport dominated by gentiles. The amiable Savitt ended our conversation by saying, "By the way, don't ever tell Vic he's Jewish. He doesn't know."

No great, or even prominent, Jewish golfers have emerged. This despite the fact that Jews, once restricted from the great golfing country clubs, have been playing golf for at least three generations. A majority of the boys I grew up with are today men who live for golf, their idea of heaven being a condominium on a golf course in Florida or Arizona.

In an interesting and intermittently amusing book called *Jewish Jocks* there is a single essay about a Jewish golfer, a man named Corey Pavin, who in mid-career converted to Evangelical Christianity. Nothing shocking about this, really. Something there is intrinsically un-Jewish, something essentially goyesque, about golf—about the clothes, the bucolic setting, the vast expenditure of time required to play a full 18 holes.

Both the editors and contributors of the fifty brief essays in *Jewish Jocks* tend to treat the appearance on earth of great Jewish athletes as slightly anomalous. Many of the essays aren't about actual athletes but about, in effect, support staff and executives: the basketball coaches Red Holzman and Red Auerbach, the boxing cut-and-corner man Whitey Bimstein, the union organizer Marvin Miller, the commissioner of baseball Bud Selig, the inventor of fantasy baseball, the philosopher Max Nordau, the owners of the Oakland Raiders and of the Dallas Mavericks, the president of the Chicago Cubs, the inventor of Ultimate Frisbee, the sportscaster Howard Cosell, sports writers, the gambler Arnold Rothstein, the transsexual tennis player Renee Richards, the chess champion Bobby Fischer, and the competitive eating champion Don Lerner. As for the last named, Jews, one would think, ought to be a cinch to win competitive eating contests after having trained in homes where throughout childhood not competitive but compulsory eating was in force: "Eat, *tsutsik*, eat!"

The usual suspects have brief essays devoted to them in *Jewish Jocks*: Luckman, Greenberg, Koufax, Mark Spitz, Benny Leonard and Barney Ross, the American bullfighter Sidney Franklin (né Frumpkin), the gymnast Kerri Strug, the pro basketball player Dolph Schayes. Essays on Jewish practitioners of lesser-known sports—handball, fencing, women's basketball, weightlifting, soccer, wrestling, martial arts, and Ping-Pong—also find a place. Jewish athletic flops are covered. There is an essay on Adam Greenberg, the man who was beaned on his single time at bat in the majors and never returned; and another on the yarmulke and tzitzit wearing basketball prospect Tamir Goodman, who wasn't quite good enough to play at the University of Maryland; and yet another on a would-be slugger in the 1920s named Mose Solomon, who was supposed to be the Jewish Babe Ruth but turned out to hit more like the Biblical Ruth. A flop of his own making, Jack Molinas, the immensely talented basketball player, was rightly accused of point shaving and barred from the game. With a few exceptions—Ron Rosenbaum on Arnold Rothstein, Deborah Lipstadt on the Israeli athletes murdered at the 1972 Olympics in Munich—the essays are written in a jaunty and jokey style. The title of the book could as easily have been *Jewish Jocks as Told by Jokey Jakeys*, for almost all the contributors are themselves Jewish.

If *Jewish Jocks* has a theme, it is that Jewish athletes tend to be unusual, if not positively odd, both among Jews and athletes. What, after all, were they, nice Jewish boys and girls, doing spending their lives on fields and courts, in rings and gyms, and other sweaty surroundings? Often in these essays braininess—at least what qualifies as braininess among athletes—is what differentiates the Jewish athlete. An interior lineman, who in the middle-1950s played for the University of Southern California and then for the Oakland Raiders, turns out in later life to be a personal injury lawyer, specializing in athletic injuries. Russian weightlifters, if Jewish, are not the brutes you might expect them to be. A Jewish martial arts guru, said to break stones with his face, has the first name Harvey and the body and countenance of a CPA.

The editors of *Jewish Jocks*, Franklin Foer and Marc Tracy—the former the editor of *The New Republic*, the latter one of the magazine's staff writers—grew up in the same professional-class neighborhood in Washington, D.C., went to the same synagogue, attended, as they write in their introduction, the same "progressive, heavily Jewish day school with a grasshopper as a mascot and no football team." From the photograph of them on the book's dustjacket, it would not be shocking to learn that such athletic glory as they might have won came not from smashing walk-off homeruns, diving into end zones, or slam dunking winning baskets at the game-ending buzzer, but instead from completing a flawless collection of baseball cards. What their book provides is for the most part a nerd's-eye view of the Jew as athlete.

The one essay on tennis in the collection, written by Lawrence Summers, the economist and former president of Harvard, turns out to be about Harold Solomon, a man who played defensive tennis through his long career, specializing in returning his opponents' drives with semi-lobs that wore them down, drove them nutty, and often ended in winning-ugly victories for Solomon. During the Connors-Borg-McEnroe era, in 1980, Solomon rode this dinker's game to a number five world ranking. Summers concludes that he was right "as a young man to latch on to Harold Solomon. His success teaches a lesson that transcends tennis and sport. Attitude and grit are more important determinants than natural ability." Maybe so, but they are nowhere near as much fun as the exercise of pure talent and simple cool.

Throughout *Jewish Jocks* Jewish athletes rely on craft, cunning, old-fashioned *saykhel* through which they overcome deficiencies in size, talent, and brutish aggression. Benny Leonard, "the archetype of the brainy boxer," in Franklin Foer's words, was a striking case in point. In and around New York in the 1920s, boxing was a sport in which a great number of Jews competed; in Foer's essay on Leonard, he cites the boxing historian Allen Bodner's estimate that in 1920 Jews comprised roughly a third of all professional fighters. Foer writes: "Jews are often credited with putting the science in the sweet science. Even the brutes of the tribe couldn't help but inject a little intellectualism into their craft." Tell it, one wants to say, to such Jewish pugs as Slapsie Maxie Rosenbloom and Kingfish Levinsky. Corey Pavin, we learn, "played 'Jewish, if there is such a thing: he thrived on brains and craftiness rather than strength and bravado." Did Pavin, one wonders, retain these qualities after his conversion to Christianity?

If no generalizations about Jewish athletes are safe, a few strong trends may be noted. Franklin Foer remarks that with the social mobility that set in for Jews after World War Two, the numbers of Jewish boxers lessened considerably. In his essay on the Met outfielder Art Shamsky, David Brooks, who owns a set of cards put out by the American Jewish Historical Society, notes that between 1871 and 2003 the number of Jews who played in the major leagues was 142, which averages out to only a little more than one for every year baseball has been in existence. In Robert Weintraub's article on the hapless Mose Solomon, John Mc-Graw, then manager of the New York Giants who was looking for a Jewish sensation for the Jewish fans in New York, is quoted claiming that "Jews stay out of baseball because there isn't enough money in it."

Doubtful whether this was ever true, but it certainly isn't true today, when the major-league minimum salary is $480,000, with some players making as much as $25 million per year. Money doesn't come up in the pages of *Jewish Jocks*, but money is of course increasingly what all sports are about.

Why do players take steroids? How is it that more players nowadays protect themselves by going on disabled lists with even minor injuries? Why do professional athletes seem to perform most proficiently at the end of their contracts? What makes sports unions the last of the strong unions in the United States? Why are the hockey and pro basketball seasons so long? The answer is, in every case, Money.

The money is there in good part through television contracts. But it is also found in the spiraling cost of tickets to sports events. Along with the increased price of going to sports events, the ethnic demography of the sports is radically changing. In baseball, where Afro-Americans once constituted roughly a third of all major-league players, that number, when last reported, was down to eight percent. The percentage of Hispanic players—from the Dominican Republic, Venezuela, Mexico, Puerto Rico, Nicaragua—is up, and Asian players are becoming more common. Professional football and basketball rosters, meanwhile, are preponderantly Afro-American, with the majority of the minority of white players in pro basketball coming from Eastern Europe, Spain, and Italy.

Your simple Jewish chauvinist—that would be me—searches for Jewish athletes playing major sports, and finds fewer and fewer of them. A pro football offensive tackle with the Italian name Gabe Garimi turns out to be Jewish. A top-twenty woman tennis player named Shahar

Peer is an Israeli. The Jewish Aly Raisman was a key figure on the past year's U.S. Olympic gymnastics team. Perhaps the most successful Jewish professional athlete now going is Ryan Braun, the left-fielder of the Milwaukee Brewers known as the Hebrew Hammer and the National League's Most Valuable Player in 2011. Eight or nine other Jews are currently playing major-league baseball, and no Jews that I know about play in the National Basketball Association.

A few years ago, the Chicago Bears had a quarterback, now with the Washington Redskins, named Rex Grossman. His father is an ophthalmologist in Bloomington, Indiana. Grossman went to the University of Florida, where he was a consensus All-American and runner-up for the Heisman Trophy. The name Grossman, the physician father, the mention of Florida—my Jewdar went whirring away, strongly suggesting that he could be a member of the tribe. Grossman had an off-and-on career with the Bears, but in 2006, he led the team to a 13–3 record. In the Super Bowl at the end of the season, alas, he was responsible for five turnovers, and seemed unable to do anything right. The Bears went down to the Indianapolis Colts in a dreary 29–17 defeat. Not long before I learned that Grossman is not Jewish. A good thing, too, else after the Super Bowl there might have pogroms in the streets of Chicago.

American Jews who were themselves never first-class athletes—me, again—are perhaps unduly delighted to have great Jewish athletes on the scene. These athletes suggest a complete assimilation in the culture of the country. They help smash the stereotype of Jews as chiefly cerebral in their gifts. They are a source of pride in demonstrating that there is no realm in which Jews cannot excel. They are a salutary reminder that, as the man said, the Jews are like everyone else, only more so.

THE THRILL OF DEFEAT

In the late 1940s and early 1950s, a less psychological age than the one in which we now live, such phrases as "self-esteem," "self-worth," and "self-image" we are not yet current, but for a boy growing up in Chicago at that time something akin to what those psychobabblish phrases only vaguely imply was at stake on the playground. Tell me your position on the playground softball team and I shall tell you your standing as a kid. For good and ill, ability at sports was pretty much the measure of the man—make that "boy." If you were not adept at sports, you did well to be a bruiser, or a poor third, someone extremely clever at amusing athletes and bruisers. Later, of course, the clever ones would have their day, but that day was a while off.

Perhaps I am unnaturally sensitive about the status of the playground, for I grew up in a neighborhood where most of the kids were a year or two older than I, and so, consequently, I was assigned all the menial athletic jobs—catcher in softball, center in football, goalie in hockey—and didn't much like it, though there was nothing I could do about it. When I was ten, however, our family moved to West Rogers Park, and suddenly, in my new neighborhood, among kids my age, I was assigned all the glory jobs: quarterback, shortstop, point guard. It was like being transferred from the field office in Paragould, Arkansas, to the company headquarters office in Paris. By high school I was finished as a serious athlete, but I have ever afterward thought of myself as a quarterback, shortstop, point guard. Freud says that a boy who is certain of his mother's love figures to go on to become a conqueror. I say that if, in addition to much mother love he grew up in Chicago and had to play right field until he was fifteen, he isn't likely to conquer a thing.

As with almost everything else in Chicago, sports, too, was organized along the lines of neighborhood. More precisely, this meant by the local park or fieldhouse—which usually had a gymnasium—in the neighborhood. The park district was an important part of growing up in Chicago. When asked where you were from, you would usually identify yourself by your local park and say you were from "around Clarendon" or "near Chase Park" or "close to Green Briar." The director of the neighborhood park organized softball and basketball leagues for grammar school kids, and sometimes arranged games between parks. One of the great social dividers in Chicago when I grew up here was between kids who went to Catholic schools and kids who went to public schools; the former rarely referred to the neighborhood but usually talked about the "parish." This division was not entirely dissolved in the park fieldhouse, but at least there Catholic and public school kids met on the basketball court or on the softball field.

Mine was a two-park boyhood, with time divided between Indian Boundary, at Lunt and Rockwell, where we played tennis and outdoor basketball, and Green Briar, at Peterson and Washtenaw, which had an indoor gym, softball fields, and a director with an already thinning crew cut named Ed Kelly. Ed Kelly went on to become head of the Chicago Park District, a job with enormous political power, and was often spoken about as the number two or three man in the Chicago political machine. Although I didn't realize it at the time, Kelly, while working at Green Briar, was building a political career, but he was also very good at what he did as a park director. He was immensely likable and always seemed fair in his dealings with us kids; he also happened to be a highly efficient athlete—a centerfielder in softball, a man with a soft long set-shot of great accuracy in basketball—which lent him even greater authority.

I was sorry to see Ed Kelly deposed from his job as head of the park district, and this for a distinctly personal reason. The reason is that when I was in eighth grade at Daniel Boone School, I entered and won a freethrow shooting contest at Green Briar, then under Kelly's direction. Shooting underhand, I made twenty-one out of twenty-five free throws (mediocre athletes recall all their records—who else, after all, is going to remember them), but, somehow, was never presented with a trophy. Had I bumped into Ed Kelly, I intended to remind him about this and ask him to cough up the trophy. So consummate a politician is he, I don't doubt that, first, he would have remembered me (or at least convinced me that he had) and, second, that he would come up with the trophy. But now, alas, it is too late. Another hope for athletic glory lost.

I don't know where Ed Kelly went to high school, but he was clearly Catholic League. In prep sports, the big division in the city was between Catholic and Public League schools. Fenwick and Mount Carmel and St. Rita's were among the powerful Catholic League football teams when I was in high school; Lane Tech and Austin were the Public League powers, though Schurz and Tilden and Chicago Vocational were perennially strong. A young reporter named Jerome Holtzman covered prep sports in those days for the *Daily News* before switching over to the *Sun-Times*.

There were always a lot of tickets floating around to the Kelly Bowl game, named after Mayor Edward Kelly, between the winners of Catholic and Public League championships. I used to trek out to Soldier Field to see them, but far and away the most exciting high school football player I ever saw in Chicago was a halfback from Austin High named Abe Woodson. Woodson went on to play for the University of Illinois and, afterward, briefly, for the San Francisco 49ers. Against a serious Lane Tech team, at Lane Stadium, I once saw Woodson run back a punt sixty yards or so for a touchdown. But the play was called back owing to an offside call against Austin. When Lane re-punted, Woodson, rather nonchalantly it seemed to me, ran it back for another touchdown. A friend of mine named Loren Singer, who played pass defense for Senn High School, used to carry a clipping from the *Sun-Times* in his wallet of a photograph showing Abe Woodson hurtling over him and carrying the caption, "Missed Opportunity."

Abe Woodson was black—one of the few blacks, it was said, to go to the then predominantly white Austin High. Rumor had it that the Austin coach used to pay Abe Woodson's car fare to travel to Austin to attend school, which even then seemed to me a good and characteristically Chicago story, with its familiar Chicago subtext that the fix was in. Woodson seemed all the more extraordinary, not to say exotic, for being black at a time when few black athletes were prominent, or at least prominently mentioned, in Chicago prep sports, outside of track and field. (Jesse Owens, after all, was one of the most famous Chicagoans.) DuSable High School's marvelous basketball team of the early 1950s would change that and for good. Basketball soon came to be preeminently a black sport. ("It's our golf," I once heard a black comedian say.) From DuSable's Charley Brown and Paxton Lumpkin through Carver's Cazzie Russell through Westinghouse's Mark Aguirre through St. Joseph's Isiah Thomas to Farragut's Kevin Garnett to Simeon's Derrick Rose the string of dazzling basketball prospects coming out of Chicago's black neighborhoods has been unending.

But before black athletes began their unrelinquished dominance of the local—and national—basketball scene, basketball in Chicago was a big Jewish sport. Bosco Levine was the coach at Marshall High, Sid Novak at McKinley and then Crane. Irv Bemoras, followed by Eddie Goldman, kept Marshall a longtime power in city prep basketball. Von Steuben's Harvey Babitch broke all sorts of high school scoring records in the early fifties. Babitch was followed at a distance of four or five years by Howard Carl, who went from Von Steuben to become, at roughly five feet, eight inches, DePaul's all-time scoring average leader until his record was broken by Mark Aguirre. Roosevelt High School, at a time when Albany Park was still heavily Jewish, was another basketball power, and had a center named Moose Malitz, who may have been the last Jew in the city of Chicago to be nicknamed Moose (also, maybe, the first). The best basketball player to come out of Green Briar was Ronnie Rubenstein, who, after making all-city at Senn, started at guard for Louisville.

Lest the above paragraph seem Jewish chauvinism—which, come to think of it, it could well be—let me quickly adduce the then annual BBYO-CYO basketball game, in which the best Jewish and Catholic players in the city met in an all-star game. In the 1950s this game was a big enough citywide attraction for its sponsors to book the Amphitheatre as the site of the game. In one such game I recall a brilliant performance by another athlete from our neighborhood, Frank Ehmann, who went to St. George High School (and later was All Big Ten at Northwestern) and whose father had a barber shop on Devon Avenue. In sports, as in so much else about Chicago, the neighborhood was the source of patriotism and pride. The city was essentially a federation of small competing villages, and one took pride in one's own village champions. And yet the city itself seemed in those days a large village. As a high school kid, I recall taking part in conversations where such high theoretical questions were posed as who could hit the longest softball in the city (Zeke Ireland, who played Windy City softball), who was the best rebounder (Howie Abrahams, of Marshall, of whom it was said, "Abrahams takes all boards"), or who was the strongest guy in town (a fellow named Phil Grandinetti, who was said to be able to lift middling-size trees out of the ground). Rich stuff.

Chicago's one distinctive contribution to sports is sixteen-inch softball, and if there were such a profession as a sports anthropologist, he could doubtlessly tell from skeletons of dead Chicagoans what positions they played in softball: stocky third basemen, wiry second basemen, heavyset catchers, slightly out of shape pitchers, and so forth. Spring and summer, kids played the game all day long and into the evening. Often on Sunday mornings the playgrounds would be filled with their fathers, who dragged out the spikes and the old softball pants, to play choose-up games. When there weren't enough kids to organize a game, we played a variant of it, with two or three on a side, known as line ball.

The best players in the city played in the league known as Windy City, and some among them were fabled. I never watched Windy City games, but I saw many of the same teams at Thillens Stadium out on the edge of the city at Kedzie and Devon, and later, at Clarendon Park, near Marine Drive. The players on teams with such names as Midland Motors, Martin Jewelers, KoolVent Awnings were mostly in their twenties and thirties, but seemed impressively mature to me in those days. Moose Skowron, before his career with the New York Yankees, played first base for (if memory serves) Midland Motors. Bato Goviderica, the former DePaul basketball star, played for Martin Jewelers, as did a remarkable man missing two or three fingers on his left hand named Petey Kuhn. I recall, too, a pitcher named Willie Phillips, who parted his carefully pomaded black hair straight up the center and looked more like a 1940s band leader than an athlete. Phillips was reputed to be able to curve the cantaloupe-size Clincher softball; he had a pick-off move in which, coming off a hesitation, he whipped the ball to first base between his legs without ever taking his eyes off the batter. It was one of those elegant athletic moves that, nearly sixty years later, I still remember in all its intricacy, as a balletomane might remember Pavlova dancing in *Swan Lake* or a devotee of piano music might remember youthful Glenn Gould playing the *Goldberg Variations*.

My guess is that, given time and a typewriter, there are tens of thousands of men who grew up in Chicago who could tell a story not greatly dissimilar to the one I am telling here. This past spring, for example, when the comedian Bill Murray was substituting for the then ill Cubs, announcer Harry Caray, Murray told of his memory of repeatedly rushing home after school to catch the end of the Cubs game only to hear Jack Brickhouse reporting yet another Cubs loss while off in the cavernous background of Wrigley Field he could hear the sound of kids stomping on empty beer cups. The dolorous echo of those stomped-upon cups, the unconvincing cheerfulness of Brickhouse's voice, anyone who heard Murray that afternoon who had grown up in Chicago knew precisely what he was talking about. Ah, Chicago, where to be a serious sports fan is to have hopelessness spring eternal. Oh, mother, hide my razor and anything else sharp in the house, for I am about to discourse upon the sorrows of being a sports fan in the town without pity (on, above all, its sports fans).

In 1949, when we were twelve years old and I first met him, my lifelong friend Robert Ginsburg was wearing a yellow sweatshirt upon which was printed, in the shape of a football, "Chicago Bears, Six Times Champion." Today, nearly sixty-five years later, the only editing that sweatshirt needs to bring it up to date is to change the number Six to Eight. My friend Robert carries in his wallet a ticket stub to a 1945 Cubs–Tigers World Series game, which he attended at the age of eight; seventy years that baby has been moldering in his various wallets, unjoined by another Cubs World Series ticket stub. The DePaul basketball team has gone to the Final Four a time or two, but always, once there, only to fizzle out. The Blackhawks, during the glory days of Hull and Mikita, were a superior team, but then I have never been a big hockey fan and have tended to view the sport as a secret arrangement whereby Canadians are provided with a warm place to stage fistfights.

One does not, it seems safe to conclude, choose to live in Chicago either for the splendors of climate or for the sustained thrill of victory the city's teams supply. Yet the loyalty of Chicago fans to their teams is unparalleled. San Francisco, for example, is a city interested only in winning teams; if its teams don't win, San Franciscans drive out to Napa for a wine tasting. New Yorkers tend to get worked up about their teams but—with the exception only of the early Mets teams to which they formed a comic sentimental attachment—New York, too, tends to be a city for winners. In Philadelphia, they hate a loser, and have no compunction about booing so great an athlete as the Phillies' Mike Schmidt when he went into a rare slump. In Pittsburgh, not even exciting baseball teams draw well. Other cities—Minneapolis and St. Louis, Cleveland and Kansas City—fade in and out in their enthusiasms. It is only in Chicago where a last place Cubs team can fill Wrigley Field on a sunny Sunday in September, or the Bears with a 5–7 record can play to a full house at Soldier Field in late December in zero degree weather. There are some who feel that such loyalty is, well, not to put too fine a point on it, a little sick.

I am sometimes among them. I am both loyal to Chicago teams and simultaneously critical of the loyalty we Chicagoans show them. As a fan in Chicago, I am both a sport conservative, who dislikes Astro-Turf, the notion of too many night games at Wrigley Field, and needs to be persuaded of every other change in the games and sports scenes of my boyhood, and a sports Leninist, who feels that, if Chicago teams cannot win, he wants them to lose ignominiously, so that revolutionary change will come about—and soon. I always thought, for example, that the Cubs and Bears would never improve so long as fans kept paying to see them play no matter how mediocrely they performed; and in their time they reached, so to speak, heights of mediocrity one might not have thought attainable. Here we come to the first of many conundrums about sports in Chicago. If you put the Cubs or White Sox in Pittsburgh, the franchises would have gone under years ago. If you put the Bulls (until the advent onto the scene of the crowd-pleasing Michael Jordan) in Los Angeles, not even Jack Nicholson would have shown up. But in Chicago they clunked along. It's a great sports town, as the boosters say. Or is it merely an odd one?

Odd, is it not, that Chicago, a town that has been variously described as brutal, tough, a city on the make, for more than three decades supported as its principal sports announcer a man named Jack Brickhouse. Brickhouse announced Cubs games and (at one time) Sox games on television, for many years did the Bears games on radio, was for a good stretch the television announcer for the Bulls games, in the early days of television did wrestling, and for all I know may have announced checkers, curling, and pie-eating contests. A number of people have told me that Jack Brickhouse is a nice man; no one has ever said that he was much good at what he did for a living, even though he ended up in the Baseball Hall of Fame along with a small number of other baseball announcers with longevity in the job. Jack Brickhouse began announcing sports for WGN-TV early in my youth and retired only in my middle age. How can I describe the experience of listening to Brickhouse announce a game, an experience I have undergone not hundreds but thousands of times?

Listening to Jack Brickhouse announce a ballgame was like being trapped on a long bus ride with a hardware salesman who believed intensely in his product and knew no jokes. This, mind you, was a bus ride that lasted for more than thirty years. Brickhouse believed in his product all right, but, one has to add, he didn't seem to know much about it. He was fond of asking whoever was in the booth with him if a batter with a three and one count on him had "the green light." The most dismal fly balls, if hit by Cubs batters, were described as getting "good wood" on the ball. Players who were traded, when at bat against a former team, would like nothing better than, to hear Brickhouse tell it, "to wreak vengeance on their old teammates." At the end of yet another dreary season, Brickhouse, as chipper as ever (he must have drawn an impressive salary), would find the Cubs "in their familiar role as spoiler."

Every Chicago sports fan has his own favorite Jack Brickhouse story. A man now living in San Francisco recalls Brickhouse announcing a Bulls game, capping Bob Love's missing a crucial lay-up by remarking that "Love is usually deadly from that range." Steve Carlton, the great Philadelphia pitcher who had severed all relations with the media, was supposed to have said that if he ever gave an interview, he would give it to Jack Brickhouse. "Brickhouse would probably begin it," a friend of mine said at the time, "by asking Carlton how he got the nickname Lefty." I, myself, recall watching television the final game of the nightmare 1969 season, when the Cubs blew a nine- or ten-game lead going into September, at the end of which kids poured down onto the field and began circling the basepaths, in a frenzy of I am not sure what (frustration, anger, hatred), causing Brickhouse, smiling that strange, slightly maniacal smile, watching those kids racing dervishly around the bases, to comment something like: "Now this is what makes America great."

"Only in America," Harry Golden used to say. But only in Chicago, and perhaps also Peoria, city of his birth, did Jack Brickhouse seem possible. In my more lucid moments I know that he did not actually bring about all those gray years of defeat for Chicago teams. But he was always there at the mike, always cheerful, always infuriating. The Brickhouse years, as I now think of them, seem like the Trojan War, with Chicago as Troy, except that we had no Hector—if you exclude Ernie Banks, who used to like to exclaim, "Let's play two," which always seemed to me a sure prescription for double depression—and Brickhouse (oh, God) was our Homer.

At one point during these years, the Cubs ran television commercials that were essentially invitations to a picnic. I don't recall the copy with any exactitude, but these ads suggested that you come out to Wrigley Field to catch a little sunshine, gaze upon grass and vines, eat a hot dog, have something cool to drink, forget your troubles—and, oh yes, almost as an afterthought, see a ballgame. These ads were not foolish. However inept the Cubs may have been during the stretch, Wrigley Field has always been an oasis within the city. (As a North Sider and hence a National League man, I went much less frequently to Comiskey Park, which remains chiefly memorable to me as the place where I was served my first beer; I was fifteen at the time and looked twelve.) I have been going to Wrigley Field, man and boy, for roughly sixty-eight years, and the pleasure never seems to wear off. Even now, at that precise moment as I mount the steps when I first catch sight of the green of the outfield grass, I feel a slight but palpable shiver of delight to be back.

I won't say that I have sat in every seat in Wrigley Field, but I have over the years sat in every section. In recent years, when I went with a now late friend then in his eighties named John Lull, we used to sit in reserved grandstand on the third-base side, because John couldn't handle too much sun. At six years old, he had been to see the 1906 World Champion Cubs play; we are talking, my man, about Tinker, Evers, to freakin' Chance. Later I mostly sat, owing to friends who have an accountant who has season's tickets, four rows behind the Cubs' dugout.

It was in those seats that I at long last caught my first foul ball in Wrigley Field. A furious line drive off the bat of Leon Durham crashed off the shoulder of a youthful *shtarker* in mustache and tank top and rolled back over two other people and came spinning to a halt in my lap. Did I, you ask, turn the ball over to the kid in the tank? Of course I didn't.

As long as I am talking about greatest thrills in Chicago sports, my fondest memories of Wrigley Field go back to the days of late adolescence, in the middle 1950s, when there was brisk gambling action in center field, in the bleacher seats and under the scoreboard. Historians will want to know that the way this worked was that, at the outset, one made a bet of from twenty to fifty dollars on the outcome of the game, and then bet from inning to inning on the pitch-by-pitch action. Home-run odds tended to be about 13–1; a popular bet was something called, with alluring rhythm, "two bucks no reach," which meant a bet on or against the team at bat having a batter reach second base during the inning. In the fifth inning a guy known as the Junk Man would show up; one of those Jewish or Italian roughnecks, a type with which Chicago has never been in short supply, he was the man with whom you could bet the other way at long odds if you happened to be winning your original bet. What a fine feeling to be out in center field on a Tuesday afternoon in July winning a bet, covered the other way by the Junk Man against any sharp reversal of fortune (or *peripeteia*, as Aristotle had it)—one had it made, absolutely made in the shade.

I was never a Bears season's ticket holder, and so went to Bears games only rarely, even less and less in recent years, so that my sharpest memory of Soldier Field is the dated one of small smart-money men who used to go to Bear games in pointed shoes, car coats, and short-brimmed checkered hats, puffing on dollar cigars and wearing blue sapphire pinky rings. Chicago Stadium has been more familiar turf, for I was an early and eager NBA fan. In the Chet Walker, Jerry Sloan, Bob Love days, I shared season tickets with an old friend. I have only to breathe in to inhale memory of that fine Stadium smell, a combination of beer, cigar smoke, urine, grilling sausages, and other life-threatening grub. Then as now blacks and Jews seemed to predominate among NBA fans in Chicago, and whenever I go to a Bulls game today I am sure to run into characters I knew in high school or used to see around city parks.

I suppose Chicago teams have a natural constituency in people like me, men who grew up playing the games they now spend almost as much time watching. In Chicago there was scarcely anything to do as a boy but play these games, for mountain, sea, and the majestic delights of nature were not around to distract one from the playground; there were no schools in our city like the Bronx High School of Science and the High School of Music and Art to filter out young boys with special talents. A boy in Chicago could scarcely avoid growing up interested in sports, and the only serious question was in which sport or sports to concentrate his interest. Nor were kids' sports organized as they are today into one or another variant of Little League. I am myself pleased to have grown up at a time when parents kept clear the hell out of their children's play. One of the ironical consequences of parents interfering in their kids' play is that fewer kids seem to have become interested in sports. If their parents were so hot for their participation, how good could it be, right?

But for those of us who did grow up playing and loving sports, that love has not greatly diminished. Certainly it hasn't among the guys I went to high school with in Chicago, no matter how wildly various their occupations or success in life. "If you're an athlete," the late Jimmy Cannon wrote, "you're trapped in a prolonged boyhood." And if you are a fan you are, too. Yet there are worse places in which to be trapped. In Chicago, as in no other American city I know, sports is a lingua franca, cutting across class and racial lines and many other barriers. It is part of our common masculine heritage and hence is part of our common language, uniting, however briefly, professor and butcher, ad man and auto mechanic.

In Chicago, we are also united in being sick unto death of teams that specialize in inducing depression in their fans. Every fan knows about injury, bad luck, and disappointment, and the lesson of sports, it has been said, is finally about losing. Yet in Chicago, I believe, we have had more than ample opportunity to learn this lesson. Speaking for myself, I think I have it down pretty well by now, having had it drilled into me for much of the better part of seven decades.

Oddly, much as I remain hooked on sports, much as my appetite for them remains unabated, most of my memories of watching Chicago teams are rather dreary ones. To be sure, there have been some glory moments: the cool elegance of Sid Luckman as the Bears quarterback; the whiplike line-drive home runs of Ernie Banks; Gale Sayers not so much running as gliding to six touchdowns in a single game; the ability of Chet Walker always to come through with that clutch basket; the clean brutality of Dick Butkus's tackles; a beautiful game pitched with intelligence and control by the vastly overweight, Wilbur Wood, a clear case of mind over matter; the fighting heart of Jerry Sloan devoting himself to defense in basketball; a perfect throw into third from right field by Andre Dawson; Walter Payton high-stepping into the end zone; the slow spectacle of Rick Sutcliffe's gradual comeback, after physical injuries and shot confidence; Michael Jordan, turning the game of basketball up a full notch to a new level of play, flying, floating, twisting through the air to deliver a 360, triple-pump, how's ya motha, in your kazoo slam yet rather refined dunk.

Brilliant and gratifying as such things have been, they seem but brief flashings in an otherwise gray sky. More emphatically do I remember scenes of desolation and gloom. Going back to my boyhood, I can recall a Cubs slugger named Bill Nicholson, whose nickname of "Swish" certainly didn't derive from any homosexual traits; a Bears end named Ed Sprinkle, whose specialty was attracting penalties for unnecessary roughness and unsportsmanlike conduct; a Bulls center named Tom Boerwinkle, who at seven feet tall had a vertical leap of roughly three inches; Abe Gibron, then the Bears coach, standing disconsolately on the sidelines, his ample stomach well over his belt, as the Bears take the pipe once more; endless athletes of great potential—Roy Smalley Sr., Dick Allen, Bobby Douglass, Shawon Dunston—who in various Chicago uniforms never found it; Ray Meyer doing his Uriah Heep bit (I'm so "umble") as yet another DePaul basketball team chokes in yet another NCAA tournament; Lee Elia caught on a tape recorder calling Chicago fans a bunch of Oedipuses Rex; Mike Ditka walking off the field as the Bears blow yet another crucial game on Monday Night Football, a picture of sullen dejection; the Bulls losing to Rick Barry and the Golden State Warriors, after blowing a substantial lead first in games, and then in the final game, of the NBA semifinals, after which Golden State goes on to beat the Washington Bullets for the championship in four straight; the White Sox gently submissive before Baltimore pitching in the American League playoffs. . . . I could go on and on, but better perhaps to end this masochistic paragraph.

After the Cubs blew the final game of a lazy playoff with the San Diego Padres, I, a teacher of youth, author of many tomes, an intellectual, a product of the Enlightenment, a man of middle years and sober mien, was for fully a week, I won't go so far as to say suicidal (I haven't the attention span for such sustained gloom), but nonetheless in a bit of a schlunk. My appetite was under control, the World Series seemed dreary (which it was), I was far from my usual ebullient Rotarian self. Watching the Cubs blow that fifth game to the Padres—with a lead and the ostensibly invincible Rick Sutcliffe on the mound—brought me more grief than watching the Bears the following year smash the Patriots in the Super Bowl brought me joy. But then anguish, disappointment, grief have tended to be the lot of the sports fan in Chicago. Yet why do we hang in there, continuing to follow teams who have almost specialized in dispensing the agony of defeat?

Because, I suspect, we were brought up to it. As Chicagoans, we combine cynicism (everything's fixed, right? everyone has his price, right?) with hopeful sentimentality (wouldn't a subway series be marvelous?). As Chicagoans, too, we grew up with a love for sports, which was a major part of neighborhood life; and for the first fifteen or so years of most of our lives, the neighborhood in Chicago, with its playgrounds, its parish, its parks, was all of life that most us knew. But I, who tend to think of myself as reasonably worldly, have long since left the neighborhood, and so why carry on this not quite rational interest in sports, cheering on and generally getting worked up over youthful millionaire athletes who have no more real affiliation with the City of Chicago than Dmitri Shostakovich?

If I could have back all the time I have spent watching sports, they might ask me to show my ID before serving me a drink. What about the time left? Every so often it occurs to me to close up shop, forget about sports, and devote the time I annually spend on it to learning to play the contrabassoon. But I am in too deep. I already have too much time invested, to get out now. If I stopped watching Chicago sports, the Bulls would be certain to win the NBA, DePaul the NCAA, the Bears the Super Bowl, and the Cubs and Sox meet in the World Series. If any one of those unlikely events were to take place and I were not there to see it, I should suffer sorely. I prefer instead to continue suffering in the manner to which I have long become accustomed. I am not one of those dopey Chicago fans who is always crying, "Wait till next year!" I can wait, all right, not to worry, but I'll be there all the same.

OPEN ANOTHER
CAN OF QUARTERBACK

Rich Cohen's *Monsters* is the best book on professional football I know—the best because the most truthful. Whatever its flaws, the book supplies a history of the game from before the founding of the National Football League to the current day, shows how the advent of the free-substitution rule changed football from a players' to a coach's game, and provides the name of the first player to spike a ball in the end zone (Homer Jones, a wide receiver for the New York Giants). What distinguishes Mr. Cohen's book, however, is his understanding that professional football is and always has been chiefly about violence.

Until 1985, the Dallas Cowboys were thought "America's Team," but that year it was the Chicago Bears who swept the boards of national attention. The team's juggernaut defense, the antics of its quarterback Jim McMahon, the stalwart play of the great running back Walter Payton, the comic phenomenon of the 325-pound lineman William ("the Refrigerator") Perry, the video the team made to a ditty called "The Super Bowl Shuffle"—all this made the Bears the media dream team.

Monsters is, in the tradition of Frederick Exley's "A Fan's Notes" (1968), about what the 1985 Chicago Bears winning the NFL championship meant to its then adolescent author. Born in 1968, Mr. Cohen grew up during lean years for the Bears and their fans. On the Bears making it to the Super Bowl, he writes: "I never had World War II; I never had V-J day; I was never a sailor and I never kissed a girl in Times Square—but I did have this." The 1985 Chicago Bears, he claims, cured him of the "defeatism of the Chicago fan" and—allow room for a bit of hyperbole here—"they had saved my life."

Frederick Exley had a drinking problem, but Rich Cohen is able to get high on his own prose. If I were a referee instead of a reviewer, I would throw the flag at various places in his book for piling on (overwriting) and delay of game (writing more than is required in an autobiographical mode). Mr. Cohen's prose resembles the famous "46" defense of the '85 Bears; he blitzes a lot. Here he is describing Detroit quarterback Joe Ferguson after having been smashed into unconsciousness by Bears outside linebacker Wilber Marshall:

> A few minutes later, Ferguson, having been revived, sat on the sideline, helmet off, hair tousled, dazed. I've seen the same look on the faces of old hobos on the Bowery, methadone addicts on withdrawal, winos with delirium tremens. If El Greco came back, he might want to paint Joe Ferguson five minutes after that hit, his eyes as wide as saucers, a fog all around him, the roof of the Silverdome rising above.

Mr. Cohen also goes in for the crackback simile, which sometimes works brilliantly but sometimes misses. He amusingly refers to the merely 5-foot-10 quarterback Doug Flutie as "the Michael J. Fox of the gridiron." But he describes Los Angeles Ram running back Eric Dickerson as "tall and lean, an exclamation point broken free from the page." He writes that Bears quarterback Jim McMahon "went through the defense like a drunk going through a bar—filled with bad intent."

In *Monsters*, Mr. Cohen finds parallels between the 1985 Bears and the city of Chicago that may exist only in his mind. "America's city," he calls Chicago, and notes that the 1985 Bears "seemed a perfect expression of the city—its character, its toughness, its heartbreaks, its history." He writes that "the Bears' smashmouth style seemed to capture the spirit of the town." I was hoping against hope that he wouldn't quote from Carl Sandburg's wretched hog-butcher-for-the-world poem, not a single word of which has ever been remotely true, but he does so, alas, extensively.

Mr. Cohen has an ear for amusing remarks, such as the defensive lineman Dan Hampton describing William Perry with his shirt off as resembling "a mud slide." The best parts of *Monsters* are its interviews, chiefly with the men who played on the 1985 Chicago Bears. The most revealing is the one with Doug Plank, a former Bears defensive back who did not play on the Super Bowl team but who speaks with candor and insight into how brutal professional football can be. Mr. Plank claims that what makes a great football player is neither size nor speed but "the ability to suppress your survival instincts."

Mr. Cohen devotes several excellent pages to pro football before the founding of the NFL. The Chicago Bears were originally known as the Staleys, because they were sponsored by the A.E. Staley Starch Co. in Decatur, Ill. George Halas, who played for the Staleys and later brought the team to Chicago, was a crucial figure in the formation of the NFL, which began in 1920 as the American Professional Football Conference. Other early franchise owners were Tim Mara (in New York), Art Rooney (in Pittsburgh) and George Preston Marshall (in Washington). Begun on what today seem derisory sums, these franchises are now billion-dollar properties.

Halas was both a clever businessman and a genuine innovator. Although not its inventor, he was the man who as coach of the Bears made the T-formation, built around a passing quarterback, work. Halas was the first coach to study game film. He took up the idea of "the eye in the sky," or having an assistant coach witness a game from high in the stadium, to gain a wider perspective. His own record as a coach was 324 wins against 151 losses and 31 ties.

Much piety surrounds the name George Halas in Chicago. Halas himself grew pious in his old age, certain a seat near the 50-yard line awaited him in heaven. He was in fact a bleak and unpleasant man. Mike Royko, the Chicago columnist, described Halas as "a tight-fisted, stubborn, willful, mean old man," which sounds about right. His favorite word, applied to opposing players and coaches, referees, and his own players when they let him down, was the more common term for fellator. His cheapness was legendary. He throws around "nickels like manhole covers," Mr. Ditka said after negotiating his salary with Halas, who owned the team until his death in 1983.

Mr. Cohen did not know Halas, but he did interview Mike Ditka, whom he also affects to admire. I write "affects" because he supplies a great deal of evidence that portrays Mr. Ditka as a crude bully. Mr. Ditka regularly humiliated his players in public, and Mr. Cohen quotes Bob Avellini, one of the less successful quarterbacks to play under Mr. Ditka, saying: "Everything he did was based on fear."

Born a century earlier in Ukraine, the country of his family's descent, Mike Ditka is easily imagined as a Cossack, riding through *shtetls* blithely raping and pillaging. In an interesting throwaway fact, Mr. Cohen reports that Mr. Ditka decided not to go to Penn State but to Pitt because the latter improved his chances of getting into dental school. Dr. Michael Ditka, DDS—the thought chills the blood and makes the movie *Marathon Man* seem as light and lyrical as *Funny Face*.

Mr. Cohen remarks that as Halas was Mr. Ditka's coach, so was Mr. Ditka his, Mr. Cohen's, coach. How so is far from clear. He didn't, surely, teach him to kick ass. (The title of one of Mr. Ditka's books is *In Life, First You Kick Ass.*) Mr. Cohen ends *Monsters* with a scene from 1994 in which, then twenty-six and working at *Rolling Stone*, he is told that the Bears had fired Mr. Ditka as the team's coach. "The blood rushed into my face," Mr. Cohen writes. "I . . . went down into the street, veins pounding in my head. I sat on a curb at 51st Street and Sixth Avenue, dropped my chin in my hand and cried." I hope this isn't true. I want to believe that Mr. Cohen, in search of a dramatic ending for his book, made this up.

On the subject of Buddy Ryan, the Bears' defensive coach in the middle 1980s, the man who invented the then-famous "46" defense, Mr. Cohen supplies much interesting information. The 46 defense was designed to do one thing: maim the opposing team's quarterback. "Let's open another can of quarterback," Mr. Ryan was fond of saying to his defensive unit. He had the endorsement of Halas, and during the years he was the team's defensive coach Mr. Ryan answered to no one, not even Mr. Ditka, the titular head coach. *Monsters* sets out the psychological combat between these two brutish men in a way I haven't seen before.

Mr. Cohen is deft at describing notable NFL massacre scenes: the destruction of Joe Ferguson, the brutal sacking of Jim McMahon by a Green Bay Packer named Charles Martin, the Wilber Marshall crackback block on Lawrence Taylor, some of Doug Plank's more vicious forays. A producer at NFL Films told Mr. Cohen that football has surpassed baseball in popularity because of its violence: "Fans love to see the player wounded and even more to see that player get off the turf and stay in the game and strike back." I once heard Emmitt Smith, of the Dallas Cowboys, asked what it was like to be a running back in the

NFL, answer that it was getting into 30 car accidents in a single afternoon, without, one assumes, the protection of seat belts.

Professional football players are our gladiators. The only difference is that we, the fans, don't, as they did at the Colosseum in Rome, put our thumbs up or down to decide a player's fate. But then we don't have to; they all but kill themselves. In each of his interviews, Mr. Cohen asks former players: "How're you holding up physically?" Everyone answers with an iliad of injuries and woes.

No one, though, topped those suffered by Jim McMahon, the team's punky QB and Mr. Cohen's favorite player among the 1985 Bears. Notable among Mr. McMahon's injuries were a bruised heart (gulp) and a sliced kidney (hope you haven't passed out here). "My shoulders, my elbows, my knees—they're all pretty much gone," Mr. McMahon reports. He has memory problems, deterioration in his upper neck from a compressed disc, and a lower spine that's degenerating. Mr. Cohen asks if Mr. McMahon, knowing then what he does now about how dangerous pro football is, would still have pursued it as a career. Mr. McMahon answers: "I'd do it all again in a heartbeat."

Some of the older players Mr. Cohen interviewed remark that everyone knows the toll charged by playing football. You work in the mines, you expect the possibility of black-lung disease. You work for the mob, you expect to be shot at. You play professional football, you expect head injuries, and it pays a lot better than working in the mines and the hours are better than working for the mob. Or so the reasoning goes.

That reasoning is deeply faulty. Decadence is what any sensible person would call paying men, even paying them stupendously well, to destroy themselves for our pleasure. I write this without any sense of virtue, for I have watched—and continue to watch—my share of pro and college football every autumn. You will doubtless continue to find me at my post (a comfortable chair before a 52-inch television set) this and every other season so long as I continue to draw breath. I'm not entirely proud of it.

Toward the close of *Monsters*, Mr. Cohen allows that, in light of the brain damage, dementia, and suicide among former professional football players, he has "come to rethink my taste for the knockout blow." He writes briefly about the prospects for curtailing the brutality of the game. But the possible turns that reform will take—better helmets, a more careful check on concussions, a closer observance of the rules, with more severe penalties for violating them—aren't very impressive.

Speaking at the funeral of the great Bears running back Walter Payton—Payton died at forty-five, of a liver ailment possibly, Mr. Cohen speculates, caused by his 13 years in the NFL—Mike Ditka said that "the game is greater than the athletes who play it." If you believe that, there is a three-flat building in the Chicago neighborhood of Englewood, scene of so many recent gang killings, I could let you have at a good price.

THE OLD BALL GAME

When Marilyn Monroe divorced Joe DiMaggio, Oscar Levant remarked that it only went to show that no man can be expected to excel at two national pastimes. Time can do terrible things, even to wit, and this superior *mot* now has a slight flaw, which is that it is no longer clear that baseball is America's other pastime. In the 1940s and early '50s, the national pastime it indubitably was, a game that captured the country's attention and enraptured the imagination of young boys and most men, who had earlier played it as boys. Just how it did and why it did and with what consequences is the subject of the intellectual historian Lee Congdon's *Baseball and Memory*, a book about the game but also about much more.

The 1940s and '50s, the years at the center of Congdon's book, are those of his boyhood, and, as it happens, also of mine. The sports menu during those years was much shorter than it is now. Professional basketball hadn't yet arrived in a serious way; professional football had a short season, and not many teams had franchises west of the Mississippi; hockey was still felt to be essentially a Canadian sport; golf and tennis were thought, for the most part correctly, to be country-club or rich people's games. Baseball was the main, the primo, the supreme American sport.

If baseball had a serious rival as a spectator sport, it was boxing, for a heavyweight title fight riveted American attention like no other sporting event. But such fights were intermittent, and baseball was played daily for six months, eight if one includes spring training. Besides, one had to be a brute to box, while baseball was a game available to every boy of normal size and decent coordination.

A Little League World Series was staged as early as 1947, but baseball for young boys remained largely unorganized through Lee Congdon's and my boyhoods, a playground game unimpeded by otiose intervention from adults. Summer days one ambled over to the schoolyard, and got into a pickup game with other kids who had the same end in mind. If there weren't 18 boys up for a game, the positions of right field, second base, and first base were eliminated, and one played something called pitcher's hands out.

As a boy, one styled one's play on one or another of the major league ballplayers one had heard about on the radio, or read about in the sports pages or in *Sport* magazine, or had seen at the local ballpark, if one lived in a city with a major league team. I played shortstop on the gravel field of Daniel Boone School with a trapper's mitt bought from Montgomery Ward, doing my best impression of the St. Louis Cardinals' great shortstop Marty Marion.

The ranks of boyhood baseball players thinned out in high school, where baseball wasn't one of the glory sports. Large crowds didn't attend high-school baseball games the way they did football and basketball games; and there weren't any girls watching from the stands before whom—hope against hope—one might look heroic. I left playing baseball in high school for a perfectly mediocre career in tennis and basketball. High-school baseball was a game for the true hard cases: boys who loved the game in and for itself.

In those days high-school baseball could be a dangerous sport. Batting helmets were not yet devised, and sixteen- and seventeen-year-old opposing pitchers threw heat, as fastballs were even then called, with uncertain control, leaving open the real possibility of being smashed in the head or face. Getting spiked while tagging a runner out was another hazard. Then there were line drives—"screaming liners," "frozen ropes," in the standard clichés—smashed back at the pitcher or third or first baseman. However pastoral some writers make baseball seem, the possibility of serious injury was part of the game.

Even if one stopped playing it once out of grammar school, baseball remained in the bones of most American males. Boys grew up knowing the rosters of the then-16 major league teams, traded baseball cards—

now, some of them, worth obscene sums of money—passionately argued the merits of various players. I probably learned more arithmetic attempting to understand batting averages and other key statistical categories in baseball than I did in the classroom. The last two words of the National Anthem, an old joke had it, were "play ball."

Baseball was American, a part of the culture. During World War II a way of identifying oneself to fellow American troops when returning from behind enemy lines was through one's baseball knowledge.

"Who goes there?"

"Staff Sergeant Bob Mahoney, Fifth Armored Division, Headquarters Company."

"Who is Ted Williams?"

"Boston Red Sox, left fielder."

"Okay. Come forward."

Not knowing who Ted Williams was might have got one shot.

Sports generally, but baseball most of all, was the lingua franca of American men in a democratic country. Baseball could nicely slice through social class and educational lines. Through their common interest in baseball, a philologist could sustain a good conversation with a garage mechanic, a butcher with a biochemist.

Baseball and Memory begins with Bobby Thomson's home run in the old Polo Grounds, hyperbolically known in the press as "the shot heard 'round the world," in the final playoff game that won the pennant for the New York Giants over the Brooklyn Dodgers on October 3, 1951. For decades afterward men marked the event, as others marked Pearl Harbor or the Kennedy assassination, by remembering where they were when Thomson hit his homer. The home run was hit at 3:58 Eastern Standard Time, Congdon notes, a fact that reminded me that I had just come out of my last class for the day at Nicholas Senn High School in Chicago, headed for the smoke-filled purlieus of Harry's School Store, where Thomson's homer was of course topic number one.

Along with Bobby Thomson's home run, Congdon recalls Don Larsen's perfect game against the still-in-Brooklyn Dodgers in the World Series of 1956. (I watched the game on a blurry television set while sitting on a couch with the stuffing coming out of it in a broken-down fraternity house at the University of Chicago.) He retells Pittsburgh Pirate Bill Mazeroski's walk-off homer against Ralph Terry to defeat the Yankees in the 1960 World Series. He sifts the evidence about Babe Ruth's supposedly calling and aiming a home run at Wrigley Field in 1932 (accuracy on the question has yet to be solidly established).

Lee Congdon has spent—I hesitate to say wasted—his youth and much of his manhood as a Chicago Cubs fan. As is well known, the Cubs have had an uncanny knack for letting their fans down—hard. The team has not appeared in a World Series since 1945 and not won a World Series since 1908.

The pages of *Baseball and Memory* are replete with Cubs pitchers with high earned-run averages and poor career won-lost records, sluggers who could be counted upon not to come through in the clutch, egregious trades of brilliant ballplayers—Lou Brock, Rafael Palmeiro, most notable among them—for now properly forgotten ones. In 1969, with, for once, a solid roster of players (five of them on that year's National League All-Star team), the Cubs, though 9½ games ahead of the Mets in August, went 8–17 in September and blew what looked like a sure trip to the World Series, proving that even when they were good they weren't good enough.

Congdon shows no signs of regret for his long years as a Cubs fan, however little punctuated by glory or triumph they have been. He does, though, have deep regrets about what has happened to the game of baseball that he was brought up on and still loves. Sports have politics: Fans line up along a liberal to conservative spectrum, and not infrequently people who are liberal in their politics are arch-conservative in their views on sports, and vice versa.

On this sports spectrum, Lee Congdon is a veritable wingnut. He feels that baseball has been diluted by the increase in the number of teams from 16 in his youth to 30 today, with a corresponding thinning-out of talent. He prefers the older vintage ballplayer, whose natural talent was reinforced by toughness and dedication and, often, amusing eccentricity. He quotes the Brooklyn Dodgers pitcher Preacher Roe saying that the best advice about pitching to the Cardinals great Stan Musial was "throw four wide ones and try to pick him off first base." He cites the competitiveness of the take-no-prisoners pitcher Early Wynn who, when asked if he would deliberately throw a ball at his own mother, replied: "I would if she were crowding the plate."

A purist in his baseball values, Congdon does not like extending playoffs to wild card teams, has no taste for interleague play, despises the designated hitter instituted by the American League in 1973—"an obscenity," he calls it—and not yet adopted by the National League. The newer baseball stadiums put him off; only Wrigley Field in Chicago and Fenway Park in Boston pass his muster. He doesn't approve the rule against pitchers deliberately brushing back hitters crowding the plate. He is opposed to better—perhaps the more precise word is fancier—food being served in some ballparks; he mentions the truffle fries and martinis served at the Mohegan Sun Sports Bar at the new Yankee Stadium.

These are extreme views, highly unprogressive, and doubtless deserve to be argued against—though not by me, who happens to share every one of them.

About the use of steroids among baseball players, Congdon is an even harder-liner. He believes that no player found to have used steroids should be allowed in the Hall of Fame, and that all of them ought to have their records wiped off the books, *tout court*—into the dustbin of history with all these audodidact pharmacists. To illustrate how widespread the use of steroids was, he brings up the almost commonplaceness of ballplayers in the steroid era hitting 50 or more home runs in a season—a feat never accomplished by such chemical-free ballplayers as Hank Aaron, Frank Robinson, Reggie Jackson, Mike Schmidt, Ted Williams, Ernie Banks, and Eddie Matthews. His paragraphs on steroids are infused, quite properly, with anger.

Congdon recapitulates the year, 1998, of the great (ultimately fake) home run derby between Mark McGwire and Sammy Sosa. For a portion of that summer I was housesitting for a friend in the village of Laconnex, near Geneva, and each morning upon arising I eagerly booted up his computer to see if McGwire or Sosa had hit any homers the day before. Both players, we now know, were jacked up on steroids. Turns out that I, along with millions of others, as the old Brooklyn Dodger fans used to say, was robbed, or at least had, and it's not a good feeling.

Growing up, as (again) did I, on the splendid boys' sports novels of John R. Tunis—*The Kid from Tomkinsville, Highpockets, The Kid Comes Back, Rookie of the Year, All-American, Iron Duke,* and others—Lee Congdon brings a moral cast to his love of baseball. While telling gripping sports yarns, Tunis's novels inculcated the tenets of the old liberalism at its finest: teamwork, courage under pressure, fair play, hatred of prejudice. All but the last-named virtue has little today to do with sports; in fact, athletes and their coaches and managers spend a good deal of time seeking out the niggling small advantage that will defeat or otherwise discourage the opponent. Sportsmanship has less and less to do with contemporary sport.

One of the results is that ballplayers have come to reflect, as Congdon contends, "our baser rather than our nobler selves." With a few notable exceptions in the contemporary era—Cal Ripken Jr., Rick Sutcliffe, Orel Hershiser, Andre Dawson, Carlton Fisk, Derek Jeter—athletes tend to be disappointing human beings. Perhaps this comes of their being men who, even as boys, owing to their much-prized physical talent, nobody ever turned down for anything. In the current era, where money from enormous television revenues and posh endorsement contracts arrive for them in wheelbarrowish quantities, the emergence of character in an athlete is even more difficult than when all he had to deal with was adulation.

For those of us frivolous enough to have put in a vast number of hours watching sports, and other concomitant remarkable physical acts, the notion of being a fan has become a more and more dubious proposition. The proposition, baldly put, is this: Why are we more loyal to, and ardent on behalf of, teams than are the men who play for them?

This is one of a series of questions that all, alas, have the same answer. Why do athletes use steroids? Why do they seem more prone to injury—or is it that they are more protective of themselves?—than athletes of an earlier era? Why are they largely devoid of loyalty? Why has an afternoon at a major league baseball game for a family of four become a $200 or $300 extravagance? A sports journalist once stopped the television sports producer Don Ohlmeyer because he had a question for him. "If your question is about sports," Ohlmeyer replied, "the answer is money."

As a historian, Lee Congdon could not have been expected to resist making parallels between the game of baseball of his boyhood and the game today. Nor was he likely to have avoided going on from there to measure the decades when the game of baseball seemed golden against those rather more tarnished—by drugs, staggering contracts, feckless behavior, ugly, electronic-scoreboard-distracting ballparks—decades of recent times.

Not merely baseball but life generally was better in the 1950s, Congdon maintains, and he makes his argument in a balanced way, taking on the worst cases. Even though racial segregation was still prevalent in the '50s, for example, he notes that black life may have been qualitatively better, with lower crime and unwed birth rates. "With far more reason to be bitter," he adds, there was less in the way of self-defeating grievance-collecting among blacks then than now. In the 1950s, families, black and white, seemed stronger, life safer, growing up less wracked by the foolish notions of psychology and sociology for too long now in vogue." Whatever its gains in personal freedom, the 1960s, Congdon writes, "has left mountains of human wreckage in its wake."

Congdon's larger argument is that baseball, when it was part of the culture, provided an important storehouse of memories, which, under current cultural conditions, soon figure to disappear. These memories, he holds, are all the more important as a stay against the thought that life is pure progress, ever onward and upward. "Fascination with the older game," he writes, "cannot be divorced from a growing recognition on the part of at least some Americans that history does not move in an ever-ascending direction."

The young, we are told, are today bored with baseball, finding more immediate—baseball fans would argue, also much less subtle—excitement in basketball and football, and even in so-called extreme sports. The number of American black athletes, who until recently comprised a third of major league players, has diminished, while the number of Central and Latin American and Asian players has risen. The day may not be far away when major league baseball is no longer a game played preponderantly by Americans.

The United States could once claim to be a national culture, with the majority of its population knowing and singing the same songs, viewing the same television shows, playing and watching and passionate about the same games. This national culture has been eroding over the past half-century, splintering off into many cultures: youth culture, black culture, Hispanic culture, and more. The result is that one can no longer confidently say that a game, an art, a phenomenon, is essentially American.

What can confidently be said is that a major trade has taken place over the decades since the 1950s: that of stability for widened tolerance, of moral equanimity for less restricting moral relativism, of a unified culture for a poly-cultured society. Perhaps, in this trade, there are players to be named later of whom we haven't yet been informed. If there are not, if this is all there is to the deal, then it has to be judged a trade that not even Lee Congdon's boneheaded Chicago Cubs front office would have made.

WRIGLEY FIELD

The *Honesty in Reviewing Manual*, a slender book long out of print, requires that I mention that George Will has thrice taken me to dinner, picking up the check each time. The theme of sports dominated all three meals. At the first dinner, his future wife was along and presented him with a baseball signed by Keith Moreland, then a Cubs outfielder, under the inscription, "From the other guy in right."

At the second dinner, Jim Frey, the former manager of the Cubs, joined us. He told about being accused of racism by Bob Gibson for the observation that it seemed to get dark early in Venezuela; about running out of patience with the mound antics of the "mad Hungarian" Al Hrabosky; and about another pitcher who had an only slightly higher than .500 lifetime win-loss percentage but wished to be treated as a superstar. All of Mr. Frey's stories ended with the refrain, "I couldn't take it anymore."

The scene of the third dinner was at Mike Ditka's restaurant, and we were joined by George Will's son Geoffrey, who had earlier been a student in a course of mine on Joseph Conrad at Northwestern University and was now in the FBI. ("Only one of us at this table," the elder Will said, "is packing heat.") Apart from our table, every size-52 suit in Chicago seemed to be in the joint. One of the starters on the menu was Pot Roast Nachos, a synecdoche if ever I saw one. I recall thinking that if Edith Wharton were still alive and came to visit me in Chicago, Ditka's would not be the first place to which I would take her.

George Will also took me to the first game of the 2008 playoffs, when the Cubs played the Dodgers. He had arranged for a skybox, in which we were joined by a gracious man who was formerly president of the Atlanta Braves. The Dodgers first baseman James Loney hit a grand slam that put paid to the Cubs' hopes. The Cubs would go on to lose the series three games to none, capping off a clean century since the team had last won a World Series.

By 2008, I had declared myself the baseball equivalent of a bisexual, rooting for the Chicago White Sox as well as for the Cubs, which in Chicago is verboten, but, like Jim Frey, I couldn't take it—the Cubs' dismal performance over the decades—anymore. So the loss that evening did not hit me anywhere near as hard as it did George Will, who was palpably demoralized, suffering in the stoical manner of the die-hard Cubs fan. We parted at the El, on which, at the Lawrence Avenue stop, I was winked at by a tall African-American transvestite.

George Will is as serious about baseball as he is about the Constitution or foreign policy. If anyone thinks otherwise, believes him a mere dilettante, I invite him to glimpse Mr. Will's excellent book *Men at Work: The Craft of Baseball* (1990). Amid a vast array of interesting arcana, the reader will there find eight alternative strategies a manager might adopt with men on first and third with one out.

How did so clever a man as George Will fall into the slough of despond that is the life of a Cubs fan? Mr. Will grew up in Champaign-Urbana, Ill., where his father was a philosophy professor. Champaign-Urbana is roughly mid-distance from Chicago and St. Louis, and the young George Will could as easily have been a Cardinals as a Cubs fan. He claims in *A Nice Little Place on the North Side* that the allure of big-city Chicago—"To Moscow! To Moscow! To Moscow!" cries Irina in Chekhov's *Three Sisters*—drew him in.

Although he does not mention it in his book, Mr. Will once told me that the reason he could not be a Cardinals fan was that the announcer for the Cardinals when he was growing up was the bilious Harry Caray, whose depression the congenitally optimistic George Will could not abide. (Such is the bitter lot of the Cubs fan, Caray would in later years become the principal, and still depressive, TV announcer for Cubs games.)

The Cardinals are the second-most successful team in the game, after the Yankees, while the Cubs have been the most futile franchise in modern baseball. Had he become a Cardinals rather than a Cubs fan, would Mr. Will have the conservative politics he now has? Did his years following the Cubs imbue him with the tragic sense of human limitation that is at the heart of conservative philosophy? But for the dampening presence of Harry Caray in St. Louis, who knows, George Will might today be a Democratic senator from Illinois.

The argument of George Will's book on Wrigley Field is that the atmosphere of nostalgia, the historical feel of the Cubs' home stadium, "is part cause and part symptom of the Cubs' dysfunctional performance." How dysfunctional it has been he sets out in dismaying detail, statistical and anecdotal. The Cubs' last World Series victory was 1908; its last appearance in a World Series was 1945. Since moving to Wrigley Field in 1916, the team's winning percentage has been a dispiriting .488, its overall record 7,478 wins to 7,833 losses. The question is: Has the antique elegance of Wrigley Field been an enticement for the team's owners to do nothing to improve the team, since the fans, allured by the field's fading grandeur, come out in any case?

Mr. Will highlights various shaming Cubs records: In 1942 the team's shortstop Lennie Merullo committed four errors in one inning; the outfielder Lou ("the Mad Russian") Novikoff, who feared that the ivy on the walls of Wrigley Field was poisoned, once attempted to steal third with the bases loaded; a Cubs third baseman named Don Hoak, in 1956, struck out six times in a 17-inning game. When Mr. Will was a boy, his father explained the concept of being "overdue" in baseball by distinguishing between Stan Musial and the then-Cubs shortstop Roy Smalley, who, with a lifetime batting average of .227, was never overdue.

Since 1916 the Cubs have had this lovely stadium; the problem has been to put good players upon its greensward. In the commercial language of our day, the "product" hasn't really been there. At Wrigley Field the flora has been far superior to the fauna. The great names that have played for the Cubs turn out to be less than legion: Cap Anson, Mordecai ("Three Finger") Brown, Grover Cleveland Alexander, the double-play combination of Tinker, Evers and Chance, Hack Wilson, Gabby Hartnett, Ernie Banks, Ferguson Jenkins, and one might toss in Ryne Sandberg and Andre Dawson, but that's about it. Two players who might have been on this list are Lou Brock, one of the game's great base runners, and Dennis Eckersley, one of its dominant closers, had they not been traded away early in their careers.

A Nice Little Place on the North Side is replete with the amusing trivia that in baseball constitutes lore. The book recounts what must be the grandest tirade in all of sports, that by a Cubs manager named Lee Elia against critical fans, in which even the prepositions seemed profane. It chronicles the contempt of Leo Durocher, when manager of the Cubs, for Ernie Banks, the team's greatest player in its modern era. It relates the sad Steve Bartman incident, in which an earnest fan interfered with a foul ball that, had it been caught, might have ended a key inning during a 2003 playoff game; the tale exhibits baseball fans, who made Mr. Bartman's life a misery, at their most repulsive.

George Will takes us through the various owners of the Cubs. The Wrigleys, the chewing-gum family, owned the team for decades before selling it to the Chicago Tribune Co., which sold it in 2009 to its current owners, the Ricketts family, whose fortune is based on Ameritrade, the online brokerage firm. Phil Wrigley, the son of the first owner, William, was a man who did not much care for baseball. His business model, as Mr. Will puts it, was: "If the team is bad, strive mightily to improve . . . the ballpark." Under his ownership, ivy was planted on the outfield walls. Advertisements were not permitted within the confines of the park. A modest green scoreboard, operated by hand, was installed above the center-field bleachers.

Phil Wrigley promoted the stadium as if it were an Elysian Field: "The idea," he wrote, "is to get out in the open air, have a picnic. . . . We are aiming at people not interested in baseball. These are the fans we want." The former major-league pitcher Jim Brosnan, who spent four seasons with the Cubs during the 1950s, captured the spirit of Phil Wrigley's plan and its consequences when he said: "Come Out and Have a Picnic—and the other teams usually did."

In my lifetime I have seen the ticket prices at Wrigley Field go from 75 cents for bleacher seats to last year's price of $100.80 (it's that damn 80 cents that stings) for box seats. Every year I buy two pairs of box-seat tickets, first-base side, 11 rows off the field, just above the visiting team's on-deck circle, from a good friend who has kept his season tickets through three marriages. Today the bleachers resemble nothing so much as a singles bar, filled with young men and women in bubbly good health and cut-off jeans and Cubs T-shirts.

I confess that, in line with Phil Wrigley's plan, I have gone to Wrigley Field more for the park than for the ragged product. I like the moment when one comes up the stairs from the concession walkway below and the greenness of the place, field and walls both, accosts the eye. I like sitting in the sun with a friend, chatting both during the game and between innings. I always leave home an hour or so early to find a parking space in the neighborhood and so save the $30 parking fee, which gives a fairly precise notion of at what rate I value my time. I only go to day games, where the sense of doing something sinful by attending is more intense. I usually go in midsummer, and since the Cubs are generally out of contention in their division by mid-May, there is a fine absence of tension in the proceedings on the field. A summer afternoon at Wrigley Field has been for me rather like going to a spa without the pedicure and white terry-cloth robe.

Across town, the Chicago White Sox have better players, a savvier front office, a more intelligent owner (Jerry Reinsdorf), and better food. They also have, as do most baseball parks in the contemporary era, a Jumbotron, the huge video screen that, in its all too regular blarings, gives a contemplative man no rest. Fan Cam, Kiss Your Neighbor, the race of the M&Ms, the Trivia Quiz, rock music, advertising—mental toxicity oozes from the thing.

One of the great advantages of Wrigley Field has been that it has no Jumbotron, though one is currently planned by the Ricketts family. The major obstacle in its way is the objection of the owners of buildings surrounding the Wrigley Field outfield, on whose roofs stands have been erected and seats sold to corporations and others who use it to barbecue and booze it up during games.

George Will sets out the claims of both sides on this issue—my own view is a plague on both their condominiums—and, the traditional conservative giving way to the free marketeer, comes out for the Cubs' owners having their Jumbotron, needing as they do the revenue from advertising that the intrusive monster will bring. His argument, not unpersuasive, is that Wrigley Field is well behind the times in its training and video facilities, and without the revenue that the Jumbotron brings in the Ricketts family most likely will not be able to afford to bring the park up to date.

"What the Cubs do is play *professional* baseball," George Will writes, and the team needs to be more efficient at generating revenue if it is ever to field a competitive team. "So, sentimentalists: Get over it," he exclaims to those who prefer Wrigley Field in its full antiquity. Alas, I cannot. No doubt the hideous Jumbotron will be installed, which will save me $403.20 a year in Cubs tickets. Jumbotron blasting away, hot dogs ordered by app, video ads emerging from the long trough that is the urinal in the men's room—in this dark advanced technological future the Cubs will have to soldier on without my tepid support.

George Will has achieved a fine balance in *A Nice Little Place on the North Side* between his heartfelt allegiance to the Chicago Cubs and his recognition of their status among sports fans as a national joke. As fodder for humor the Cubs have been inexhaustible. The morning after the Cubs lost the 1984 National League Championship Series to the Padres, owing in good part to Leon Durham, the team's first baseman, allowing a dribbling grounder to go through his legs, I was shopping in my neighborhood grocery store. The owner asked if I had heard about Leon Durham's attempted suicide. "Really?" I asked, genuinely shocked. "He stepped out in front of a bus," the man said, "but it went through his legs." Lots of laughs, those Cubs, and, as George Will neatly puts it, "a lifelong tutorial in deferred gratification."

RED SMITH

The best writing in newspapers, it used to be said, was in the sports pages. Variously known as the toy department or the playpen or the peanut stand, its interest restricted to matters of supreme inconsequence, the sports pages allowed the people who filled them more latitude for the prose equivalent of fancy footwork. In sports, after all, not that much was at stake: men in funny costumes batting a ball around— or, as in football and boxing, batting one another around—or running round tracks, on foot or in machines or atop horses. Sportswriters, not lashed to journalism's deadly troika of *when, where,* and *why,* had the latitude to be jokey, dramatic, stylish, even gaudy.

Sportswriting was lent a certain literary imprimatur by some of its former practitioners. Ernest Hemingway began his newspaper career on the sports pages, and Ring Lardner went from writing about sports for newspapers to writing novels about the uneducated that often had sports as their background. Many American writers carried unrealized sports fantasies as part of their psychic cargo their life long. F. Scott Fitzgerald claimed that the two biggest disappointments in his life were not having seen combat overseas in World War I and not having been big enough to play football at Princeton.

Most of us who grew up with athletic aspirations will understand Fitzgerald's disappointment about not playing football in college. I myself would rather have been an all-city high school basketball player, or won the Illinois state singles tennis championship, than have written "Moon River" or turned out a flawless translation of Dante—which I didn't do, either. Most men who have not achieved the athletic glory they longed for would, I suspect, feel much the same way. In sad compensation, we watch games on television or read about them in our local newspapers.

I long ago reached the stage of jaded sophistication in watching sports on television where having the sound turned on is not required. The few bits of information or rare insights offered by sportscasters, as they are called, are not worth the heavy price they exact in cliché or empty babble. I only read the sports pages in the local press when I go to the barber shop, and I now check scores online or on television crawls on ESPN.

Reading about sports has become dispiriting. Endless are the stories of that continuing sad saga of athletes cheating through chemistry. Contract negotiations, with their vast sums being bandied about, are another glum-making regular item. Articles about concussions in football figure to sweep the boards (to use a basketball metaphor) this autumn—and perhaps for years to come. The never-ending personal scandals, from wife-beating to murder, of young men unable to cope with the heavy cash and adulation that come their way, do not lighten the spirit. Hold that Tiger, as Mrs. Woods might say.

As a boy, the first newspaper sportswriter I read was Jerome Holtzman, who covered prep sports for the *Chicago Sun-Times*. I later came to know Jerry Holtzman, who arranged to have me invited to a dinner that included James T. Farrell, an ardent White Sox fan and author of the *Studs Lonigan* trilogy, and another Chicago sportswriter named Bill Gleason. Holtzman, who later wrote for the *Tribune*, became the official historian of baseball, which meant that every year he wrote a lengthy article for the *Sporting News* summarizing the past baseball season. Holtzman invented the category of relief pitching known as "the save." He was also a nice man.

The one sportswriter considered indispensable throughout my boyhood, and well beyond, was the columnist Red Smith (1905–1982). Smith didn't begin his professional life as a sportswriter, but drifted into it as a reporter on the *St. Louis Star*. His editor, after canning half the six-man sports department for being on the take from a local boxing promoter, asked Smith to shift to the sports desk. He never saw it as a demotion. "Sports constitutes a valid part of our culture, our civilization," he would later write, "and keeping the public informed and, if possible, a little entertained about sports is not an entirely useless thing."

After stints on papers in Milwaukee, St. Louis, and Philadelphia, in 1945 Smith was brought to the *New York Herald Tribune* by Stanley Woodward, the paper's legendary sports editor. Of Smith, Woodward wrote that "he was a complete newspaper man [who] had been through the mill and come out with a high polish." After the *Herald Tribune* went under in 1966, Smith transferred to the *New York Times*. His columns were widely syndicated.

Red Smith was considered the thinking man's sportswriter. He abhorred clichés. He commanded an impressive, sometimes bordering on the ornate, vocabulary. He specialized in striking similes. He called in irony when the occasion required it, which in sports was frequently. And he did all this within the confines of plain style—without the excessive use of subordinate clauses or dashes, and without any semicolons whatsoever.

Unlike so many of the talented newspaper writers among his near-contemporaries—James Thurber, E.B. White, John O'Hara, A.J. Liebling—Red Smith had no wish ever to rise above writing for newspapers. He thought of himself as essentially a reporter. He once claimed that he'd rather go to the dentist than write a book. Of the difficulty of writing, he remarked that "all you do is sit down at a typewriter and open a vein." When asked how long it took him to write a column—and it is estimated that he wrote roughly 10,000 of them—he answered: "How much time do I have?"

Walter Wellesley Smith was born in 1905 in Green Bay, Wisconsin, 14 years before the Packers came to town and put the place on the map. He went to Notre Dame and then directly into journalism. A Midwesterner by birth and upbringing, he eventually became what I think of as a naturalized New Yorker: one of those people who, whatever their geographical origins, found their spiritual home in New York and, with it, a comfortable seat at the bar at Toots Shor's.

Red Smith wrote on all the standard sports, following the calendar of the country's sports seasons and major events. Every fourth year he broke his normal rhythm by going off to the Olympics. He wrote a lot about boxing in the day when no sporting event had greater interest than that of a heavyweight title fight. He thought boxing "a rough, dangerous, and thrilling sport, the most basic and natural and uncomplicated of athletic competitions, and—at its best—one of the purest of art forms." (Today, of course, boxing is considered the purest form of barbarism, and attracts minimal interest.) He was also excellent on thoroughbred racing, and he wrote a fair amount about fishing for trout and bass, a sport he loved and the only one in which he acknowledged participating.

He wrote most on baseball, which he loved, and on which he was splendid. He was good on track and field and golf, but not quite so fine on football. His view of hockey was implicit in the old joke: "Went to a fight last night and a hockey game broke out." Basketball he loathed, once remarking that he would rather drink a Bronx cocktail (a martini with orange juice and maraschino cherry added) than go to a basketball game. He was wrong about this, I believe, and might have felt differently had he lived into the era of the graceful giants, the Magics and Michaels and LeBrons.

How does the best of Red Smith's writing, all written for the next day's paper, ultimately to be used for wrapping fish, hold up? *American Pastimes*, handsome collection of his writings—the earliest of which is dated September 30, 1934, the latest January 11, 1982, or four days before his death—has been assembled with skill and care by Daniel Okrent. A literary man of all work, Okrent has supplied a useful introduction to the volume; the author's son, Terence Smith, a former CBS and *New York Times* journalist, has written a gracious afterword. With the exception of an opening article called "My Press-Box Memories," none of the columns in this book runs to more than 800 or 900 words. (What might the result have been, one wonders, if Red Smith had extended himself to compositions of 5,000 or 10,000 words?) Some of the columns are organized by decade, some by particular sport, and others by simple chronology.

Of the legendary American sportswriters—Grantland Rice, Jimmy Cannon, Frank Graham, John Lardner—Red Smith holds up best. Part of this is owing to his temperament: He knew how best to distance himself from his subject; he understood that he was writing about sports, not the world economy. And unlike A. J. Liebling writing about boxing, Smith, in his coverage of sports, never seemed to be slumming. When he came up against hypocrisy or chicanery—the former on the part of baseball owners, the latter on the part of basketball point-shavers and others—he was properly stern in his condemnations. When he was sentimental, as in describing the installation of old ballplayers in the Baseball

Hall of Fame, he recognized it. "Even a toad would be moved," he noted in describing the privilege of election to the hall.

Reading Red Smith's columns in bulk, as opposed to having read him in the regular rhythm of his daily columns, one gets a firmer notion of his strengths, weaknesses, and general point of view. He was a man of good sense. One finds nothing nutty, over the top, or in the least outré in any of the columns collected in *American Pastimes*. In his writing, he generally maintained the detachment bordering on skepticism proper to an observer of events in which he had no true stake.

Smith could use his impressive vocabulary to comic effect:

> Joe DiMaggio relaxed in the home club's gleaming tile boudoir and deposed at length in defense of Pete Reiser, the Brooklyn center fielder, who had narrowly escaped being smitten upon the isthmus rhombencephali that day by sundry fly balls.

He referred to boxing legends and wisdom as "the cauliflower gospel," called Wembley Stadium in London "a cooked gaboon of concrete," cited the use of water to "emasculate scotch."

It's difficult to know how educated Red Smith was. Often writing as many as six columns a week, and attending the various events that served as the fodder for these columns, he couldn't have had much time for reading serious books. In one of his columns, he mentions "David Wark Griffith, Federico Fellini, and Ingmar Bergman." In another, he quotes Ernest Newman, the London *Times* music critic, on the subject of genius. In a column on the fuss made when Carl Yastrzemski got his 3,000th hit, he notes that when Cap Anson (1852–1922), the Chicago Cubs first baseman, got *his* 3,000th hit, little fuss was made because "in those days Media was where the Medes and Persians came from." Baseball, he declares in one column, is "as ceremonious as a Graustarkian court." He had, in short, a wide enough culture to elevate his column and give it tone.

The charming little touches in Smith's writing caught his more careful readers' attention and gained their admiration. The British middleweight Randy Turpin, late in his fight against Sugar Ray Robinson, "was weaving like a cobra dancing to a flute." The knees of the heavyweight Archie Moore, in his fight against Rocky Marciano, "were wet spaghetti." He called the Yankees pitcher Allie Reynolds, a member of the Creek Indian nation, "that estimable aborigine." The fight promoter Don King shows up in a pair of "brown pants with a crease that could draw blood." There is scarcely a column in this book that is without one or more of these fine touches.

Sometimes, true enough, they go awry. The Yankees pitcher Bob Turley comes out of a game "like a loose tooth." In a fight against Sugar Ray Robinson, the welterweight Carmen Basilio's left eye closed up "like a purple clam." Joe DiMaggio catches a Gene Hermanski long line-drive "like a well-fed banquet guest." A lake is described as "flat as a fried egg"; fog at the 1978 World Cup tournament in Fort Lauderdale looks as if "a grey soufflé garnished the fairway." He refers to a 12-pound trout he himself caught as "broad-shouldered, magnificently colored, and splendidly deep, like Jane Russell"—which, even if it doesn't quite work, is amusing nonetheless.

Many of these columns were written before the age of television, when sportswriters could not assume that readers had already seen the game being written about, so Smith had to expend much of his space on recounting games. In a column from 1944, he felt the need to describe every touchdown in Army's 59-0 win over Notre Dame. He chronicled action more than personalities. Thus, he spells out the trajectory of a Jim Hickman homer in a 1963 Mets-Braves game: "A high fly to left, curling toward the foul line, arching toward the stands, sailing, sinking—in for a grand slam."

Many of his best columns were tributes to older ballplayers: Walter Johnson, Lefty Grove, Honus Wagner, Napoleon Lajoie, Babe Ruth. Some turned on an anecdote or joke. One such tells the old story about the punter who reverently asks God's help to bring the horse he has bet on in a winner. As the horse comes down the stretch, leading by two lengths, the punter says, "Thank you, Lord. I'll take him from here. Come on, you son of a bitch!"

A newspaper column is primarily an instrument of opinionation. Red Smith was never short of opinions, some of them unpredictable. He thought banning the beanball from baseball took an important weapon out of a pitcher's arsenal. He had memories of Ty Cobb, whose violence on the basepath made Attila the Hun look like Mother Teresa, and felt that removing high slides and other rough play from baseball was in part responsible for the game's declining attendance. The advent of the designated hitter, he thought, took the element of managing out of the game. He knocked the hype of Super Bowl games, and thought the baseball All Star game a non-event and "a sorry exercise in huckstering."

He admired Curt Flood, the man who made free-agency in baseball possible, and sided against the owners in every dispute they entered into with players. He felt much the same about the International Olympic Committee, whose insensitivity and instinct for always making the wrong decision was flawless. He was never blind to the corruption in college sports, and, quite properly, blamed "the college presidents, the coaches, the registrars, [and] the alumni, who compounded the felony."

Although he wrote with great admiration for Joe DiMaggio and Yogi Berra and called Willie Mays "the most exciting player of his time," Red Smith's candidate for the greatest athlete of his day was the jockey Willie Shoemaker (1931–2003). Smith thought thoroughbred racing the most dangerous of all sports, with the possible exception of rodeo, which he called "the world's most violent sport." Shoemaker brought not only bravery but intelligence to horse racing; he was also an all-round athlete, unbeatable at tennis and golf. He also happened to be a gent, which always counted significantly in Red Smith's reckoning.

He doesn't come out and say it, but Muhammad Ali may well have been Smith's candidate for the most overrated athlete of his time. "The boy braggart," Smith called him. He disliked Ali's running at the mouth, degrading his opponents, pumping himself up. "If there is any decency in him," Smith wrote in connection with Ali's third bout against Joe Frazier ("The Thrilla in Manila"), "he will not bad-mouth Joe Frazier again, for Frazier makes him a real champion. In the ring with Joe, he is a better and braver man than he is with anybody else." When Ali elected conscientious-objector status in 1966, Smith wrote, in the one jarring political note in the more than 500 pages of *American Pastimes*, that he made "himself as sorry a spectacle as those unwashed punks who picket and demonstrate against the war." What Smith would have made of Muhammad Ali today, dragging his Parkinson's-benumbed body to the Olympics and other sporting spectacles, would have made the subject for a powerful column.

Among the pleasures of *American Pastimes* is the tour of sports history—in effect, a decade-by-decade highlights show—that the book provides. Red Smith wrote during a time when sports fans knew not only the names of the great racehorses—Whirlaway, Seattle Slew, Citation, Secretariat, War Admiral—but knew their athletic personality as expressed through racetrack performance. His columns record the great prizefights and prizefighters: Joe Louis, Rocky Graziano, Tony Zale, Jersey Joe Walcott, Archie Moore, and others. Writing out of New York, he often wrote about the Yankees and their winning ways: "The dreary, weary, yawning ennui of it."

The older columns remind one how vastly the money in sports has changed. First prize for the Masters golf tournament in 1946 was $2,500. Smith's column on Walter Johnson includes a reference to the 1912 Philadelphia Athletics' "hundred thousand dollar infield," whereas today, two season box-seat tickets to Yankees games would cost that much. Had he been alive, Red Smith might have put the astonishing sums now earned by athletes in perspective, if that is possible. And it is hard to believe that he would have been anything other than unflinching in his denunciation of athletes who use steroids and other drugs.

Smith was said to have been highly irritated when, in 1956, the first Pulitzer Prize for sportswriting went to Arthur Daley of the *New York Times*. The Pulitzer Prize committee must have been puffing on the same stuff the Nobel Prize committee did when, in 1901, it passed over Leo Tolstoy for the prize in literature and gave it to Sully Prudhomme. Smith won a Pulitzer Prize in 1976. But he also won something much greater. Through his carefully crafted prose, always turned out under deadline pressure, he won for his best columns a life that has lasted long after he, much to the regret of his readers, departed the planet.

JOCKS

JOE DIMAGGIO

Where'd He Go?

The best criterion of fame is when a crazy person imagines he is you. In his full-court-press biography of Joe DiMaggio, *Joe DiMaggio: The Hero's Life*, Richard Ben Cramer does not say whether this ever happened to his subject, but it is difficult to think that it did not. DiMaggio had, after all, first-name fame—fame of the kind that exempts headline writers from even mentioning your last name, like Frank (Sinatra), Johnny (Carson), Barbra (Streisand), Marilyn (Monroe), Michael (Jordan), Jerry (first Lewis, now Seinfeld). It is a small club, and Joe DiMaggio was a charter member.

Fame was DiMaggio's portion, and it was served to him early, often, and throughout his long life. He received it in all its forms, high, mass, and squalid. No doubt he loved it, but it also made him, quite properly, paranoid. "Even paranoids have real enemies," the poet Delmore Schwartz insisted, but it is their friends of whom the immensely famous must really beware. Fame can easily be coined, and, though DiMaggio himself proved excellent at this, turning his mere presence into cash, his signature into gold, he was always leery of others trying to make a buck off his name.

Joe DiMaggio was what is nowadays called an icon. (Once understood to mean a small religious painting, the word "icon" has been called into service in recent years to accommodate the national language inflation, which finds mere "superstar" insufficient.) One of the best reasons *not* to be an icon is that it brings out iconoclasts, often in the disguise of biographers. "The story of DiMaggio the icon [is] well known," writes Richard Ben Cramer. "The story of DiMaggio the man has been buried." His self-appointed task is the indelicate one of exhumation, and his *DiMaggio* leaves plaster shards and shattered glass everywhere.

Cramer begins his story in 1930, when Joe was fifteen. He was one of nine children, the fourth of five sons, born to a Sicilian fisherman illiterate in both Italian and English who lived in the North Beach section of San Francisco. He was, in Cramer's telling, an oddly detached boy, the sort who was not in need of the approval of his pals. People, somehow, came to him. He also had none of the standard marketable skills. He did not want to work on the fishing boat with his father and older brothers; he hated, in fact, the smell of fish. He had no interest in school, and dropped out at fifteen (his elder brothers had done so even sooner). Instead, he hung out, scuffled for a few bucks a week selling newspapers, playing poker, finding something that could be resold.

But there was one thing Joe could do: he could hit a baseball, really cream it. Whence this talent? Cramer does not, probably really cannot, say. What can be said is that it did not come from relentless early training or deep determination. DiMaggio entered baseball many decades before Little League came along with its early coaching, which is to say long before play for children, for better and worse, was organized. Kids just met on the playground, chose up sides, had established positions, and played the game. Joe played it supremely well and without great effort.

As a boy, he apparently had no special passion for baseball. He became more interested later when he discovered he could make a few dollars playing on semi-pro teams. At eighteen, he signed with the minor-league San Francisco Seals, where his brother Vince played. (A younger brother, Dominic, also played for the Seals and, later, for the Boston Red Sox.) That first season with the Seals, he had a 62-game hitting streak, batting .340 for the year.

He broke into baseball as a shortstop, a position at which he was not much good. The Seals also tried him at first base, at which he was not much better. After joining the New York Yankees in 1936, he would eventually become, along with Willie Mays in the National League, the greatest centerfielder to play the game, Mays having a flair for the dramatic, DiMaggio a flair for making every catch look as graceful and as easy as a thoroughbred trotting into the winner's circle.

Joe DiMaggio's competence at baseball touched on the profound. He could do six of the seven things required by the game: run, throw, field, hit, hit for power, and—here the sixth, magical quality entered in—do all of the above at times of maximum pressure, "in the clutch," when the game was on the line. The only aspect he never mastered—chiefly because he was never called upon to do so—was pitching. (Babe Ruth began as a pitcher, and, during his years with the Boston Red Sox, was a good one.) DiMaggio also had great sports intelligence, intelligence of a kind that, in my experience, is connected to no other, and which entails the instinctual certainty that prevents one from ever making the kind of mistakes that other players make fairly regularly.

At the plate, DiMaggio was a classic of quiet elegance. "The guy was a *statue*," Lefty Gomez, his Yankee teammate, once said. Tall (6'2"), smoothly muscled, he stood, stock still, all concentration, fearless during an age when the vocabulary of pitchers included such happily menacing phrases as "a little chin music" and "smoke him inside." He had the sweetest stroke in the game, and was often photographed—as he is on the back cover of *DiMaggio*—at the end of that great follow-through that left him, stride complete, weight on the left foot, bat on the left shoulder, ball (one assumes) either rolling away out of reach in one of the power alleys or in the delighted hands of a fan in the stands.

A DiMaggio strikeout was a rarity—the New York saloonkeeper Toots Shor, one of his pals and hangers-on, said Joe looked better striking out than other men making a hit. In more than 6,000 times at bat over his career, as we learn from Cramer, he was two-and-a-half times more likely to hit for extra bases than to strike out. On the subject of his superior hitting DiMaggio was not much of a theorist; he believed it came from the same place that Aristotle thought the power of making metaphors derived: God.

In his era—roughly from 1936 to 1951, with two years out for stateside service in World War II—DiMaggio's only rivals as pure hitters were Ted Williams, Stan Musial, Hank Greenberg, and, later, his teammate Mickey Mantle (to whom DiMaggio rarely spoke, telling another teammate, "He's a rockhead"). He was especially rivalrous toward Williams, who may have been the better pure hitter and who was the last player in the major leagues to bat .400 in a season. (DiMaggio probably would have matched it in 1939 if he had not been forced to play the last three weeks with an eye infection, which caused his average to drop 30 points to .381.) "He throws like a broad," DiMaggio said of Williams, "and runs like a ruptured duck." Besides, he would add later, Williams never won anything.

DiMaggio won everything. In his thirteen seasons in the majors, the Yankees were in ten World Series, and victorious in nine of them. He was among that small number of athletes who, through the main force of ability combined with attitude, can make a team produce winners. Others have been able to do this in basketball—Michael Jordan most recently—but basketball involves only five men on the court at one time. In football, a quarterback—Joe Montana comes to mind—can sometimes do it, but since there are two separate teams in football, offense and defense, the feat is highly unlikely. It is rarest of all in baseball, where nine men are on the field and no one but the pitcher dominates, and pitchers work only one game in five.

DiMaggio seems to have accomplished it not only through amazing play but also through an Olympian contempt for anyone who contributed to his team's defeat or failed to meet his personal standard. His teammates were in awe of him, in awe of his skill, and no less in awe of his determination to play even when in deep pain. In 1949, he led the American League with 39 home runs, had 155 runs batted in, hit .320, and was in the lineup in 153 of 154 games—playing, as Cramer reports, "hurt in almost every one of them."

A lonely man with no gift for gregariousness, DiMaggio always kept apart from his teammates. Occasionally he would take a young player in hand—the relief pitcher Joe Page is an example Cramer mentions—and build up his confidence. But he dressed for the field in a corner off by himself and spent the half-innings in which he would not be batting near the tunnel to the locker room, alone with a Chesterfield and half a cup of coffee. (A reserve outfielder named Hank Workman had the job of lighting DiMaggio's cigarette just before he arrived in the dugout from centerfield.) He usually made the trip back to his hotel with a friend who was not a team member. A measured aloofness was everywhere part of his style.

Great timing marked not only DiMaggio's playing at the plate and in the field but his larger career. He started with the New York Yankees a year after the great Babe Ruth retired, which seemed to put him in a direct line of succession as the greatest player in the game. When he arrived, the Yanks had gone four years without a pennant; in his rookie year he helped take them to the World Series, which they won.

John Gregory Dunne was no doubt correct to observe in the *New Yorker* that DiMaggio would not have achieved the same fame had he played for St. Louis, Cleveland, or Detroit. New York had its own cachet. With its heavy concentration of high-powered sportswriters working the then more than twelve city dailies, DiMaggio's every move was chronicled in highly colored prose. Besides, television was not yet on the job when DiMaggio entered the majors, exposing players day in and out, subjecting them to inevitably disappointing interviews, everywhere erasing whatever aura their on-the-field performance might bring. The burden of description was left to sportswriters and radio announcers, who could make a duel between, say, DiMaggio and the Cleveland fastball pitcher Bob Feller seem like a battle between Achilles and Hector.

Along with all this, DiMaggio had somehow, as Cramer notes, "grown into his face." He became—with his gap-toothed smile and wide nostrils—if not handsome, then, in a masculine version of the *jolie-laide*, a "beautiful-ugly" man. In the realm of sobriquets, he also had two of the best: Joltin' Joe (for his hitting) and the Yankee Clipper, which felicitously suggested his stately presence in the ocean that was centerfield in Yankee Stadium. A great sobriquet requires a definite article—Red Grange had the Galloping Ghost; Ted Williams, the Splendid Splinter; George Herman Ruth, the Babe—and the Yankee Clipper for DiMaggio seemed a perfect fit.

Raw to the point of being a rube when he came up, DiMaggio did not take long to learn how to fulfill the role of a quiet hero, the epitome of grace under pressure. Although he played as hard as anyone going, he never caused consternation afield by arguing with umpires, badgering opponents, or getting into fights. When an otherwise obscure Brooklyn Dodger outfielder named Al Gionfriddo made an amazing catch on a ball DiMaggio expected to be a World Series home run, DiMaggio, already rounding the bases, kicked the bag at second, an incident so out of character that it is remembered even now. In press interviews he gave little away, and if he had any secrets, the press was not yet devoted to uncovering and exposing them. His taciturnity translated itself as reticent dignity. He came off as a gent: a Hemingway hero in Yankee pinstripes.

Such, at any rate, did the Clipper appear from the outside.

Richard Ben Cramer proposes to show us the less than elegant inside. Not to put too fine a point on it, *DiMaggio* makes Joe out to be a drip, a jerk, a bore, and a creep, with nothing good to be said about him off the baseball field. Early in the book, Toots Shor, whose most honored customers included Jack Dempsey, Ernest Hemingway, and Joe DiMaggio, is quoted offering a definition of class—"a thing," says Toots, "where a guy does everything decent." In Richard Ben Cramer's pages, Joe DiMaggio does almost nothing decent. He is a bad father, a worse husband, a poor friend, a cheapskate, selfish, humorless, a prude operating on a sexual double standard, a solipsist of the highest order.

In his bachelor days, Cramer tells us, DiMaggio was happy to dance between the sheets with any woman who was ready and willing; and, fame being a great aphrodisiac, more than a few were. He was a guest (nonpaying, surely) at the cat-house of Polly Adler, *madame extraordinaire* and author of *A House Is Not a Home*, where he complained that the shiny sheets did not allow him to get enough traction. As did most bachelors of the day, he referred to women as "broads," though in their company he tended to be quite formal. In later years, he was known (here comes the double standard) to send male friends home for a change of clothes if they showed up in mixed company at restaurants neglecting to wear a jacket and tie.

That Joe was not much of a husband also appears on the bill of complaint. What he was was a husband on the Sicilian model. He married his first wife, an actress named Dorothy Arnold, in 1939, in a wedding in San Francisco that required police crowd control. They had a son, Joe Jr. Conflict did not take long to get under way. The new Mrs. DiMaggio wanted both her marriage and a career in the movies. Joe did not see much point in the latter. Something had to give, and soon enough the marriage did.

In the middle of this marriage, DiMaggio had his 56-game hitting streak, still unsurpassed in the majors, which ran from May 15 to July 17, 1941, when it was stopped in Cleveland by a negligible pitcher named Al Smith. (The next day he began a streak that lasted for an additional fifteen games.) Once under way, the streak put him in the headlines every day, taking people's mind off the war in Europe. His teammate Lefty Gomez said, "He seemed like a figure, a hero, that the whole country could root for." And they did, except at home; in 1944 his wife sued for divorce, charging mental cruelty. Translation: indifference.

DiMaggio's second marriage, to Marilyn Monroe, has been more exhaustively chronicled than the relationship between Romeo and Juliet. When they first met, she, sweet ditz, was perhaps the only person in the country who had never heard of him. He had been out of the majors for a few years, and their courtship put him back in the headlines. "They are folk heroes, Marilyn and Joe," wrote the sports columnist Jimmy Cannon, "a whole country's pets." They were the best athlete and the sexiest girl, the king and queen of the prom, with the whole nation as high school. They married in 1954, when she was twenty-seven, he thirty-nine. They had only their fame in common.

The marriage was unrelieved hell. She thought he did not care enough about her career; he was jealous and discouraged by her willingness to play the national bimbo. On their honeymoon in Japan, she went off to entertain the troops in Korea. Lots of other men were always sniffing around. She was rumored to wear no underwear, and then, in the famous photograph of her skirt blowing up while she stood on an air grate for the movie *The Seven-Year Itch*, she showed the entire world that this was not so. Joe was on the set the day the scene was shot. Cramer quotes the director Billy Wilder, who recalls "the look of death" on his face. Murder may have been more like it. He roughed her up that night, and three weeks later she filed for divorce. The marriage lasted nine months.

The children of the famous do not, for the most part, have uncomplicatedly joyous lives, and Cramer, by more than implication, accuses DiMaggio of making things even worse for his son by being an indifferent father. To be the child, especially the son and namesake, of Joe DiMaggio, and not oneself a good athlete, was to draw a very difficult card in life. Joe Jr.'s second bad card was being the child of divorce. Prep school, Yale, the Marines, businesses his father set him up in, connections he made for him—nothing seemed to work. He lapsed into drink and drugs, and ended up a middle-aged man with a gray ponytail and false teeth. Left an annual stipend of $20,000 in his father's will, Joe Jr. died of an overdose of heroin and crack cocaine six months after his father's death in 1999.

That $20,000 stipend leads inexorably to the subject of DiMaggio's cheapness, about which Cramer rattles on endlessly. We are told about the hanger-on who gave him a free Cadillac, to which his response was, "Did you fill it with gas?"; about his habit of carrying his wash to a local Laundromat because the machines were fifteen cents cheaper than in the building where he had a free condominium; about how, apart from a single check for $100, he never gave anything to the Joe DiMaggio Children's Hospital in Hollywood, Florida, where he lived out his last years; and, especially, about how he was disinclined to pick up any restaurant check—he was after all known as the Yankee Clipper, not the Yankee Tipper—or in fact pay for anything, even though he had millions tucked away, including a safe-deposit box jammed with $100 bills.

The final major item Cramer puts on DiMaggio's rap sheet is his connection with the mob. The Boys, as we used to call them in Chicago, cultivated the great Italian hero. Every time he went into one of the Boys' restaurants or nightclubs, which in those days included most places in New York, they put a couple of hundred dollars in a special account for him in the old Bowery Bank. One of Joe's greatest patrons among the Boys was not an Italian but a Jew named Abner "Longy" Zwillman, who, Cramer claims, gave DiMaggio three boxes of cash to stash for him before he was murdered—money that DiMaggio later rescued from his house in San Francisco during the earthquake of 1989.

When material of this kind comes up in *DiMaggio*, one especially feels the want of footnotes. Where did Cramer get all this dish? Pete Hamill, the veteran New York journalist, has suggested in a review that Cramer probably got it from third-level mafiosi, adding that "mob guys, particularly low-level hoodlums, are notorious bullshit artists." But even if it were all true, it is unclear how else DiMaggio was supposed to behave. Tell Longy Zwillman and the others that he was too high-principled to accept their kindness? Nothing, after all, was ever asked of him, nor does Cramer claim that DiMaggio was ordered to appear in mob-owned places, let alone do anything that was against the law. Was he supposed to have been saintly enough—or perhaps brave enough—to turn down the money, which was not even handed over directly?

The fact seems to be that the mob was no less caught up in the mystique of Joe DiMaggio than everyone else. Whenever he flew, American Airlines upgraded him into first-class, assigning him a seat, D5, corresponding to his initial and his old Yankee uniform number. Throughout his life, DiMaggio had guys to run his errands, do his bidding, smooth the way for him. He never asked favors; he didn't have to. Toots Shor, Jimmy Cannon, a man-about-town ticket agent named George Solotaire, a foot surgeon named Rocky Positano, and others rushed to do them for him. They did so not because he commanded or conned them, but because they wanted to—because their friendship with the Clipper came to seem the most significant thing in their lives.

As for his cheapness, even Cramer allows that DiMaggio picked up checks when out with his teammates. So if any principle was in operation here, it would seem to be that he let people pay who were themselves making a profit by being with him, of whom there were more than a few. If Joe DiMaggio ate in your restaurant, lived in your condominium complex, wore the clothes you manufactured, such would be the rush of other people wanting to do likewise that it all meant money, fairly serious money, in the bank. Because of the magic of his name, and the even greater magic of his presence, he was visited by a plague of leeches all his life. The last seventy or so pages of *DiMaggio* showcase the work in this line of a Florida attorney named Morris Engelberg, who eventually sold, through Sotheby's, DiMaggio's canceled checks, license plate (DiMag5), MasterCard, driver's license, hundreds of signed baseballs, shirts, and other paraphernalia, and just about everything but the tumor in his lung that killed him.

"I'm not great," DiMaggio told the writer Gay Talese in 1966, attempting to put off a request for an interview, pleading to be left alone. "I'm just a man trying to get along." Years later, when first acquainted with the lines from Paul Simon's song "Mrs. Robinson"—"Where have you gone, Joe DiMaggio? / A nation turns its lonely eyes to you"—he is supposed to have responded, "I haven't gone anywhere. I'm employed." Yet if he was not the deep creep presented by Cramer, neither will it do to make him out to be just a dumb jock. He was more complicated than that.

Although a lousy husband, for example, DiMaggio proved an excellent ex-husband to Marilyn Monroe. He looked after her as best he could, coming to her aid whenever needed. This was fairly often, for she needed a lot of looking after, not least when she landed in Payne Whitney for mental problems and he bailed her out. He always despised Frank Sinatra and Peter Lawford for pimping her, and the Kennedy brothers, John and Bobby, for treating her like a whore. Cramer reports that Joe and Marilyn planned to remarry, and when she was found dead in her apartment in 1962 an unfinished letter to him lay beside her body. He went to his own grave believing they—"the fucking Kennedys," as a friend reported him calling them—had killed her.

Nowhere did DiMaggio seem so gallant, or so tragic, as in the aftermath of Marilyn Monroe's death, when he stepped in to take care of all the details of the funeral, seeing that it was conducted in dignified privacy and arranging that fresh roses be sent to her crypt every two weeks "forever." At the time, I remarked on the impressiveness of this to Saul Bellow who knew Arthur Miller, who was Monroe's husband after her divorce from DiMaggio. According to Bellow, Miller had said DiMaggio used to beat her up fairly regularly. "You know," he added, "brutality is often the other side of sentimentality."

Only two beatings of Marilyn Monroe by DiMaggio are recorded in Cramer's biography, however. I say "only" and "however" because, such is the relentlessness of his attack, if he had known about more he would surely have reported them. Nor, for all his digging in secret sexual places, is Cramer able to report any instances of DiMaggio fooling with another man's wife. Monroe herself, when asked later if Joe hit her, said, "Yes, but not without cause." And she is not the only one who has ever wanted to come to DiMaggio's defense, or to find extenuating circumstances for his behavior. Any reader of *DiMaggio* will feel much the same way.

Henry Kissinger, whose admiration for DiMaggio began at age ten, when he watched him play in Yankee Stadium, and who later became a friend, has said: "If you had told me in 1938 that I would be Secretary of State, and I would be friends with DiMaggio, I would have thought that the second was less likely than the first." At *Time* magazine's 75th anniversary dinner, when they wanted DiMaggio to sit at the head table with President Clinton, he refused. He despised the Kennedys as sexual predators, and he despised Clinton on the same grounds. He sat instead with Kissinger and his wife.

In most contests between a biographer and his subject—and contests they often come to seem—it is difficult not to find yourself rooting for the subject. The reason is that the contest is an inherently unfair one, for the biographer has not only hindsight but can bring virtue—if he pretends to it—to bear on his side.

Richard Ben Cramer, cool and with-it though he strains to be, plays the virtue card throughout. If DiMaggio uses the word "broad," or cannot make a go of marriages to two very difficult women, he is a misogynist (a touch of political correctness thrown in at no extra charge). If he fails to tell members of the mob to stick it in their ears, he is practically a member of the mafia himself. If his son does not turn out to be an astrophysicist, he is a rotten father.

In scoring off DiMaggio in all these various ways, in smoking him inside, Cramer's own position is implicitly one of moral superiority. But if the biographer is the morally superior man, why does he seem so much less interesting than his subject and finally so unconvincing? The short answer is that his moral superiority exists only on paper.

MICHAEL JORDAN

He Flies through the Air

Forget it. It'll be close at the end, and then with about twenty
seconds left, Michael will have the ball and he'll keep his eye
on the clock, and then with a few seconds left he'll go for a
jumper and hit it. The Bulls will win, and the legend will live.
It's who he is, and it's what he does.

—Chuck Daly, NBA coach

When I was thirteen, my father allowed me to put up a wooden
backboard and basket in our backyard in Chicago. The yard was
small, mostly grass, the only concrete being a narrow sidewalk leading to
the alleyway. I used that basket in all seasons, including insultingly cold
Chicago winters when I would daily shoot a hundred free throws with my
gloves on. At other times, I would play fantasy games. Since I have always
been of the realist school, in personal life as in literature, I would limit my
scoring to anywhere between 24 and 33 points a game, usually winning for
my team by popping in two free throws after the clock had run out. Not
in my sweetest fantasies could I ever imagine myself doing what Michael
Jordan, the now long retired star of the Chicago Bulls, would do in actual-
ity some 40 years later. If I was a realist even when grounded in fantasy,
he, Michael Jordan, was a magic realist, soaring in life.

In *Playing for Keeps*, his book about Michael Jordan, David Halberstam uses the phrase "Jordanologist" to describe close students of the
great player, marketing phenomenon, and international celebrity. Only
now do I realize that, since 1984, when he left the University of North
Carolina after his junior year to play with the Bulls, Jordanology has
been, as the professors say, my subspecialty. Over this period of time I

must have seen Michael—as we in Chicago refer to him—play perhaps a thousand games; even though I watched most of them on television, I feel that I know his facial expressions, his moods, his verbal responses at least as well as I do those of most of my oldest friends. When I acquired cable TV, I did so not chiefly but exclusively in order to see more of Michael before he closed out his career. The prospect of seeing him at night could lift my spirits during the day, actually watching him play— even through the cool medium of the screen—brought me the kind of ephemeral but never-to-be-gainsaid pleasure of a fine meal or a lightish aesthetic experience.

Maybe not so lightish as all that. Having had the chance to observe so much of Michael Jordan in performance may be the equivalent, in sports, of having had tickets to the early years of George Balanchine's New York City Ballet. If this reference to Balanchine seems too elevated, the law of carefully measured accolades has long ago run out on Michael Jordan. By now he has been compared with nearly every genius the world has produced, with the possible exceptions of Goethe and Proust. In many quarters, he has become the standard by which genius in *other* fields is measured. "Frank Galati," I heard a former president of Northwestern University say about a theatrical director who happens to teach there, "is the Michael Jordan of the contemporary theater."

When Michael retired, Jerry Sloan, coach of the Utah Jazz, whom the Bulls twice defeated in the NBA finals on their way to winning six championships in eight years, said that he should be remembered "as the greatest player who ever played the game." Sidney Green, a journeyman player and briefly a teammate, asserted that Jordan "was the truth, the whole truth, and nothing but the truth, so help us God." Jayson Williams, the power forward for the New Jersey Nets, called him "Jesus in Nikes." Bobby Knight, the coach of Indiana University, once remarked that we would not see his equal in our lifetimes and neither would our children or our grandchildren in theirs. Later he pushed things up a notch by stating that Michael Jordan was the greatest player of all time, not just of basketball but of any sport. My own view is that in Michael we had the reincarnation of Achilles, but without the sulking and without the heel.

Chicago has not been notable for its winning teams. But we have had a splendid run of gentleman black athletes, beginning with Ernie Banks and moving chronologically through Gale Sayers, Walter Payton, Andre Dawson, and Michael Jordan. These are men who, like a much earlier generation of black jazz musicians, have brought a high degree of quality to their craft and much dignity to their personal bearing. Alas, with the exception of Michael, all have had to settle for playing on losing teams, while Michael, by contrast, after a few early years in the NBA desert without capable teammates, triumphed with an astonishing completeness.

In part because I grew up in Chicago, in part because of the mysteries of temperament, I identify in sports almost exclusively with the losers. The poor guy who misses a crucial field goal that costs his team the Superbowl, the pitcher who allows a game-winning home run late in the World Series, the nineteen-year-old kid who blows two free throws and knocks his team out of the Final Four—these are the athletes whose long, melancholy off-seasons I ponder, not those who, champagne dripping from their hair, announce they are off to Disney World. Having an athlete like Michael in my life, an athlete who is so clearly a winner, has been a switch, and of a radical sort. Yet in retrospect even Michael's winning has seemed of the dramatic sort, that is, winning against the odds, coming from behind, pulling it out of the fire—which was, of course, his specialty.

I am a Jordanologist of sufficiently long standing to have seen Michael actually *not* come through, even to see him blow a few games with poor passes or by having the ball stolen from him. But the more lasting impression is of the surging Michael, the Michael who could put together a dazzling 24-point fourth quarter before a television audience of twenty million. Even in 1995–96, when the Bulls won 72 of 81 regular-season games, more than any other team in the history of the National Basketball Association, it seemed—whether true or not—that the vast majority were won by coming from behind, as often as not with Michael scoring at the buzzer.

In this as in many other respects, Michael Jordan was very much a basketball player of the modern era. As a fan, I myself go back to the game in its medieval phase, being old enough to remember when Jews were still a strong presence. I recall the elegant Dolph Schayes, of the Syracuse Nats; and Nat Holman and, later, Red Holzman, two of the great names in coaching; and Abe Saperstein, the founder and original owner of the Harlem Globetrotters. In the Chicago Public League of my youth, there were coaches named Bosco Levine and Sid Novak, and many of the All-City players had names like Irv Bemoras, Harvey Babetch, and Eddie Goldman. One of the great annual sports events in the city was the game between the Catholic Youth Organization and the B'nai B'rith Youth Organization.

As for the game itself, when I first came to it the great offensive weapon was the two-handed set shot, and free throws, more often than not, were still shot underhand. The set shot elided into the one-hander, the one-hander into the jump shot. The slam dunk would come later—specifically, with the extraordinary and sudden advent of excellent coordination in large men, which seemed to have happened, quite mysteriously, in the late 1950s.

But the really dramatic change occurred with the integration of black players into big-time college programs and the NBA. As late as the 1950s, Harry Coombs, coach at the University of Illinois, and Branch McCracken, coach at Indiana, did not trouble to recruit blacks players; and Adolph Rupp, at the University of Kentucky, was said to have no compunction about expressing his own racist sentiments. The first black in the NBA was Nat (Sweetwater) Clifton, a former Globetrotter. As everyone knows, basketball turned out to be a game at which blacks excelled and soon came to dominate.

The game has been further jazzed up in recent years by such innovations as the outlawing of the zone defense, the installation in 1954 of the 24-second clock, and the three-point shot. The NBA has also lost the scruffiness that old-line fans like me used to love. I recall seeing a Boston Celtic player named Togo Palazzi play a game, on national television, wearing shorts of the wrong color, which suggests not only that he was a careless packer but that NBA teams in the 1950s operated on a very slim budget. Between then and now, the really huge difference has been made by money. In his last season, Michael Jordan's salary was $36 million, and he is said to have earned another $40 million or so through endorsements—for McDonald's, Gatorade, Hanes underwear, Nike, etc.—as well as from royalties and personal contracts.

★ ★ ★

Professional basketball has run in waves of success and failure, athletic and commercial. When I first began to watch, the Boston Celtics, with players such as Bob Cousy and Bill Sharman and then later Bill Russell and John Havlicek, were indomitable, magnificent to watch, and downright irritating in their refusal to lose championships. A new phase set in with the sleek New York Knicks of Willis Reed, Earl Monroe, Walt Frazier, Bill Bradley & Co. and the Los Angeles Lakers of Jerry West, Elgin Baylor, and Wilt Chamberlain. But then the play dipped badly. I recall going to a Bulls-Knicks game at some point in the mid-1970s with Jerome Holtzman, the sports columnist for the *Chicago Tribune*. "They need four or five more balls out there," he remarked as we watched the two teams pound drearily up and down the floor. "One ball isn't enough for these selfish jerks."

Things picked up again with the entrance into the NBA of Larry Bird of the Celtics and Magic Johnson of the Lakers, two players who revitalized the game. Others worthy of a connoisseur's interest—Pete Maravich, Julius Erving, Isiah Thomas, Paul Westphal—came on the scene. Michael Jordan arrived toward the close of Bird and Johnson's careers, and he clearly represented something new. He took things to a higher level, and brought an excitement of a kind the game had never quite known before.

Power in the NBA is demonstrated in a number of ways. But only a very small number of stars have had the authority, in effect, to appoint their own coaches. In practice, this has meant the power to fire any coach who does not run the team the way the star wishes. Magic Johnson, for example, was able to have Paul Westhead canned because his run-and-gun offense was not Magic Johnson's kind of offense. Larry Bird might have been able to do the same, though under the strong management of Red Auerbach it is unlikely he would have tried.

But Michael Jordan outdid them all: he was able not only to insist on the retention of Phil Jackson, the Bulls' coach during their championship seasons, but to elevate Jackson into serious money—roughly $7 million—during Michael's and Jackson's final year. The alternative was watching Michael retire early or otherwise take his golden-egg-making apparatus away with him, and there could be no mistaking the goldenness of those eggs: David Halberstam reports that, in 1993, with Michael

playing, the NBA finals for the first time achieved higher television ratings than the World Series—and when he was not playing the audience
dropped by eight million viewers, or roughly a third. In June 1998,
Fortune estimated the reverberating effect of Michael on the national
economy, including tickets, merchandising, television revenues, endorsements, and the rest, at "just about $10 billion—and still counting."

As for what gave Michael Jordan all that allure, commercial clout, and
bargaining power, it was, to begin with, his performance on the court.
He was a natural—with preternatural strength and speed, huge hands,
astonishing leaping ability, amazing stamina. Adding to Michael's leaping ability was his capacity to maintain himself in the air; "hang time"
is the term of art here, and at moments—when leaving from the free-
throw line for a slam, say—he did seem as if attached to an invisible
hang-glider. When Hersey Hawkins, another player, asked him how he
executed a certain shot, Michael replied: "When you get up, you hang
for three seconds and let the defender fly by and then you release it."

If Michael was a natural, he was a natural who worked hard to
improve his game, and who possessed, along with great court savvy, an
indomitable, a really quite fanatical, will to win. He began as a slashing,
driving player, able to elude defenses and then arrange to score in some
inventive way. Later in his career he developed one of the game's great
jump shots, which he released high in the air and fading away—a thing
of beauty and a joy, if not forever then till the next time he did it. In *The
Jordan Rules*, a more critical book than Halberstam's, the journalist Sam
Smith records Phil Jackson's continual amazement at Michael's ability
to score pretty much at will against even the best players in the world:
"It was a curse in some ways to be a comet racing across the game with
everyone light-years in your wake."

On the court, finally, Michael was the complete player—as brilliant
on defense as on offense. Led by Michael and two teammates, Scottie
Pippen and Ron Harper, the Bulls had what was known as the Dober-
man defense. That is exactly what it must have felt like to play against
these guys—as if one were being pursued by a pack of lean, mean Do-
berman Pinschers.

David Halberstam argues that the great NBA players over the past
twenty years have not only had a will to win but have been able directly

to transfuse this will into their teammates. Not *all* the great players have been able to accomplish this: Julius Erving, one of the most elegant offensive players in the history of the game, could light a fire only under himself; Kareem Abdul Jabbar, one of the most consistently efficient players, could not lead; Wilt Chamberlain, one of the strongest athletes in any sport, was so lacking in this capacity that it seemed a team could not hope to win *with* him (though the Philadelphia 76'ers did, once, in 1963). But three players who did have it—and of whom Halberstam provides lengthy accounts—were Magic Johnson, Larry Bird, and Isiah Thomas.

Did Michael? He certainly had the will to win, and to the highest power. But sometimes this worked to the detriment of the team itself. He practiced so hard that he often tended to wear his teammates out. He was a specialist at baiting other players on his own team. If he did not think a newly arrived player fit, he would stay on the guy's back until he either remade himself to Michael's specifications, asked to be traded, or simply disappeared from the league. He had a nice taste for vengeance, never forgetting either a slight or an injury.

Basketball began as a non-contact sport, but it has not been one for decades. So violent can the rebounding become that the area around the basket is known among the players as the alligator-wrestling pit. Everyone in the NBA now does weight training. Superior coordination and endurance and style are important, but, at the highest level, without the muscle to back it up they do not come to much. The Detroit Pistons, who dominated the league before the Bulls, did it on sheer physical intimidation; the New York Knicks, under the coaching of Pat Riley, attempted the same thing, though without comparable success.

When Michael Jordan first came into the league it was understood that his then-teammate Charles Oakley was his bodyguard. Anyone roughed up Michael, Oakley would find a way to repay him later in the game. It is dangerous out on an NBA floor, where one's masculinity is regularly tested. Michael himself eventually muscled up. He came in at 6'6" and 185 pounds; he ended his career 30 pounds heavier—all of it muscle, carefully acquired with the help of a personal trainer so that the added weight would not slow him down.

But the largest problem that Michael presented, especially to his own team, derived not from his weight or his manners but from his extraordinary ability, with which he dominated every game. One of his teammates, a now-forgotten center named Dave Corzine, complained that when the team won it seemed it was Michael's doing but when the team lost it was everyone else's. A man with so much talent tends to render the concept of teamwork beside the point, if not wholly to derogate it.

When the Bulls first attempted to install their complicated Triangle offense, which would, among other things, have taken some of the pressure off Michael's having to score so frequently, he described it derisively as "an equal-opportunity offense." In *The Jordan Rules*, Sam Smith reports that once, during a time-out, Phil Jackson was designing a complex play in a tight spot. Cutting him short, Michael told him, "Give me the fuckin' ball." The temptation to do just that in each and every tight spot had to be great. Basketball writers took to calling the Bulls "Michael and the Jordanaires," and Michael himself referred in a press conference to his teammates as "my supporting cast"—not a smart move in a man who made few bad moves, on the court or off.

Off the court, one of the reasons Michael was able to garner so much endorsement money is that he gave off the solidest of vibrations. Bill Russell, the great center of the Boston Celtics and then for a few years coach of the Seattle Supersonics, is said to hold a low opinion of most contemporary professional players. Yet he thought Michael an exception, a young man of good character. Halberstam notes in him "an innate elegance and coolness." He could make baldness look good, he wore clothes splendidly, and if there are still best-dressed-men lists he must be atop most of them. "I wanna be like Mike," was the tag line from his Gatorade commercial, and many people did.

He also had a way of making people forget about race. "As Jordan smiled," Halberstam writes, "race simply fell away." In good part this was owing to his absolute refusal to whine, complain, or show moodiness of the kind too many black athletes are susceptible of whenever things do not go their way. Unlike many of them, Michael never fell back on white racism as an excuse to justify poor performance or broken contract negotiations. No less impressively, he kept himself well away from the drug and easy-sex scenes that in recent decades have been part of the world of NBA players, young men with the dangerous combination of too much money and too much free time on their hands. The closest he came to scandal was when he lost serious-sized bets to a golf hustler with a criminal record.

Michael has also kept himself free from politics. When the Nike company was found to be manufacturing its products at low wages in southeast Asia, brave columnists in the *New York Times* proclaimed that Michael ought to denounce the practice and perhaps threaten to break with the company. But he chose not to speak on the matter—or on any other, similar matter. After one of the Bulls' championships, he even declined to attend the team meeting at the White House with George Bush, preferring to play golf. Whether he thinks politics bad for business, or just does not care, nobody knows for certain; perhaps a combination of the two keeps him apolitical. "Even Republicans," he once said, "buy gym shoes."

Halberstam refers to Michael as "very well-spoken." I disagree. I would say he is half well-spoken. Certainly he has mastered the jock jabberwocky that passes for analysis in post-games interviews: "I thought we had a nice flow of energy out there, especially in the second half, when the momentum seemed to shift. But it was a question of whether we could keep our focus down the stretch and if our bench could step up, which they were able to do." He can also do the false-humility bit as well as anyone: at his retirement press conference, with journalists from all over the world gathered in a huge hall, he began by reminding everyone of a recently murdered Chicago policeman whose funeral was taking place the same day, noting that this was the real story of the moment.

Michael is more believable when his natural and controlled—and, I would add, earned—arrogance shows through. The genuine Michael is the man who replied, when asked what advice he might give to his then-teammate Dennis Rodman, who had taken to having himself photographed in a wedding dress: "I'd advise him to wear pants as often as possible." This is also the Michael who is said to have regularly driven the better part of the 30-mile trip from his suburban home to Bulls games in Chicago on the shoulder of the Kennedy Expressway. Typically, the police, if they stopped him, would recognize him and let him go; when necessary, he gave them tickets to the game or a signed basketball before driving off.

★ ★ ★

Une saison en enfer, Arthur Rimbaud titled one of his two books of poems, but Rimbaud did not know the half of a season in hell of the kind
Bull fans have undergone without Michael Jordan.

Without Michael, professional basketball itself has come to seem, at
least to this fan, flat, devoid of drama, without magic. Still, one counts
one's blessings. Having spent too many hours watching boys and men
hit, kick, and throw balls, and having been born too late for Babe Ruth
or Bobby Jones or the prime of Joe Louis, I am grateful that I was
around to see my share of Michael Jordan. A fine rousing spectacle,
watching this magnificent athlete who turned his sport into an art—the
art of coming through in the clutch, which he did, splendidly, time after
time after time.

HANK GREENBERG

Designated Mensch

Baseball trivia quiz: (1) Name a Methodist first baseman who won the triple crown. (2) Name a Baptist right-hander who led the National League in ERA in five different seasons. (3) Name two Catholic outfielders—one from each league—who hit more than 450 home runs and had lifetime batting averages above .330. Are you having trouble coming up with the names Jimmie Foxx, Christy Mathewson, Babe Ruth and Stan Musial? Maybe it's because the religion of athletes strikes you as superfluous? And so it should, unless they happen to be Jewish ballplayers and you happen to be Jewish.

Only among Jews is there a set of baseball cards, put out by the American Jewish Historical Society, devoted exclusively to Jewish players. Only Jews bother to discover, and then take exuberant pride in, the fact that such un-Jewishly named ballplayers as Shawn Green and Kevin Youkilis are members of the tribe, by which I don't mean the Cleveland Indians.

Is there something a bit parochial and chauvinistic and also unconsciously condescending in this interest on the part of Jews in Jewish ballplayers? Samuel Johnson's remark about lady preachers and dogs that walk on their hind legs, that "it is not done well, but you are surprised to find that it is done at all," often, alas, applies to the delight that Jewish fans take in their athletes. This exaggerated interest is partly owing to the relative paucity of Jewish ballplayers who made it to the majors. Between 1871 and 2003, there were only 142 of them, which averages out to roughly one a year. Perhaps a dozen Jews are playing major-league baseball at present, the best among them being Ryan Braun, the Milwaukee Brewers' star left fielder.

Of the Jewish ballplayers who played major-league baseball, a small number were truly standouts; the Indians' third baseman Al Rosen and the Cubs' pitcher Ken Holtzman come to mind. Many more were journeymen, like the catcher Moe Berg, who was said to be able to speak six languages and was unable to hit above .240 in any of them.

Two Jews were genuinely great ballplayers. One is the Dodgers' Sandy Koufax, who between 1961 and 1966 compiled some of the most astonishing records in baseball; in three of those years he won the Cy Young Award and the triple crown for pitchers: leading the league in wins, strikeouts, and ERA.

The other is Hank (born Henry, called Hymie by his family) Greenberg, who played only nine full seasons in the majors and—owing to injury and the nearly four years he served in the Army during World War II—parts of three others. Greenberg is best known for driving in 183 runs in 1937 (one short of Lou Gehrig's American League record), hitting 58 home runs in 1938 (two short of Babe Ruth's record) and twice winning the American League's Most Valuable Player award while playing for the Detroit Tigers. Yet Greenberg may be quite as famous for being Jewish as for what he did in the batter's box.

Undeniably Jewish by name and by countenance, Hank Greenberg (1911–86) was not avid in his religious practice. Though brought up in an Orthodox Jewish home, he was, as a Jew, more respectful than devout. Early in his career he did not play baseball on the Jewish high holidays, though he did so later. (Koufax, by contrast, never played on them, including famously choosing not to pitch Game One of the 1965 World Series when it fell on Yom Kippur.) Greenberg's first wife, Carla Gimbel, was a nonpracticing Jew; his second wife was a Christian. He raised his own children without religious observance. Still, as a Jew in baseball in the 1930s, he was an anomaly. When an Irish cop once stopped him for speeding and asked what he did for a living, he answered that he was a baseball player, causing the cop to respond: "Who in the hell ever heard of a professional baseball player named Greenberg?"

A new biography of Greenberg, written by John Rosengren, offers much interesting information admixed with hyperbole. The book's subtitle, "The Hero of Heroes," is characteristic of the approach. The

English call exaggerated expression "over-egging the pudding"; of Mr. Rosengren's biography, centered on Greenberg's Jewishness, we might more accurately say that he over-eggs the kugel. "Hank had not bettered Ruth and he had not stopped Hitler, but he had single-handedly succeeded in changing the way Americans saw Jews. . . . A single word that could stand up to any form of prejudice: Greenberg." Wouldn't it, as Jake Barnes says in *The Sun Also Rises*, "be pretty to think so"?

Mr. Rosengren is fearless in his use of clichés. In his pages "fans go wild" and "crowds thunder their approval," then sometimes "solemnly file out of Briggs Stadium." Scores tend to get "knotted," "scribes" "pen" articles, photographers "snap photos," and losing teams "take comfort in John Barleycorn." Hank Greenberg, you should know, "was not master of his own destiny," though he would "bask in the glory of his return" to baseball as the story of his first marriage "crackled over the wires and dominated the front pages of Detroit's newspapers."

The unconscious comic touches I think of as empty historical montage also play through Mr. Rosengren's pages. A hypothetical example of empty historical montage might run: "As Big Bill Tilden served his last ace at Wimbledon, a mere four hundred miles away in a quiet laboratory in Berlin Max Planck failed yet again to discover quantum physics." Or, to quote an example from Mr. Rosengren: "Two days after a U.S. B-29 dropped the first atomic bomb on Hiroshima, Hank collected three hits, including two doubles, in the first game of a twin bill at Briggs Stadium against the Red Sox."

The question arises whether an entirely successful biography of an athlete can be written. At its best, biography entails a tripartite view of its subject: as the world sees him, as his family and friends see him, and, perhaps most important, as he sees himself. In this last aspect most biographies of athletes fail, for introspection is a rare quality among athletes and may even be a hindrance to them. Some biographies of athletes are iconoclastic; most are idolatrous. In any case, the literary net is lowered for biographies of sports stars.

Hank Greenberg was intelligent but, on the evidence Mr. Rosengren provides, without keen self-knowledge. For himself, as my sainted mother used to say, he was smart. He was a near genius at salary negotiations with Walter Briggs, the parsimonious owner of the Detroit Tigers, and in the final years of his career was the highest-paid player in baseball.

He was smart, too, in knowing his own weaknesses as a ballplayer. Unlike his near contemporaries, Ted Williams and Joe DiMaggio, Greenberg was not a natural athlete. He was large—6-foot-3 by the age of seventeen—and klutzy, with flat feet. Apart from his great strength, he had no special gifts for the game. But he put in vast hours to improve his fielding, initially as a first baseman, then as a left fielder, going so far at one point as to take dancing lessons to sharpen his coordination. He paid people to pitch to him and others to shag balls for long stretches of early-morning and postgame batting practice.

Hank Greenberg was thirty when he was drafted into the Army in 1940 and thirty-four when he came back to baseball. He could have returned to baseball after a year but chose to serve until the war was over. He never saw action, but, unlike so many of the 470 major leaguers drafted during the war, who played on armed-services baseball teams, he had serious administrative positions, which he performed ably.

Greenberg's courage was called upon more during his baseball days than during the war. When he began his professional career, anti-Semitism, rife in American life, was especially virulent in Detroit, where Henry Ford published the *Dearborn Independent*. Ford had the Jew-bee in his bonnet. He blamed the advent of jazz ("Moron Music") on Jews and claimed that Jews were natural traitors: "The Jewish Associates of Benedict Arnold" was a characteristic *Dearborn Independent* headline. Father Charles Coughlin, the radio priest and another professional anti-Semite, broadcast out of suburban Detroit.

Then there were the major-league players, many of them uneducated Southerners, for whom Jew-baiting was a second national pastime. Greenberg heard ethnic slurs not only from the stands but also from opposing teams' dugouts. Mr. Rosengren's book contains a number of anecdotes about Greenberg facing down anti-Semites on the field and in the locker room. After taking abuse from the bench of the Chicago White Sox during a game in 1939, Greenberg walked into the Sox clubhouse and announced: "I want the guy who called me a 'yellow Jew bastard' to get to his feet to say it to my face." As Mr. Rosengren recounts: "No one moved. Hank walked slowly around the room and looked at each of them. . . . Not one of them dared stand up. Hank walked out, paused at the door to look back, then left."

One comes away from Mr. Rosengren's biography with a firm notion of Hank Greenberg as a decent human being, a man of integrity and honor, what Jews call a mensch. He seems only rarely to have been swept away by his own fame and good fortune. He was invariably kind to young fans. Traded to the Pittsburgh Pirates in 1947, his final year in baseball, he tutored the rookie Ralph Kiner, who attributed much of his success as a slugger to Greenberg. He encouraged Jackie Robinson, when Robinson, under extreme pressure, broke the color line in major-league baseball that same year.

Would Hank Greenberg be as well known today if he weren't Jewish? Although he was inducted into the Baseball Hall of Fame in 1956, his statistics, owing to his war-shortened career, are not as impressive as they might otherwise be. He hit 331 career home runs and had a lifetime batting average of .313, numbers that are respectable but less than dazzling. Statistically he resembles Johnny Mize and Chuck Klein, both deserving hall-of-famers but not the sort of ballplayers who get their biographies written. According to the Society for American Baseball Research, had Greenberg enjoyed a full career he would, to quote Mr. Rosengren, have ranked "26th all-time for home runs (502), 11th for RBI (1,869), and tied for 54th for runs scored (1,554)." The baseball sabermetrician Bill James believes that, given the poor quality of wartime pitching, had he not gone off to the Army, he would have hit more than 600 home runs. But all this is extrapolation, not reality.

On any all-time all-star baseball team one's first baseman would not be Greenberg but, indubitably, Lou Gehrig. Clumsy afield, neither would Greenberg find a place in the outfield. Hank Greenberg's place on this all-time team, for which he has no rivals in major-league baseball, would be that of designated mensch.

BOB LOVE

The Unknown Superstar

The scene was the third game of the first-round playoffs of National Basketball Association championship between the Los Angeles Lakers and the Chicago Bulls in 1971. The Bulls had had an uphill but overall magnificent season, finishing with the third-best record in the NBA, but now they were down two games to none in a beat of seven series. Earlier, the Bulls' coach, Dick Motta, for using what is euphemistically called "improper language" and then refusing to leave the court, was thrown out of the game. The score was close but things nonetheless looked bleak. A rebound off the Lakers' backboard sent Bulls' forward Bob Love and Lakers' guard Keith Erickson high into the air, bodies entwined. They landed with fists flying. Love got in two solid shots to Erickson's face, Erickson came back with a couple of his own, and the flurry of blows was quickly broken up as Chet Walker, the Bulls' other forward, grabbed Love and pulled him away.

Although professional basketball can be a very rough game, its meaning is not to be found in its violence, as is the case with professional football and often with hockey, yet there was something wonderfully exhilarating about Bob Love swinging out at Keith Erickson. In fact, it wasn't a very smart move; and if Motta hadn't been ejected a short time before, no doubt Love would have been. What was exhilarating about the fight—which probably lasted less than a minute—was that Bob Love, the least assertive, the least pushy, the least violent of athletes, seemed in those few seconds to have announced that he was a man who would take no guff and one who, after a nearly flawless season, had now arrived as a full-fledged pro. As it turned out, the Bulls

155

went on to win the game. The next day Chet Walker, underlining the irony at his friend and teammate's fracas of the day before, referred to him in the press as "Muhammad Bean"—a double-barreled allusion to Love's nickname of Butterbean and Muhammad Ali.

That Bob Love had arrived in the NBA is no longer subject to doubt; that his status as a professional basketball player was that of a superstar, albeit of a rather unspectacular variety, might have startled many people, and not the least, Love himself. But then Bob Love was a superstar with a difference, and to get at that difference perhaps it would be well to first get at the conventional notion of a superstar in sports.

In pro basketball a superstar is a player whose level of play goes beyond simple mastery of the rudiments of the game. There is an element of inspiration to his play. He raises the standards of excellence, making what once might have seemed brilliant now appear merely competent. The Milwaukee Bucks' Kareem Abdul-Jabbar is justly deemed a superstar because of his ability to dominate a game—intimidating on defense and able at any time to blow a game wide open by scoring seven or eight quick baskets in three minutes of play. The Los Angeles Lakers' Jerry West was a superstar, in part because his all-around play has a perfection that was classical in his execution and, even more important, because he was a clutch player who could be depended upon to be at his very best when the pressure was greatest. But then all-around play alone doesn't necessarily always define a superstar. The Boston Celtics' player-coach, Bill Russell, was a notoriously inept offensive player; there must have been thousands of high school kids who shot a basket with greater style and effect. Yet Russell happened to be a defensive genius and, moreover, a man of—old fashioned word though it is, no other fits quite so well— extraordinary character.

Love, on the other hand, did not come anywhere near dominating a game the way Jabbar did. His moves on the court had little of West's elegance, nor did he appear to have anything of Russell's generalship. Far from it. Love's presence on the court often seemed hardly noticeable. But after a game, sitting in your car in the parking lot, waiting for the postgame traffic to begin flowing, you turn on the radio. You learn that Love had 29 points to lead all scorers on both teams. You learn that he had 14 rebounds. And you learn something else—that the other team's leading scorer—Billy Cunningham of the Philadelphia 76ers, or

Connie Hawkins of the Phoenix Suns, or Gus Johnson of the Baltimore Bullets (for Love, as a standout on defense, always drew the toughest assignments)—was held to well below his average output of points. And you said to yourself, My God, did Love play a helluva game! And you wondered why you didn't happen to notice.

Bob Love was the most deceptive player in the National Basketball Association. His ability did not elude everyone, however, and in 1970 he finished seventh in the balloting for the NBA's most valuable player, while at the beginning of the following season his fellow players in the league voted him among the most underrated players. The most cursory glance at the Bulls' statistics for the 1970–71 season conveys something of the nature of his true performance. For starters, Love led all Bull scorers with an average of 25.2 points per game, sixth best in the NBA. He put in more court time by some 300 minutes than any of his teammates. He was second in team rebounds, behind only the 7-foot Tom Boerwinkle, and led his team in free throws made with 690, shot at an accuracy clip of .829 percent. Again, in that year's NBA All-Star game, he led all scorers at half time with 13 points, playing for the West squad which went on to win the game. That year, too, Love was chosen to play in the NBA All-Star game; this time as a starter.

Despite all this, Bob Love's talent, his really prodigious abilities, remained relatively obscure. Why? There are two reasons: the particular nature of the team he played for, and his own rather subtle style on the basketball court.

Sports teams, like children, quickly acquire personalities. In football, the Green Bay Packers under Vince Lombardi personified the strength in the fundamental virtues of discipline, hard work, and authority. In baseball, the New York Mets of a few years back were thought of as amiable bumblers—losers everybody loved. The 1969–70 NBA champion New York Knicks, fast-moving and stylish, all flash and brilliance, seemed to reflect the best qualities to be found in Manhattan itself.

And the Chicago Bulls, what was their team personality like? At first glance the Bulls were best characterized as plodding. The team was not known for its speed or great flash and was without (except in isolated instances) notable style. It seemed to win all its games going uphill. Little came easily to the Bulls, yet as the season wore on, the team just kept on winning—coming from behind to win one night, blowing a comfortable lead then having to bust their heads to pull out a game the next, scrapping down to the wire on a third. The Chicago Bulls were a team whose quality emerged only over the haul of a long season, and only then did it become evident that they played better than they looked—better, possibly, than they really were. The Bulls were something of a Harry S Truman of pro basketball teams.

The Bulls were also wholly the creature of Coach Dick Motta's basketball imagination. Motta, 1970's Coach of the Year in the NBA, is something of a Truman-like figure himself. A man of compact build, he is outspoken, dedicated, and wholly business-like in his approach to the game. The press' favorite adjective for Motta was "feisty," In fact, Motta was not all that feisty. He is, however, a tremendous competitor.

In his approach to basketball, Motta, unfeistily enough, was what might be termed a pragmatic conservative. He is a man who shaped his teams around what talent he had, and did not dream impossible dreams. The Bulls have never been noted for speed, nor have they ever had any consistent outside shooting or scoring power at center. Therefore, Motta organized the Bulls' offense around half a dozen set plays, with a number of variations, all of which were calculated to set up an easy shot or hit an open man near the basket. The Bulls' defense, on the other hand, was not spectacular but sedulous. They had no one, for example, like the Knicks' brilliant guard Walt Frazier, noted for lunging steals of the ball well in the back-court followed by dramatic solo flights to the basket for smooth layups. But as on offense, so on defense, the Bulls hung in there.

Whatever the Chicago Bulls weren't, one thing they very much were was a team—and a team in a sport that is more given over than most to featuring individual performance. An Earl Monroe wriggling and writhing aloft, then letting fly with a perfect 20-foot jump shot; a Wilt Chamberlain stuffing the ball into the basket with such gusto that the backboard is left in a state of palsy for a full minute afterward; an Oscar Robertson threading his way through an entire defense with an undeniable dribble, then tossing up a classical jumper while getting fouled for a three-point play—these are the high, the lyrical, moments of professional basketball. And yet they are moments of individuals, virtuoso moments, great solo flights. Not that the Bulls did not provide their fans with such moments. But for the Bulls these were almost beside the point. The point, instilled by the relentless coaching of Motta, is the more humdrum business of winning games.

Under Motta, the Bulls were not primarily dedicated to the cultivation of great individual performers. The concept of the superstar was not so much alien as it was uninteresting to Motta, who believed that the main point about any basketball player, apart from his talent, is his determination to win. If a player really wants to win, Motta held, he could work him into the Bulls' style of play. As a coach, Motta was not wedded to any one brand of basketball, nor to any one type of basketball player—only to the idea of winning.

In Bob Love, as in Dick Motta, you sense a man for whom the game of basketball is as important as life itself. In large part this came through in Love's concentration—at practice sessions, in a game, even when merely talking about the sport. Even Love's physique seemed shaped to the game. He is 6-foot-8, muscular in a slender way—with long arms whose elbows seem to jut out slightly more than normally, making them all the more effective as weapons to be used under the backboard and for rebounding. Love wore a basketball uniform as if born into it; so natural did it seem on him that it was difficult to imagine him in street clothes.

Yet for all that Bob Love was a natural, a man born to play basketball, his skill was a long time in being recognized. Love was born in Bastrop, Louisiana, near Baton Rouge. He learned his basketball there, and in high school, along with basketball, played on the same football team as Luke Jackson, the powerful rebounding center of the Philadelphia 76ers. (Although basketball nowadays is more and more thought of as a city game, the rural areas always provided a large number of ball players for the pros. Along with Love and Jackson, Willis Reed, the great center of the Knicks, is also from a small town in Louisiana.) After high school, Love went to Southern University in Baton Rouge. His size attracted the attention of the pro scouts, but their reports on him were not all that favorable. The Bulls' scout of those days reported that he didn't think Love could make it among the pros.

Nevertheless, when it came time for the NBA draft the year he graduated from college, Love was a fourth-round pick of the Cincinnati Royals. Since the competition merely to get on an NBA team was ferocious—maybe eight or ten rookies could break in in any given sea-son—the odds against Love's making the Royals were considerable. He would have to prove himself spectacular at the Royals' training camp merely to avoid being cut. When the Royals' training camp ended and the cuts were made, Love was out.

Love faced a decision. Should he hang it up and return home, or stay with the game, hoping to break into the NBA at a later time? Love was married, had a child, and could not afford the life of a basketball bum. Still, to give up the game meant to give up the dream—and to give up the dream meant to give up any hope of making the pros and earning his living doing the thing he did and loved best. But to keep the dream was costly, and not for himself alone; it involved sending his family back home—a difficult thing to do for a person who was by tem-perament a family man—and supporting them from a distance during the basketball season by playing minor league basketball while working at a full-time job.

Not much is known about the minor-league Eastern League, but to get a rough sense of what is involved, one must imagine the condi-tions surrounding the lowest-level minor-league baseball team in the country, and then be prepared to grasp the fact that next to the Eastern League, the conditions are positively Jet Set in luxuriance.

In the Eastern League, in the days Bob Love played in it, one got paid only when one played. If you caught a cold and missed a game, you also missed a paycheck. Not that you missed so very much, even then, for the size of one's take depended upon the size of the crowd, and the crowds more often than not were small. Although some players received more, an average night's work paid somewhere around $50; yet a team might only play two games a week, and some weeks only a single game. The conditions of the game itself were lousy. One dressed in dank locker rooms to play in drafty gyms. On the floor itself a basket might be a few bare feet from a concrete wall, making the prospect of a driving layup a bad insurance risk. Teams piled in cars in Trenton to drive to a game in Allentown, and after the game piled back into the cars for the drive back. All of which was far from the good life of the professional athlete.

Looking back on those years, Love remarked, "It was a hard life, and I hated being away from my family, but there was no other way."

Still, the competition was good, for there were a great many fine ball players who for one reason or another fell just short of landing on an NBA team. Love played two seasons in the Eastern League, using the time to polish the rough edges off his game, develop his shot, build his confidence, and acquire a good deal of experience playing against tough competition. To support himself and his family back in Louisiana, be got up at 6 a.m. to work as a dietitian at a Trenton hospital. Such a life could scarcely have been other than a grind—dreary, lonely, exhausting—and there was no reason to be confident that it would ever pay off.

At the end of his second season in the Eastern League, Love made the Cincinnati Royals, but only to take up a frustrating and what looked to be permanent residence on the bench. The Royals had a strong though not winning team; Oscar Robertson was its main man, and he dominated the style and tone of the Royals' game. Love got in little floor time, and ample opportunity for his confidence to rot out in the role of substitute. Before long he went into the expansion pool and was picked up by the Milwaukee Bucks. But his situation was not greatly changed in Milwaukee either, for he still spent most of his time sitting. At this point in his career, Love looked to be one of those dim figures in professional basketball, the superfluous athlete who fills out the roster, is used as fodder for trades, and after four or five dismal seasons fades into oblivion.

"Those were frustrating years." Love concedes. "Especially since, given half a chance, I still felt I could make it among the pros."

Love's seeming journey into oblivion was interrupted in the middle of the 1968–69 season when the Bucks traded him to the Bulls. To say that he was traded, though, is somewhat imprecise; in fact, the Bucks threw him into a trade whose main deal involved an exchange of guards, with the Bulls sending Flynn Robinson in exchange for Bob Weiss. Love was, in effect, a sweetener, or what in the trade is known as a "throw-in." As Dick Motta explains it, accepting a throw-in is often a pro basketball team's way of hedging its bet on a trade. If a trade looks a bit shaky to begin with, then turns out to be a full disaster, a team's front office can at least justify the bad deal by saying, well, hell, we got two players for one, and we never expected neither would work out.

From a fan's seat in Chicago Stadium, the trade that brought Weiss and Love to the Bulls looked at the time to be a tremendously bum deal. (Two years later, of course, it would seem a work of sheer trading genius.) Flynn Robinson was a guard with an exciting repertoire of outside shots who could occasionally come up with a 30-point game. Even to the most intense followers of pro basketball, Weiss was relatively unknown and Love, well, Love was a total obscurity. Nor did the Bulls, a then floundering and fairly characterless club, particularly want Love, even as a throw-in. "They practically had to beg us to take him," Pat Williams, the Bulls' executive vice president and general manager, recalls. "Our scouts told us not to. What did we want him for, they asked? Thank goodness we went against what was then thought to be the best informed judgment."

Upon coming to Chicago, Love's already hapless career took an ugly turn for the worse. Within the first week of his arrival, he was involved in an auto accident; his wife was badly cut up and his infant child suffered bone damage. Nor did things immediately improve with the Bulls. Even so astute a basketball eye as Motta's failed at first to grasp what the Milwaukee trade had brought him. As Motta freely acknowledges, practice sessions don't always reveal all that much about a player. Watching Love in his first few weeks of Bulls' practices, Motta noted that his new forward could play good defense, but he had little idea of the sort of offensive player who had practically strayed onto his team. For most of the remainder of the 1968–69 season, Love was the Bulls' fourth forward, playing behind the starters Bob Boozer and Jimmy Washington and the team's No. 3 forward, Barry Clemens. Bulls' fans' primary view of Love was of his back, draped in a warmup jacket that rarely came off, leaning against the bench.

The following season the Bulls made a number of trades, easily the most significant of which was acquiring Chet Walker, the 6-foot-7 All-Pro forward from the Philadelphia 76ers, in exchange for Washington. In the shuffle of trading, Love moved up to No. 3 forward, behind Walker and a promising rookie named Bob Kaufmann. In the exhibition games and at the beginning of the regular season, Kaufmann seemed not to be living up to promise. As a result, Love was getting in a good deal of playing time. Then one day while the Bulls were on the road on a western swing, Motta happened to be studying his team's statistics, when be noticed an extraordinary fact—Bob Love, the perennial substitute, was scoring at the phenomenal clip of roughly a point for every minute he was on the court. On that same road trip, against the San Francisco (now Golden State) Warriors, Motta put Love into the Bulls' starting lineup, and from that game on he was never supplanted.

Reflecting on Love's ability on the basketball court, Motta noted that he was probably the most deceptive performer in the NBA. "He was really not much of a jumper, or at least he never appears to get much more than 12 inches or so off the ground. And you hardly even noticed when he's scoring. There are some players in this league who have shots that never cease to amaze everybody. Jimmy Washington, for example. At least once each game it looks as if he's come down from the rafters to stuff the ball. Or Flynn Robinson, who every so often hits on an outside shot that looks as if it had a 30-foot trajectory. When a ballplayer does this sort of thing, it electrifies the crowd, it stands out in everyone's mind, to the point that they tend to forget all his turnovers, forced shots, or the fact that he may not have contributed a thing for a full quarter.

"With Love it was just the reverse," says Motta. "Bob was hustling every second, contributing something every minute he's in the game, and he had more playing time than anyone else on the team. His total contribution may not always have been apparent during the game, but it showed up unmistakably in the statistics. And, where it's more important, in the team's record."

"I admire Bob Love more than any professional athlete I've ever known," said Pat Williams. "His approach to the game, his seriousness about it, and the obstacles he's had to overcome to get where he did—all these things are involved in my admiration for the man.

"It's sometimes difficult to know precisely what it is that made him so tremendous a performer. I'd say two of the things he does best were play tough defense, night after night, and against the NBA's most potent scorers, and then, on offense, he moved so well without the ball."

Moving well without the ball, a pro basketball jargon phrase simply means that a player never stands flat-footed on the court but is always feigning, picking, or cutting for the basket in anticipation of a pass that will set him up for an easy shot. This Love did do extremely well. And full-time. But a player can move well without the ball from now till the Second Coming and it won't mean a thing if he doesn't have an ability to get off his shot—and the eye and touch to make the shot count.

There were certainly more glorious shots in the league than Bob Love's. Dick Barnett, the Knicks' starting guard, for example, had a jump shot which, for total motion, was unsurpassed outside the windmills of Holland. Barnett went up high in the air, arms bent, torso twisting, legs kicking out, giving the overall effect of a perpetual motion machine. Cazzie Russell of the Warriors shot a jump shot which, in its streamlined motion, resembled nothing so much as a missile at launching, and which he concluded, when the shot went in, with a fist raised in the air, rather as if he were Lenin arriving at the Finland Station. The Bulls' forward Howard Porter had a jump shot of classical proportions. He leapt well off the court, arched his back perfectly, and from behind his head released a lush, soft shot of high trajectory. When the ball went in, it was a shot of great beauty and, as such things go in pro basketball, a joy for about a second and a half.

Love's shot was of considerably less interest to basketball aestheticians. It was merely simple, quick, and deadly. But to say this is equivalent to saying that Rembrandt painted good faces; it is, in short, to miss the subtlety of the thing. In taking his shot, Love seemed rarely to get off the ground more than 6 or 8 inches. But he made up for this by having a very high release; the shot itself was taken with his arms nearly fully extended over his head, which, given his height, his short jump, and the length of his arms, meant the ball started on its way to the basket from a height of roughly 9 feet. It was a shot quite without flourish: no twists, no wriggles, but an absolute economy of motion. Up, release, and in. Such fakes as he employed seemed perfunctory at best. What made his shot so effective was not its trickiness but its astonishing quickness. So far as is known, no one has ever put a clock to Love's shot, but the entire execution could not have taken more than a half second. What's more, because he did not jump high off the ground to shoot, as soon as his shot was released, Love was back on the ground racing toward the basket to garner his own possible rebound. The whole operation was as smooth and economical as it was unspectacular.

But none of this would be of any account if Love didn't have one further (and quite uncoachable) attribute, and that was a great eye for the basket. Not only did he command a basic accuracy, but he also had an excellent soft touch to his shot, the effect of which was to cause many of his slightly off-center shots to roll in where harder shots would crash against the rim or backboard and back out on the court. Love was accurate within a range of roughly 18 to 20 feet; his shooting range, that is, from a half-circle drawn from both corners of the court and meeting around the free-throw line. As an offensive player, this was his turf; he could let fly from anywhere on this imaginary half-circle and the percentage was great that the result will be two points. Unlike the other pros, he didn't seem to have one or two favorite spots on the court from which he preferred to shoot, and consequently you rarely saw Love dribbling in the attempt to maneuver over to a favorite spot. Whole games went by in which he might not dribble at all. Get him the ball anywhere within his range and, with a little daylight, up he went for his shot. No dribbling, no rococo moves, not much to talk about.

Love had a very strong sense of how deceptive his own abilities were. "I'd make a little layup here, drop in a hook a bit later, then maybe a couple of jump shots. Usually not many people notice that the points are piling up." Publicity about his play didn't much matter to Love—certainly nowhere near as much as the quality of his play—but after a game with the Portland Trailblazers, he showed a rare instance of pique. Asked by reporters what it was like to guard Portland's excellent rookie forward, Sidney Wicks, Love suggestd that they ask Wicks what it was like to guard him. Since Love had outscored, out-defended, and generally outplayed Wicks, it was a fair question.

Bob Love had still another offensive ability, and this one, ironically, had in some quarters actually diminished his reputation. Along with everything else, he was a ball hawk. He had an uncanny way of picking up a stray rebound or a loose ball in a position for an easy basket. This involved a combination of instinct and hustle, both of which Love had in abundance. But, because of his ball hawking, Love could usually be counted on every night to score two or three "crips" (baskets so easy, even a cripple could make them), which, in some fans' eyes, gave him a reputation as a "garbage" player. This is, of course, a piece of stupendous bad judgment and an injustice to boot, for it overlooked Love's superior outside shooting, his marvelous defensive play.

On his own emergence as an outstanding pro basketball player—as the game's quietest superstar—Bob Love had little to say: "It was mostly a matter of getting in enough floor time to prove myself." And perhaps that's all that can finally be said about it: Love had the ability all along, and when his chance arose to prove it after long years of waiting, his confidence had not drained away and he was ready to demonstrate just how good he is.

How very good he was was on ample display one Saturday night at the Stadium against the Boston Celtics, who came into Chicago leading the Eastern Division of the NBA and suffered a solid trouncing at the Bulls' hands, 123 to 106. It was a characteristic Bob Love performance: he had his high-point night up to that point in the season, he was all over the court on offense and defense both, put in more playing time than anyone else, yet somehow didn't, in the view of most fans, emerge the hero of the game.

Love took the Bulls' first shot in the Celtics game, and missed it. A short while later, he went up for another and looked somewhat foolish, for the ball had been blocked out of his hands on his way up, sending him into the air for his shot without the ball. A lesser player would probably have cooled it and not taken another shot for three or four minutes. Love came right back to drill a jump shot from the right corner. He next missed a jumper from around the key, then, a few moments later, made good on the same shot from the other side of the key. His next five shots in the first quarter of the game missed, though he did swish a 15-footer from an angle off the corner as the buzzer went off to end the quarter. He had 6 points, or three baskets on 11 shots, and it didn't look like his night.

At the end of the quarter the Celtics were leading, 24–21. The Bulls, however, outscored them, 41 to 21, in the second quarter. Love contributed 10 points in 10 minutes of play. His first two came on a crip layup, when he picked up a loose ball batted away from a Celtics player by Jerry Sloan. A short while later, Love connected on a shot as sensational as the earlier one had been garbagey: a soft, looping hook off an angle from the corner about 12 feet out. He was next fouled in the act of shooting, making both free throws. He then made a turnaround jumper from the corner, and another from the other corner before being taken out for a two-minute blow. When he came back in the game, the Celtics had inserted 7-foot Henry Finkel into their lineup, so Love switched his defensive assignment to the Celts' regular center, Dave Cowens, who scored 25 points for the night. For the three minutes that Love was defending against him, Cowens stopped scoring.

Love came out to the third quarter to miss two shots, one from each corner. Then he grabbed a rebound, went up for a layup, missed, grabbed the rebound from his own missed shot, and put it in. After missing a turn-around jump shot from the free-throw line, he made his next three shots—a layup off a rebound, an elegant fade-away jump shot from the corner, and an 18-footer from near the end of the key. He closed out his third-quarter performance by making two free throws. In case anyone was keeping score, he now had 28 points for three quarters of play. But it is probable that not many people noticed, for everyone in the stands was excited over the play of the Bulls' guards, Bob Weiss and Norm Van Lier, whose outside shooting and passing were blowing the game wide open. When Van Lier fouled out, in fact, be got a standing ovation from the crowd.

In the fourth quarter Love's first basket came on a conventional (for him) jump shot from the corner. A crip layup followed off a nice assist pass from rookie center Clifford Ray. The Bulls went into the fourth quarter with a comfortable lead. But the Celtics are an explosive team and midway in the fourth quarter they started to eat into the lead, reducing it from 24 to 9 points. Love, along with Chet Walker, now went to work. Love made four of his last five shots of the game, giving him six out of seven for the quarter. One of the baskets came after picking up a loose ball under the basket—very garbagey but, at that point in the game, very necessary, for it put the game on ice for the Bulls. When it was over, the Bulls had won their fifth game in a row, and everyone left the Stadium talking about Van Lier. Love, meanwhile, walked off the court with a 40-point performance.

Love was a finesse athlete. His skills as a player were those of consistency, cohesion, and defensive ability—when what most fans want, in their preoccupation with style, is leaping, flashing, and exoticism. Love was a team man in a sport that features individuals. Because of the special way he played the game, he never received the popular recognition he deserved, and his name was never firmly linked with superstardom. Still, a superstar, albeit an unknown one, is what he was.

STORIES

THE GOLDIN BOYS

Even though the coffin was closed, I couldn't bring myself to walk in front of it and greet the Goldin family in condolence. I thought about it on the drive over to the Piser Funeral Home, but given the circumstances of Buddy Goldin's death, I could think of nothing condoling to say. I signed the visitors' book on my way in, so that, in a week or so, the family would see that Dr. Philip Hirsh had been among the mourners, but that was the best I could do.

I took a seat twenty or so rows behind the family—Buddy's parents, his wife who was still in her thirties, his two young daughters. Staring at their backs, I considered how sorrow destroyed posture. Sid Goldin wore his *yarmulke* at an odd angle at the back of his head, and his expensive suit seemed, in his grief, a poor fit, riding up on his shoulders. Jean Goldin seemed to have shrunk with age and the year-round suntan that she always had now gave her a leathery look that came across as hard and unsympathetic. Sid and Jean Goldin, whom life seemed so singularly to have favored, now drew this most bitter of life's cards: the death of a son as they were approaching old age.

The rabbi, a small man a little too pleased with his powers of enunciation, was sermonizing not very convincingly upon the mercifulness of death. He referred to Buddy, whom he had pretty clearly never met, as Bernard, with a strong accent on the second syllable, which made it feel as if those of us who were Buddy's old friends had never met the man the rabbi was talking about, either. Of course, at no point during this sermon, or during the entire service, did he mention that Buddy Goldin was a suicide.

The other item that went unmentioned in the rabbi's sermon was the absence of Buddy's twin brother Eddie. Twins though they were, Buddy and Eddie Goldin were very different in temperament and, even though unmistakably brothers, also in looks. Both were dark, but Buddy's hair was straight and Eddie's curly. Buddy, at 6'2", grew to be two inches taller than Eddie, who was stockier, more muscular than his brother. As kids, Buddy had had bad skin and Eddie a chipped front tooth (later capped). Buddy always seemed cool and a little detached, while Eddie was hot-tempered, a battler. Yet they always got on well together, at least as far as anyone knew. I never saw them argue, or heard either brother ever say anything against the other—and I used to see a lot of them. Their junior year in high school their father bought them a two-tone Oldsmobile convertible—a Starfire, I think it was called—with a dramatic red-and-white paint job and leather seats, and they shared the car without argument or any kind of quibbling whatsoever.

I knew that there had been a serious falling out between Eddie Goldin and his parents, and that Eddie had broken with them. He was variously reported as teaching in Thailand, Taiwan, or Zimbabwe—nobody seemed to know for sure. Nor was it clear if he even knew about Buddy's leap from his twenty-third-floor law office at One North LaSalle two days before, late on a sunny Tuesday afternoon. My own guess is that, had he known, despite his trouble with his parents, Eddie would have managed to be here.

I went to grammar school with the Goldin boys at Daniel Boone School, in West Rogers Park, and afterward the three of us were the only kids from Boone to cross the line at Howard Street separating Chicago from Evanston and go to Evanston Township High School. Buddy and Eddie Goldin were sent to Evanston because they had already established themselves as extraordinary athletes and E.T.H.S. offered coaching of a kind not available in the Chicago public high schools. My father, who was a pharmacist, sent me to E.T.H.S. because he was intent on my becoming the physician—which I am today, an internist—that he would have been had the Depression not intervened. It cost six hundred bucks a year in those days to send a kid from Chicago to E.T.H.S. I knew this represented a serious expenditure for my father, who ran his drugstore on Devon Avenue with a careful eye for small economies. Even now I can remember him carting the bundles of newspapers into the store at seven on deathly cold Chicago winter mornings. For the Goldins the extra twelve hundred to send both their sons to high school was of no real concern. Money, for them, was never a problem.

We lived in a six-flat building on Washtenaw Avenue, less than a block from the drugstore, which made it easier for my father to open at seven o'clock seven mornings a week and close at nine-thirty every night but Sunday, when he closed at five, and still be able to slip home for a half-hour at lunch and a full hour or so at dinner. We ate in the kitchen, except for Friday night and Jewish holidays. I had my own bedroom and so did my sister Sheila, who is two years older than I, and so of course did our parents. We all shared one bathroom. We had in our living room, among other furniture, a white couch covered in plastic; we went into the living room only when we had company, which, given my father's work schedule, was rarely.

The Goldins lived only six or seven blocks away, on Lunt, between Francisco and Sacramento, but in what seemed to me another world. Theirs was an eleven-room house, built since the war, red face brick all the way around, with two large bay windows and a connected garage, set out on a triple lot. A crew of Mexicans took care of the lawns and shrubbery. A black woman named Jessie, who lived in a maid's room off the kitchen, did the cooking, and did it extremely well. The double garage held Sid Goldin's blue Fleetwood and his wife's cream-colored Chrysler Town & Country convertible with wood paneling on the sides. Along the inside walls of the garage were golf bags with pastel-colored covers for the woods, tennis and badminton racquets, an archery target, and other sports equipment, all of it of the best quality.

Inside, the Goldins' house gave off a feeling of elegant, expensive, yet somehow casual comfort. Had it belonged to us, my mother, I am sure, would have had all the furniture in the house covered in plastic, or else had herself and her family laminated, and I know for a certainty that none of us would have been allowed to walk on the plush white carpeting with our shoes on. The largest portion of the basement, painted a cool white, was a den and trophy room. Green leather couches and chairs were set around the room. A bar was at one end, a large television set at the other; off in a corner was a slot machine. Glass cases were arranged around the walls at various points in the room. These contained athletic trophies. Some had been won by Sid Goldin, who lettered in both football and basketball at the University of Illinois in the 1930s; above one of the cases there was a picture of him, posed with a football in one hand and with the other arm in what passed in such corny photos of the day for a stiff arm, and another photo of him, the lone Jewish face, seated among the members of the 1934 University of Illinois basketball team. Most of the trophies in the room, though, belonged to Jean Goldin, who was a serious amateur golfer—serious enough, I was told, to have had a national ranking when in her twenties. One glass case was given over to the athletic achievements of the boys, Buddy and Eddie, who were then only fourteen. Before they were through, they would need several more cases to hold all their trophies.

The Goldin boys were not merely good but spectacularly good athletes. They had both come into their full growth fairly early, but even before that their athletic precocity was marked. By the age of thirteen they were already playing in the Sunday morning men's softball games at the Boone schoolyard, and not just filling in, either, but playing significant positions: Eddie at shortstop, letting damn little get by him; Buddy in centerfield, racing back to catch fly balls over his shoulder or up to make shoestring catches, but somehow making it all look easy. Did they inherit their athletic ability from their parents? I don't know what the best scientific opinion on the subject is, but if they didn't I wish someone would explain how they came to be such wonderful athletes.

And yet they were very different kinds of athlete. Eddie Goldin seemed to come by his accomplishments through fierce hard work—unrelenting hustle, in the old sports cliché—and considerable courage. I have never known anyone physically more fearless. If the occasion called for it, Eddie would slide head first on a gravel field, would take a brutal charge on the basketball court, and cross-body block a man twice his size without the least hesitation. Questions of hustle or courage didn't seem to come into play for Buddy Goldin. He was what we used to call in those days "unconscious." On a court or a field everything seemed to come so naturally to him. Even when running very fast he appeared to lope. Like his brother, he had innate athletic intelligence; he seemed instinctively to know what to do and always made what he did look easy. Neither of the Goldin boys ever fumbled or bobbled or dropped the ball; neither seemed to be affected by pressure; neither ever made a mistake in a game, at least none that I ever saw. They were— how else describe it?—gifted, early and richly gifted.

But then there was something gifted and blessed about the entire Goldin family, or so it seemed to me when I was a kid. Food looked and tasted better at their table. Handsome cars seemed always to be backing out of their driveway on the way to immensely interesting places. Such surprises as their lives contained all seemed pleasant ones. What for the Goldins was an everyday matter often tended to knock me off my feet. One day I came home from school with Buddy, and followed him down to the cool white and green room of the basement, where his father was playing gin with three other men. Buddy quickly introduced me to the three men, one of whom was Sid Luckman, the recently retired quarterback of the Chicago Bears. "Nice to meetcha, Phillie," he said in a high, slightly whiny voice with a New York accent, not looking up from his cards. Another time, glancing out from Eddie's room down onto the driveway, I noticed Sid and Jean Goldin getting into the blue Fleetwood with a woman who looked very familiar. "Is that woman who I think she is?" I asked Eddie, who came over to the window. "Yeah," he said, "that's Myrna Loy. She's a client of my Dad's."

Sid Goldin was a lawyer, the senior partner in the firm of Goldin, O'Connor, and Corzinowski. But he was a lawyer of a particular kind. As I later learned, he scarcely ever entered a courtroom and he certainly didn't waste his time or eyesight composing or studying legal documents. He was instead a fixer and a smoother, a man with connections and clout, who knew everyone and so was regularly called in to bring together otherwise distant parties for the mutual profit of all. He was the man who knew the man who knew the man who could do what was needed: get you points in a sure-hit Broadway play, have a large parcel of real estate rezoned, call off the unions from organizing your shop. His clientele was generously studded with celebrities, including many former athletes, show-business characters, and Chicago politicians. His own name would on occasion appear in the local columns as "powerhouse attorney Sidney Goldin."

After the University of Illinois, Sid Goldin had gone to law school nights, at John Marshall, and worked days selling furniture for his mother's brother, who had a store on the western rim of the Loop. While working for his uncle and going to law school, he met, courted, and married Jean Goldstein, the only child of Judge Irving Goldstein. It was the middle of the 1930s, a time when local judges were powerful figures in Chicago. Sid remembered once getting caught in a traffic jam on the way to a Bears game with his then future father-in-law, who called over a motorcycle cop, announced that he was "Judge Goldstein, goddammit," and demanded a police escort to Wrigley Field so that he wouldn't be late for the game. Without any hesitation, the cop said, "Follow me, sir," turned his siren on full blast, and Sid and the Judge, following the cop on the wrong side of the street, drove directly to the game without even stopping for red lights.

The Judge loved his daughter and approved of her choice of a husband. He liked having a son-in-law who had been a Big Ten athlete; he recognized that this young man was ambitious and no dope. Sid Goldin's marriage enabled him to avoid the time-wasting error of starting at the bottom. Right out of law school, he was put on to a number of good things by his father-in-law. That he was connected with as powerful a man as the Judge brought him clients without any effort on his part. The Judge looked after his own. In 1942, with America in the war, he arranged to get his son-in-law a commission as a major and a job in the Judge Advocate's office at Fort Sheridan, twenty miles north of Chicago. Sid Goldin slept at home every night and emerged from the war a full-bird colonel. The Judge, it sometimes seemed, could arrange anything, except to avoid choking to death, in his sixty-seventh year, on a piece of porterhouse steak at a restaurant in the Loop called Fritzel's. A tough columnist on the Chicago *Daily News*, writing about the passing (and good riddance, he seemed to feel) of types like Judge Irving Goldstein remarked that he died of good living. A widower, he left his only daughter an estate estimated at roughly $1.5 million, and this was in 1957.

The Goldins were never money mad. As Judge Goldstein's daughter, Jean Goldin had grown up with lots of money around. Sid Goldin, even though he came of age smack in the middle of the Depression, earned big money early enough in life not to be nervous about it. No, the Goldins assumed that they would always have enough money not to have to worry about the absence of it interfering with their going through life absolutely first-class. And this they did, with an ease and sportiness that flabbergasted me, a boy whose father worked seven days a week and worried about kids stealing gum and candy from him and a mother who was apparently attempting to save a white couch for eternity.

It was at the Goldins that I first ate a club sandwich, rare roast beef, a salad served after the main course, strawberry shortcake. I don't think they ever had a bad, or even a mediocre, meal, at least not in their own home. It was through being around Jean Goldin that I, then a boy of fifteen, first arrived at the extraordinary insight that someone's mother could be sexy. All other mothers I knew seemed to be receptacles for anxiety who went about for the better part of the day in something called housecoats. Jean Goldin was not a beautiful woman; her teeth were rather too prominent and her features were neither delicate nor refined. But she wore her straight black hair short, in a European cut, always had a deep tan, and dressed in expensive clothes of dazzling colors. She moved wonderfully well and had the shapely, slightly muscular body of a woman who had spent vast amounts of time on golf courses and tennis courts at the best clubs. As their sons' guest at the Royal Oaks Country Club in Winnetka, I recall once watching her in her one-piece black bathing suit poised in concentration on the diving board at the club pool about to execute a complicated dive; Sid Goldin was at the same time applying suntan oil to his large former athlete's body while stretched out on a chaise longue listening to a Cubs game on a portable radio. At that moment the thought struck me, as it had never before struck me about any other parents I knew, that, my God, these two people must have terrific sex together.

I may have gone with the Goldins to Royal Oaks five, maybe six times during the four years I went to high school with Buddy and Eddie, but those times remain among the most vivid memories of my adolescence. I recall the ride down Sheridan Road, Buddy and Eddie sitting up front and I alone in the back, the top down on the Olds Starfire, the leaf-heavy elm trees meeting to form a high tunnel across Sheridan, the mansions along the lake whirling by, the power of the Olds's engine humming, the breeze in my hair. The easy opulence of the country club freshly astonished me each time we drove into the large parking lot with not an old or modest car in sight. I recall the thickness and fine smell of the towels in the locker room; the young Filipino men in white shirts and blue trousers with two thin gold stripes running down the outer leg whose job it was to fetch drinks, cards, fruit, or sherbert, and anything else members might desire, and to shine the members' shoes while they were out on the golf course or having a swim or in the steam bath; the whap-whap-whap of balls being hit off the practice tees mingling with the slower tempi of the pock, pock, pock of balls being hit on the tennis courts; the slender gray-haired mulatto maître d' whose excellent posture lent him an impressive dignity and a slight distance that always made me a touch nervous; and the food, the largeness of the shrimps and the crispness of the beautiful vegetables and the perfection with which the roast beef (which I always ordered) was cooked and the lusciousness of the desserts, the ice creams and raspberries and rich yet somehow delicate cakes and custards. The Goldins usually dined at seven-thirty—everyone I knew in West Rogers Park had supper at six—and I remember once rising from the table at Royal Oaks with them at nine-thirty and thinking, with a vague sense of betrayal, that my Dad was just then checking the back door and getting ready to lock up the drugstore.

Neither Buddy nor Eddie Goldin played golf in those days, though Buddy, I learned, would later in life play in high-stakes match games. (Someone was always organizing a "Nassau" or "skins" game at Royal Oaks in which thousands of dollars changed hands, and dollar-a-point gin games were available in the card rooms for those with a taste for serious indoor action.) When they took me to the club, we swam, sunned ourselves, ate, and played half-court basketball, three on a side, against the caddies who had come in after finishing a round or were waiting to go out on a second round. When your team lost, you gave up the court, which we three, since we always won, never had to do. I was the least of the reasons for our never having to relinquish the court. Eddie Goldin, though not that tall, was well built, a rugged defender, an intelligent rebounder, and a tireless hustler all over the court. And Buddy, Buddy could do everything. He was beautiful to watch. His performance on the court was pure, sure instinct, he didn't have to think about what he did; his body knew what was required and seemed automatically to supply the fakes, the cuts, the quick swoops to the basket, the effortless, perfectly timed leaps, the pull-up dead-on jump shots. "Next," Buddy would call out, after having scored the eleventh basket for our side and thus eliminated yet another threesome of caddies.

In basketball, Buddy Goldin, that great natural athlete, had found his natural sport. At Evanston Township High School he was second-team all-state in his senior year, and later started as a guard at the University of Iowa. Eddie played baseball at E.T.H.S.—he was a ninth-round draft pick of the St. Louis Cardinals as a shortstop—and junior and senior years started at quarterback on the football team. In those years—the middle 1950s—E.T.H.S. was regularly featured in polls as among the top ten schools in the country, often as the very top school. My father read and believed in such polls; they must have comforted him, for he had to sell a lot of newspapers and gum and fill a lot of prescriptions to send his son there. Insofar as one can tell about these things, I guess it was a pretty good school: it gave me a solid grounding in math and chemistry that was later useful in helping me get into medical school. It was a large and competitive place, E.T.H.S., full of bright kids and with a serious atmosphere.

In its sports program, though, the school was really impressive. Its athletic department resembled that of a middle-sized college and one with a winning tradition. All equipment, no matter how minor the sport, was superior; great expense was lavished on facilities, and a modern new fieldhouse was built during my last year there. The contracts of losing coaches were not renewed. Basketball and football games drew thousands; a few college scouts were always in the stands. I remember one afternoon after school watching Eddie Goldin being taught how to execute the bootleg play under the eye of the backfield coach and three assistants who were physical-education majors from Big Ten schools doing their practice teaching at E.T.H.S. (The last E.T.H.S. quarterback before Eddie was now starting at the University of Michigan, where Eddie himself would go on a football scholarship.) Over and over they ran Eddie through this relatively simple play, each time making some small refinement in their instruction. (I never had such careful teaching in med school.) Buddy Goldin told me that the basketball coach would shrink the nets on the game baskets to slow down visiting teams with effective fast breaks. The Goldin boys not only came through the intense pressure of such competition intact; they took it all in easy stride, flourishing under it, starring in it.

I admired Buddy and Eddie Goldin and was proud to be thought of around school as their friend. What they saw in me, I really don't know. I don't think they ever gave much thought to other people's standing, so secure were they in their own, but instead took people as they found them. I was a neighborhood guy; we were all growing up together, however wildly different the circumstances. I was, by the standard of the day, "a good guy," which is to say not a liar or a prig or vicious or mean. That I wasn't in any other way outstanding wasn't a problem for the Goldins or their parents. They weren't, in any sense, snobs. If they had been in the least snobbish, they would have excluded me.

For my own part, I don't think I hung around the Goldins for snobbish reasons, though God knows I was excited by the luxury of their lives and the ease with which everything seemed to be taken care of for them. Then there was the glamor. I never saw Sid Luckman, not to mention Myrna Loy, emerge from a six-flat, or any other building on Washtenaw Avenue. But beyond all this I know I was in awe of the Goldins, all of them, but especially Buddy and Eddie, for their talent. Despite my father's best efforts—he was always supplying me with information about Albert Einstein and other great Jewish scientists—I grew up with no real appreciation for intellectual talent; and among the crowd of kids I ran around with, artistic talent, if any existed, hadn't shown up and I'm pretty sure I wouldn't have recognized it if it had. But athletic talent of the kind the Goldin boys had was not only unmistakable but admired by nearly everyone. I know I admired it. A part of me, even though I am now in my middle forties, still does.

Buddy and Eddie Goldin may have inherited much of the means of their prowess—their coordination, their reflexes, their musculature— from their athletic parents. But where did Buddy come by the ability, which he possessed at sixteen, to pop in two free throws in the last seconds of an overtime to win a game in a state tournament with some 12,000 people screaming at him to miss—and pop them in authoritatively, with no doubt or hesitation about it? Where did Eddie acquire the knack for throwing a football with perfect accuracy into the hands of a receiver forty yards away while freezing rain was blowing in his face and six or seven bruisers going at full speed were trying to crush him? The Goldin boys could do such things because they had talent, and it's called that because few people have it, and if you don't have it to begin with you aren't likely to get it. I knew I didn't have it, and I knew that I never would—I knew that everything I would get in life would come from plodding and from hard work, which was fair enough. But this put me in a different category from the Goldins, who were, for me, extraordinary characters.

Christmas vacation of our senior year in high school, Sid Goldin took his family off for a week's holiday in Barbados, and Jean Goldin asked if I would mind coming in twice a day to walk and feed her dog, a white standard poodle named Francesca, whom she didn't want to put in a kennel. Jessie, the cook, had been given the week off and I let myself in at eight in the morning and then returned at seven at night to walk and feed Francesca again. Under the pretense of keeping the dog company, I would remain in that wondrous house for an hour or so in the evening, feeling the thick carpeting under my feet, drinking in the soft and subtle coloring of the furniture and the draperies. Sometimes I would sit in the white basement, with its green leather furniture and glass trophy cases, turn on the television, pour myself a ginger ale from the bar, and wish I had a room of my own here—wish, guiltily, that my own last name was Goldin and that I was a member of this family.

After they returned from Barbados, Jean Goldin called my mother to tell her that she had a fine and responsible young man for a son. When I next came over, Sid Goldin said, "Good job with the dog, Phillie. We're grateful." He shook my hand, and when he had removed his hand, a crisp new fifty-dollar bill was in my own.

Senior year was a good one for us all. Eddie got his offer from the Cardinals and a football scholarship from the University of Michigan; Buddy made all-state and had some thirty-odd offers of basketball scholarships, from which he chose the University of Iowa; and I was accepted by Yale, though because of the tight money situation at home (my sister was going into her junior year at Wisconsin), I decided instead to do my pre-med at the University of Illinois at Champaign-Urbana.

The Saturday night after graduation, Sid and Jean Goldin threw a party in honor of their sons. An enormous yellow-and-white striped tent went up on their ample back lawn. In one corner of the tent the Ramsey Lewis trio played; in the corner across the way, a black man in a white jacket and a chef's hat stood with a large carving knife and fork before a huge prime-rib roast, a turkey, and a ham. Three small bars were working, two in the tent and a third in the basement of the house. I noticed Sid Luckman in the crowd and, later, Ernie Banks, the Cubs' shortstop, showed up. There were a few local columnists, the guy who did the evening news on Channel 5, and the wife of the man who was the head of Standard Oil of Indiana. Buddy Goldin pointed out a somewhat withdrawn looking man who turned out to be Burr Tilstrom, the puppeteer; he was talking to a man who had been in prison for allegedly kidnapping a syndicate figure named Jake ("The Barber") Factor. Waiters brought around trays of canapés and others trays of champagne in wide-mouthed glasses. The women seemed light and dazzling in their summer dresses. I found myself at one point talking to one of them, a beautiful young woman who asked me who the Goldins were. She was with a touring company playing *My Fair Lady* at the Blackstone Theater and had been brought here by a man who the year before had won twenty games for the Chicago White Sox.

Whether any speeches were made, or gifts given, or how or at what time the evening ended, I have no idea. For me it was over around ten o'clock, when, I was later told by Eddie Goldin, I passed out after what must have been eleven or twelve glasses of champagne, while singing the Whiffenpoof song to Jean Goldin and a man named Grolnik who was a big real-estate operator on the Near North Side. At their mother's bidding, Eddie and Buddy carried me to the guest room upstairs, where I slept in my clothes until six-thirty the next morning. Rumpled, grubby, foggy-brained, walking up the stairs to our apartment, I met my Dad coming down, on his way to open the store. "You okay, Phillie?" he asked, placing the back of his hand lightly across my forehead. I mumbled something about its having been a long night. In my small dark bedroom, standing over the beige chenille spread on my bed, I peeled off my clothes, letting them fall to the floor, thinking, sadly, that a crucial chapter in my life was finished.

That summer marked the beginning of the end of my friendship with the Goldin boys. Nothing went wrong; there was no falling out. It was just the natural drifting apart that takes place when boys turn eighteen and must act on the pretense that they are now young men. Two days after graduation, Eddie Goldin reported to a Cardinals' farm club in

Sarasota, Florida, where he learned the hard but undeniable lesson that he couldn't hit curve balls, which forced him to decide that he had to put his energies into football in the fall at the University of Michigan. Buddy Goldin became a counselor at Ray Meyer's summer basketball camp, where he was able to work out with the guys who played for DePaul, Loyola, Illinois, and other major Midwest basketball schools before he went off to Iowa in the fall. As for me, I worked a forty-hour week at the drugstore, handling the front register, doing stock work, making deliveries, and listening to my father tell me how good life was going to be once I became a physician.

Looking back on my friendship with Eddie and Buddy Goldin, I am a bit amazed at how little intimacy there was in it. For three of the four years we went to high school, we drove there together every morning. What did we talk about? About sports we talked a good deal. About girls a certain amount. Friday nights we often went to the movies together. Sometimes they would take me along with them to some major sports event, for tickets were never a problem for Sid Goldin. None of us dated much. As Jews we were a minority at E.T.H.S., which we wouldn't have been had we gone either to Senn or Sullivan high schools in Chicago. Neither of the Goldin boys talked much about his parents, and I'm not at all sure that they did when they were alone. What I took to be the glamor of their life at home, they took as perfectly natural, and why not, since they hadn't ever known anything else. I thought they were the luckiest kids in the world, and I felt a little lucky myself—maybe "privileged" is the better word—to be hanging around with them.

Eddie was second-string quarterback his freshman year at Michigan, and he ran back punts and kickoffs and did both very well. Buddy started as a freshman on the Iowa basketball team. He was not yet the star he showed signs of becoming in his sophomore year, but from the beginning he made his presence felt—he averaged something like fourteen points a game—and was completely at ease playing Big Ten basketball. I went to the Iowa-Illinois game at Champaign that year and felt real pride at Buddy's poise on the floor. He looked to have put on ten or so pounds, all of it muscle, which made him seem sleek and more in possession of himself than ever. Both he and Eddie always looked born for the athletic uniforms they wore, so much so that, like certain high-ranking military officers, they sometimes seemed a little disappointing out of uniform. Iowa beat Illinois that night when, at the buzzer, Buddy popped in an eighteen-foot jump shot from the top of the key. All that was missing, I thought at the time, was for him to call out "Next," as he used to do with the caddies. I had hoped to spend an hour or so after the game with him, but it turned out that the Iowa team was getting back on its bus to Iowa City that night and that there would be no spare time. I was sorry to have missed him. Michigan went to the Rose Bowl that year and the Iowa basketball team was playing in a holiday tournament in North Carolina, so I didn't get to see either Eddie or Buddy that Christmas vacation.

Games and glory and expensive travel somehow seemed natural to the Goldins. It was what Buddy and Eddie were born into and grew up with. I always assumed that once spikes and cleats, helmets and balls were set aside, they would settle into a life of easy comfort, with powerful contacts and beautiful wives and children who were themselves splendid athletes. Short of a major illness or some inconceivable financial reversal, how could it ever be otherwise? Or so I believed, until one day in my junior year—I recall I was studying for a big midterm exam in organic chemistry—when I called home and my father asked if I had read about the fix my friends Eddie and Buddy Goldin's dad had gotten himself into. I never read the newspapers in Champaign, and told my father I had no idea what he was talking about.

"Apparently Sidney Goldin is connected with some kind of black-market baby ring," my father said. "It looks like pretty serious stuff."

"Is it getting a big play in the press, Dad?"

"Front-page headlines in both the *Trib* and the *Sun-Times*," my father said, "with photos of Mrs. Goldin and your friends Buddy and Eddie. It's also the lead story on the evening television news."

My father went on to ask if I was prepared for my organic chemistry exam, and my mother got on the phone to give me some bits of family and neighborhood news, but my mind was elsewhere and I couldn't wait to get hold of that day's Chicago newspapers. When I did, I found that it was every bit as bad as my father had suggested. The *Sun-Times* headline read, "CELEB ATTORNEY SELLS INFANTS"; the Chicago *Tribune* ran, "POWERFUL LAWYER BABY BLACK

MARKETEER" and beneath that, "Sidney Goldin, Former University of Illinois Athlete, Counselor to Famous, Linked to Baby Ranch." On page three, the *Sun-Times* had photos of Sid and Jean Goldin in evening clothes at a fund-raising dinner for Adlai Stevenson; lower down on the page were blurry photos of the Goldin boys, Buddy in his University of Iowa jersey, Eddie in his Michigan football helmet. The *Trib* ran a smaller picture of Sid Goldin alone, a head shot in which he looked dark and prosperous and rather beaky. Staring at this photograph, which appeared on the front page, I found myself muttering a line I had often heard my father use, "This doesn't look good for the Jews."

What I was able to gather from the newspaper stories—which held the front page for three days—was that Sid Goldin had operated here in his familiar role of middleman. An OB-GYN man on the Northwest Side named Dr. Howard Peterson was really the main figure. Peterson placed unmarried pregnant girls in homes during their pregnancies, paying their room and board and giving them an additional $3,000 at the termination of their pregnancy, for which they signed their children over to him—or at least they believed they did, since the deal was obviously illegal. Working through lawyers around the city, Peterson turned infants over to couples wishing to adopt children but unable to do so through the ordinary, and in those days extremely rigorous, child-adoption procedures. To obtain a baby in this way cost $20,000, with $15,000 going to Peterson and the remainder to the lawyer.

Sid Goldin had evidently brokered at least seven of these illegal adoptions. The last of them was arranged for a prominent Irish politician, an alderman married to a Jewish woman who was unable to have children. The politician had enemies, and one of them turned the press loose on the story of how the politician, with his mixed marriage, was able to adopt a child when state-run agencies at the time all but categorically refused children to homes where parents did not share the same religion. One thing led to another—or perhaps it would be better to say that one thing led to another which led to Sidney Goldin which led to scandal.

Why did Sid Goldin get mixed up in such stuff? He couldn't have needed the money—though, true enough, lots of people who don't need it will still pick up an easy five grand if they don't have to do much work for it. Apart from the money, my guess is that it gave Sid

Goldin pleasure to be the swing man on something so crucial to important people—and all of his clients in these adoptions were important people—as their getting a child. Arranging, after all, is what Sid Goldin did—was what he was famous for—and arranging to get someone a child, a live human being, was in some sense the ultimate arrangement. I'm not sure that Sid Goldin thought about it in this way. He probably viewed it more simply. Some couples needed a child; he knew a man who had children; the people who got the child would be happy; the children would go to prosperous and, as far as anyone could tell, good homes; he, Sidney Goldin, would be the man who made it all possible; and there was an easy five grand in it besides. What was so wrong?

The Illinois Bar Association felt there was enough wrong to disbar Sidney Goldin for a minimum of ten years; and since he was in his late forties at the time, this just about finished him as a lawyer. His law partners bought him out and removed his name from the firm. His rich and famous clients almost uniformly deserted him as a friend. He didn't have to go on trial, and thus risk jail, and he still had all the money he would need to get him through the rest of his life, but the humiliations, small and large, continued for some time. In neighborhood gossip, he was known as the man who sold babies. When it came time to pay his annual dues at the Royal Oaks Country Club, where he and Jean Goldin chose not to show their faces for nearly a year, his check was returned to him by the executive secretary with a curt note saying that the club was cutting back its membership, especially among people who hadn't been making much use of the facilities in recent months, and therefore could not accept his dues; a second check, this one for his original membership fee, was included in the envelope. I currently belong to Royal Oaks, am in fact on the club's board of directors, and I pulled the old Goldin file where I found this letter. I don't like to think about his wife's reaction when Sid Goldin showed it to her.

As for the Goldin boys, both of them soon developed troubles of their own. Buddy was having a brilliant season at Iowa, averaging twenty-one points a game and leading the Big Ten in assists, when in a game at Purdue he felt the ball getting away from him and the floor rushing up to meet him, and the next thing he knew he was on a stretcher on the way to the hospital in West Lafayette. His left knee had given out, ligaments had been torn, and, more significant, cartilage had been destroyed. Buddy was through for the season. When he came back for his senior year, he played with his left leg in an awkward harness of tape and plastic braces. He was never again the same athlete. His former quickness was gone; his instincts, built upon absolute confidence in that quickness, were shot. He lost his place as a starter; and sensing that he would never regain his old form, which meant that he would never again play big-time basketball, he chose to drop out of the University of Iowa for the rest of his senior year. He went back to Chicago, finishing his schooling at Loyola University and after that at the Loyola Law School.

Buddy lived at home when he returned from Iowa, and contin-ued to live there until his last year of law school. He took up golf, at which—no surprise—he was marvelous right off, shooting in the mid-dle seventies by the second year he played. He and Sid Goldin played together at public courses. A few years later, when the scandal had been pretty much forgotten, the Goldins joined another country club, Twin Orchards, whose pro told Sid Goldin that, if Buddy really gave golf his full attention, he could be good enough to play on the pro tour. If his father's scandal threw Buddy in any serious way, there was no obvious evidence of it.

As for Eddie Goldin, I heard that, though he stayed at the Uni-versity of Michigan, he had dropped off the football team, giving no other explanation than that the sport now bored him. I also heard that he had become very earnest about his studies. Eddie was always a better student in high school than Buddy; I don't recall his being in any way exceptional, but then their athletic ability cast everything else about Ed-die and Buddy Goldin into the shade. In any case, Eddie, I heard, was no longer a business but now a philosophy major.

When I ran into Eddie on Devon Avenue in the summer between our junior and senior years, I'm not sure I would have recognized him if he hadn't spoken to me first. His dark, curly hair, usually cut short, had grown out and was uncombed. Where before he had been a tidy dresser, there was now something fundamentally rumpled about him: his flannel shirt was unironed, his Levi's soiled, his Frye boots caked with mud. In later years he would top off some variant of this standard outfit with a parrot named Crackers who, from his perch on Eddie's shoulder, croaked out political slogans mixed with rich obscenities. Just now he was accompanied by a thin, rather drab-looking girl whom he introduced to me as "Reb." When she shyly said she was pleased to meet me, I thought I detected an Appalachian accent. The three of us walked up the block to a corner restaurant, run by Greeks, called Kofield's.

"My mother's fine," Eddie answered, when I asked about his parents, "and my dad is the same asshole he has always been."

The use of that word rocked me. I used my share of profanity as a kid, and I find enough occasions to use it nowadays, but the word Eddie used to describe his father is one I have always hated. The shock of hearing it from Eddie was compounded by the fact that, among their other qualities as All-American kid athletes, the Goldin boys, neither one of them, ever swore. Meanwhile, that word lay there between us.

"What's the problem with your dad?" I asked.

"There's no big problem," Eddie said, "except that he's a phony, a complete fraud."

"Are you referring to his troubles of a few years ago?"

"Tip of the fuckin' iceberg," he said. "The way we live, the way Buddy and I were brought up, the whole thing through and through is rotten. And of course the fuckin' joke is my old man hasn't any notion how rotten it all is. Like all real immoralists, he hasn't a clue that there's anything wrong with the way he lives."

Eddie's friend Reb couldn't have had the least clue about what he was saying. I noticed she had a small, homemade heart tattooed on her thin upper arm. She said nothing, but sipped a Coke through her small, gray, somehow immensely sad teeth. I was sure that Eddie had already brought her home to meet Sid and Jean Goldin—just to let them know that his days of adding to the trophy cases were over for good.

What do you do when an old friend sitting across the table from you attacks his own father? I mumbled something about Sid Goldin's always having been nice to me, but it was pointless. Eddie wasn't really interested in hearing any defense of his father. He was still in the early stages of formulating his own distaste for him, convincing himself of the righteousness of his anger, building his case. When it was completed it must have been some case, for more than twenty-five years later Eddie was still relentless in his hatred of his father.

We graduated in the summer of 1961, and that autumn I began medical school at the University of Illinois in Chicago; Buddy started law school at Loyola; and Eddie, who was among the first round of people accepted for the Peace Corps, went off to teach rudimentary construction techniques to villagers in Central Africa. It was in Africa that he acquired the parrot. He liked Africa, for all its heat and insects and desolation, and when his Peace Corps tour was finished he visited Albert Schweitzer, in the hope of staying on and working for him at his hospital mission at Lambaréné on the forested banks of the Ogooué River. Eddie was apparently able to get a personal interview with Dr. Schweitzer, though he was not offered a job. I later heard that, when someone asked him what Dr. Schweitzer was like, Eddie answered that he, too, was an "asshole." At least no one could say that Albert Schweitzer and Sidney Goldin had nothing in common.

After his return from Africa, Eddie went back to Ann Arbor to begin work on a doctorate in philosophy. It took him eleven years to get it. The 60s intervened. Ann Arbor in those days was Berkeley Midwest, and Eddie Goldin was in the thick of it. The boy athlete who had been so fearless at ten and twelve wasn't likely to go in for halfway measures at twenty-five. He was SDS; there was talk of his leaving the United States for Sweden in support of those who fled the country to avoid the draft. As Eddie's friend, even though I scarcely saw him, I was glad it never came to that.

"My son Eddie," said Sid Goldin, seated across from me on the green leather couch in my office in Wilmette at the Plaza del Lago, "has wasted his entire life hating his father. It makes me sick to think about it."

Perhaps Sid Goldin was so openly dour because I had just given him the depressing if far from disastrous news that he would need a gallbladder operation. He had come into my office for a second opinion, which all the insurance companies nowadays require before they will pay for major surgery. My name had been recommended to him by his regular internist, Howie Levine—with whom I had gone to medical school and whom I see socially—chiefly because my office is located close to the Goldins' current home in Winnetka. (Once they turned sixty, Jean and Sid Goldin began to spend their winters near Palm

Springs, in a condominium they owned at Rancho Mirage.) I was a bit disappointed but not surprised to discover that he didn't remember, until I reminded him of it, that I was the same Philip Hirsh who had run around with his sons in high school. Why, after all, should a man who had had movie stars and professional athletes for clients, who had played in the fast track long before that phrase was even coined, remember a not very interesting boy of sixteen whom he hadn't seen for more than twenty-five years?

I, on the other hand, would have recognized Sid Goldin anywhere. He still had the look of the high roller: the deep sun tan, the expensive clothes comfortably worn, the general air of a man for whom all the more trivial details and little bothers of life—from shoeshines to shopping and tax worries—have always been looked after by hired hands. He had kept his satiny black wavy hair, which now had only touches of gray at the temples. Apart from his gall-bladder problem, his health was good. At sixty-four, he wasn't carrying around any extra weight, his heart was sound, his muscle tone was extraordinary.

"Eddie never really took hold," he continued. "By the time he got his Ph.D. degree, he was in his middle thirties. His *meshuggena* politics took up most of his time and energy, at least as far as his mother and I could tell. Anyhow, he never got a permanent teaching post. One year, he's teaching at Geneseo, New York, the next year he's at Irvine, California, one year his brother gets a card from him in Taiwan. The kind of life he leads, he might as well have stayed in minor-league baseball. He never married, you know, and my guess is that he never will."

I wondered if Eddie ever thought of himself as locked forever into the academic equivalent of minor-league baseball. Having once been a first-rate athlete, he could not have found it easy to reconcile himself to being a fourth-rate philosophy teacher. At least I don't think such a thing would have been easy for me. But then I wasn't Eddie Goldin.

"We never hear from Eddie directly," Sid Goldin said. "All we know of his whereabouts is from his brother, whom he calls once or twice a year. The last time Eddie and I were together—it's almost twenty years now—he told me off. Called me a phony and a four-flusher and living a lie. Said that everything I had was built on cheating and deceit. His mother, he said, was no better, since she lived so comfortably with my corruption. But he was damned if he was going to. He wasn't going to take another penny from me, and some day he hoped to pay back every cent I had ever spent on him so that he would be free from any contamination from my crummy life. That's what he called it, you know, 'my crummy life.' My own son."

There was an unbearable silence. "How are things going with Buddy?" I asked, hoping to get the conversation on to a less painful subject.

"Buddy's got his own troubles," Sid Goldin said. He shifted his weight, resting an arm along the back of the green couch. I noticed dangling from his wrist, beyond his cashmere sport jacket and the monogram that showed on the cuff of his shirt, a thin gold chain bracelet. Odd little touch of foppery, I thought, in a man his age. "Your old friend Buddy has a serious gambling problem. It started about fifteen years ago. He wasn't making his nut as a lawyer, so he tried to make up his personal and business expenses through betting on ball games, cards, his own golf games. Twice now he's enrolled himself in Gamblers' Anonymous. His wife threatened to leave him if he didn't go into therapy, which he's in currently. It's a damn mess."

"How bad does it get?"

"All I know is what he's come to me for to bail him out. Whether he's into other people also, I don't know. At first he came for small dips—five and ten grand. Then he jumped it up to twenty, twenty-five, once forty. 'Buddy boy,' I said to him, 'you're going through your inheritance mighty quick.' After each time he comes to me, there is a quiet period, lasting maybe three or four months. But it's waiting for a bomb to go off. The last time he came to me it was for ninety grand. He was into heavy juice with the boys, if you know what I mean. He told me they would kill him if he didn't come up with the money. He wept, my beautiful All-State son, he put his head on my shoulder and clung to me and said, 'Dad, you got to help me, you got to.' Of course I did. I'm his father."

I don't know why Sid Goldin chose to talk so openly about his sons with me. Maybe it was because I was a stranger who nonetheless had known him and his sons in their glory days. I wouldn't be at all surprised to learn that he couldn't talk to old friends with the same candor that he used in talking to me that afternoon, sitting on my green leather couch—a couch that, when I came to pick furniture for my office, I chose because it reminded me of the green leather furniture from his own house on Lunt.

"Dr. Hirsh," he said (and to have him, at whose home I was once introduced to Sid Luckman, address me as doctor seemed very strange), "were my sons once really extraordinary boys, or have I just dreamed it? Wasn't there a time, Doc, when the world seemed to belong to Eddie and Buddy? Or is it all something I imagined? They were such wonderful kids. Respectful. Disciplined. Never in trouble."

"Mr. Goldin," I said, "your sons were the best. They were great kids, gifted and decent and without any meanness of any kind. Being their friend was one of the nicest things about my boyhood."

"What do you suppose went wrong, Doc? Was it my fault? Was it the way we brought the boys up? To this day my wife and I, when we talk about it together, don't really know how to account for what happened. Did we spoil them? You probably don't remember, but I had a little trouble with the press when they were in college, a little scandal—could that have been the problem? What has to happen, Doc, to turn two swell kids into a rebel and a weakling? The more my wife and I talk about it, the less we understand. Beats me," he said with a sigh and rose from the couch.

It beat me, too, and I had no solacing platitudes to offer. I could provide a clear second opinion on Sid Goldin's gall bladder but not on what had happened to his sons. Instead I told him that I would send along my report to the Blue Cross and that a man in his general good health really had little to worry about from this operation. I asked to be remembered to Mrs. Goldin. He thanked me, we shook hands, and the next time I saw him was at Buddy's funeral service in the Piser chapel in Skokie.

That was roughly six months after Sid Goldin had sat in my office. Buddy, I learned from his friend Lloyd Brodsky in the Piser parking lot after the service, had gone into the tank for more than a hundred grand and was being threatened by syndicate collection men. In the suicide note he left in his office, he wrote that he was too ashamed of himself to go back to his father for more money and too ashamed to go on living. He thanked his parents for standing by him as long and as well as they had, and asked that they look after his wife and young daughters, to whom he apologized for what he was about to do—which was to hurl himself from his office window twenty-three floors above LaSalle Street—and whom he asked to try always to remember that he loved them dearly.

I had appointments lined up in the office that afternoon, and so didn't drive out to the Waldheim Cemetery on the West Side. On the fifteen-minute drive back to Wilmette I thought further about the Goldin boys, but with no better results than Sid and Jean Goldin. Buddy and Eddie were blessed with talent—of a small and limited kind, agreed, but real talent nonetheless—and it set them apart, made them different. At least to me, who was without talent, it made them seem radiant and even a little magical. Were their sad endings—Buddy's on the pavement in downtown Chicago, Eddie's to wander all his life unattached and without consequence—somehow connected to their brilliant beginnings? Did the blessing of talent always carry its own inexplicable curse? These were deeper waters than I was accustomed to sail, and it was probably best that I clear my mind, for awaiting me in my office were people who wanted my authoritative assurance that they need not fear death by stroke, heart attack, or cancer, at least not for the present, and from every indication could go on living for years to come, which all of them would be perfectly happy to do without any thought of talent whatsoever. The Goldin boys, my old friends Buddy and Eddie, weren't so lucky.

DANNY MONTOYA

Baffled in the large section of Home Depot devoted to lighting fix-
tures and bulbs, Jerry Mandel has spent the last six or seven minutes
trying to find small frosted 40-watt bulbs for the fixture over his wife's
and his bathroom mirror. Finally, he asks a young guy with a shaved
head and a complicated tattoo on the left side of his neck wearing an
orange Home Depot apron for help. "Mr. Montoya is the lighting guy,"
he says. "I'll call him over."

A minute or so later, a small man, dark, bald, chunky, wearing
black-framed glasses and with a walk that has a bounce to it, arrives to
ask Mandel what he's looking for.

"Sometimes they hide these things pretty effectively," he says, after
Mandel tells him. "But we'll find 'em for you." The name tag on the
pocket of his apron reads "Daniel." Mr. Montoya. Daniel. Daniel Montoya. Danny Montoya. It takes a moment for it all to register.

"Danny! Danny Montoya!" Mandel says. "Are you the same
Danny Montoya I played tennis with back in the early 1950s at Senn
High School?"

"I did play tennis at Senn," he says. "Sorry, but I'm not sure I
recognize you."

"That's all right," Mandel says, "these days I often don't recognize
myself. I'm Jerome Mandel. Me. Jerry."

As Danny Montoya stares at him, Mandel can see that he still hasn't
picked up on his name. "Oh, yeah," Danny says, at last. "It's been a
long time."

"Only half a century or so." Mandel puts out his hand, and Danny Montoya shakes it. "What've you been doing?"

"Long story," Danny Montoya says. "I've got a break in roughly half an hour. What say I buy you a cup of coffee at the lunch joint at Target next door? We can catch up then?"

"I'll meet you there," Mandel says.

"Meanwhile, let's find you those bulbs," says Danny, which he quickly proceeds to do.

Fifty years ago Jerry Mandel would have traded his life for Danny Montoya's without a second's hesitation. Danny was the number one ranked boys-fifteen-and-under tennis player in Chicago and its suburbs. The suburbs are important to mention, because tennis in those days was very much a suburban game, dominated by country-club kids with names like Vandy Christie and Gaylord Messick. Nationally, most of the main figures in tennis had names like Gardner Mulloy and Billy Talbert and Hamilton Richardson, though the two Panchos, Gonzales and Segura, were also on the scene. Like the Panchos, Danny Montoya, too, was everywhere taken for Mexican; or so at least Mandel thought before he first saw him. In fact, Danny's mother was white and his father, who worked at the post office, was Filipino. He was a city kid—inner-city, we would now say—and played most of his tennis on public courts. His coach was his father.

Danny was small and quick, graceful and savvy, knowing how to get the very most out of his game. He had dazzling footwork, and nearly perfect anticipation, so that he always seemed in the right place, his Davis racquet perfectly positioned to slap home winners with an ease that encouraged a sense of hopelessness in his opponents, making them wonder if learning how to play tennis in the first place had been such a hot idea. He made the half of the court on which he stood seem no larger than a ping-pong table, his opponent's side larger than a football field. He was always in perfect control; he never beat himself.

This was in the days before metal racquets and tank tops and baseball caps worn backwards, and Danny, like everyone else then, wore all-white tennis clothes, which made his dark skin stand out all the more vividly. He had fine features, a winning smile, and glistening black hair that he brushed straight back. Standing at baseline, awaiting service, Mandel remembered how Danny would twist his racquet, sometimes giving it a double flip by slapping it at the handle, the way a cowboy might twirl his pistol before returning it to its holster, shuffle his feet, seem just a touch bored, and then take a high-bouncing serve and flick it cross-court with his amazingly accurate backhand or slash it forehand down the line for another winner. Without breaking into a smile, he would do another double flip of his racquet and walk over to take the serve in the ad court.

Haughty didn't describe Danny on the court so much as jaunty. He commanded the court, floating, gliding, seeming to dance—an intricate smooth Latin dance of his own devising—over to whack the ball precisely where he wished. He had textbook-perfect strokes and all the shots, including a drop-shot of such delicate deceptiveness that his opponents usually never saw the ball coming, and those who did weren't able to get anywhere near it before it died after a spirit-deflating low bounce. His topspin lobs left opponents at the net to feel pure dejection as they watched the ball sail over their heads. His serve wasn't overpowering but always well placed, and he never double-faulted. He appeared to be without sweat glands; in his combination of nonchalance and authority on the court, he was aristocracy in motion.

Jerry Mandel discovered that he and Danny Montoya were born two months apart, and Mandel, as a boy tournament player who usually went out in the first or second rounds of local tournaments, watched Danny with an admiration bordering on worship. Mandel had taken up tennis at thirteen—much too late, as he would discover—and for the next three years found that playing tennis was all he really wanted to do. He longed to be brilliant at it. Mandel was well coordinated, with a strong instinct for imitating style. Sport was all that was on offer when he grew up in West Rogers Park, and, like all the boys in the neighborhood, from the age of ten or so he played the current seasonal sport—baseball, football, basketball—and played them all reasonably well but none dazzlingly.

Indian Boundary Park, six blocks from the Mandels' apartment, had four concrete tennis courts, lined up vertically, back to back, each enclosed within cyclone fencing, and one day Mandel and his friend Harvey Resnick, who lived only a block from the park, walked over to swat a few tennis balls. Mandel didn't own a racquet, and used Harvey's older sister's. They played in gym shoes and jeans.

Mandel wasn't particularly good at the game at first, but that very first time out he watched some older boys rallying the ball back and forth, with smooth powerful strokes, and thought this was something he would like to be able to do. He liked the rhythm of the game, the sound of the ball against the racquet when it was hit solidly in the sweet spot, the clothes, the graceful elegance that playing it well brought. There may even have been an unconscious social motive behind the thirteen-year-old Jerry Mandel's ardor for the game. Tennis, with its English, WASP-y feel, suggested a significant jump from his own middle to the upper-middle class, from the Jewish to the gentile world.

Harvey and Mandel played a few more times, and then Mandel bought a racquet of his own and a pair of Jack Purcell tennis shoes. He would wander down to Indian Boundary on weekends and watch the better adult players. He concentrated on picking up technique: their serving motion, the way they positioned their bodies before striking the ball, the short blocking stroke of the volley. He began to acquire a sense of the angles of the game, he picked up the chatter—"Let, take two," "Ad out," "Too good"—the hand movements, various ways to pick up a loose ball off the ground with one's racquet without having to bend down for it.

One day early in the summer of his fourteenth year, Mandel took the El to play with a friend on the clay courts of Northwestern University. The clay was a café au lait color, freshly rolled and relined every morning by a man who looked as if, in another life, he might have been a hard-drinking naval chief petty officer. In the small clubhouse, where they assigned courts, collected court-rental fees, strung racquets, and sold equipment, a sign read "Pro's Helper Needed." He inquired about the job. What it entailed was going out with the pro, who was also Northwestern University's tennis coach, and collecting the balls he used when he gave lessons to children and housewives. The pay was $1 an hour, and you got to use the courts free, and a ten percent discount on tennis clothes and equipment. Mandel applied for and got the job.

The pro was a heavyset man, who in the late 1920s had had a national ranking. He had a gruff voice and a kind heart. Mandel went out with him four or five times a day as he gave his half-hour lessons, collecting the loose balls the people taking lessons hit, picking up what he could from the fairly fundamental instruction: forehand, backhand, volley, half-volley, three kinds of serve: American twist, flat drive, slice. After a few weeks, the pro used Jerry to demonstrate the strokes he taught.

When Mandel wasn't shagging balls and demonstrating strokes, he played with people whose partners were late or failed to show up. Sometimes he hit balls with older guys who played on the Evanston Township High School team. He saved his small earnings and used them to buy a new Jack Kramer model Wilson racquet, a few white Lacoste shirts, tan-colored Fred Perry shorts.

Mandel began to develop a wider repertoire of shots, hit a harder second serve without too often double-faulting, developed a stronger backhand. Each night he took the El back to Chicago, a fine brown clay dust on his Jack Purcells. Daydreaming, he imagined himself brilliantly winning the fifth and deciding match of the Davis Cup for the United States or playing on Centre Court at Wimbledon. He must also have been undergoing a sexual awakening at this time, but now, in his memory at least, thoughts of tennis crowded out all others.

That same summer Mandel began to play in local tournaments, in the public parks as well as at tennis clubs in Oak Park and River Forest. He didn't have much success. He might win a round or two, but even players less good than he—who had less stylish strokes, less of a feel for the game—often defeated him. Mandel was too enraptured in his own fantasy of style. He wanted above all to be an elegant player; his opponents were content merely to win.

That summer, too, Jerry Mandel first saw Danny Montoya, of whom of course he had heard; with fewer sports on offer in those days, Chicago papers covered prep and other junior sports more thoroughly than now. When he first saw Danny—in a tournament from which he, Mandel, had been eliminated in the first round at the River Forest Tennis Club—he recognized the game he himself longed to have. Danny had the style Mandel dreamed of, though in Danny's case style didn't keep him from winning. Danny won this particular tournament, beating a kid named Esteban Reyes who had come all the way up from Mexico 8–6 in the third set. He met Reyes at the net, shook his hand cordially, flashed his brilliant smile, and walked over to his father, a small pudgy man who looked a lot like the Danny Montoya Mandel had met fifteen or so minutes before at Home Depot.

Mandel played on his high-school tennis team, which was no big deal, for tennis in the public schools of Chicago in those years was strictly a minor sport, at most an afterthought, like fencing or speed skating. The good junior tennis players were at New Trier or Evanston Township or from the western suburb of Hinsdale, where Claire Reissen, the father of Marty Reissen, who was later nationally ranked and would play Davis Cup, was the coach. Mandel played number four singles his sophomore year, and most of the kids he played from other schools—Roosevelt, Sullivan, Fenger on the far south side—wore black gym shoes and gym shorts with their boxer underwear sticking out at the bottom; black socks under PF Keds were not uncommon. All this was a long way from center court at Wimbledon.

Senn High School had a tennis coach who worked summers as the pro at the River Forest Tennis Club, a tall, white-haired, pink-faced, taciturn man named Major Singleton, known to everyone as Maj. Rumors had it that he had been a young flying ace in World War One. (Mandel's friend Barry Grolnik, in later years trying to describe him to a group of people who didn't go to Senn, said, "You have to imagine a gentile John Wayne.") The coach's own tennis past was a bit unclear, though everyone who played tennis in the middle-west seemed to know Maj Singleton. One afternoon, decades later, Mandel heard Tony Trabert, on television, remarking that Stephen Singleton, in the umpire's chair, was the son of Major Singleton, "one of the great gentlemen in the game."

Maj Singleton must have been the reason behind Danny Montoya's transferring from Crane Tech, in the middle of the city, to Senn High School on the far north side in his junior year. The Montoyas lived a few blocks south of Madison near Western Avenue, a tough neighborhood even then, and it may have been that Danny's parents were worried about their son's going to a school where gangs had begun to form and violence was more and more part of daily life for adolescents. Crane had no tennis team, but was noted for black basketball players, one of whom, Leon Hilliard, had recently replaced Marquis Haynes as the dribbling wizard of the Harlem Globetrotters.

"Jerome," the Maj said to Mandel one day in his office, "Danny Montoya is transferring to Senn. When he arrives, I want you to keep an eye out for him."

"I'll do everything I can, sir," Mandel said. He played tennis for three years for Maj Singleton, and this may have been his longest speech to him, though once, in a doubles match against two kids from Roosevelt wearing brown Keds he gave Mandel and his partner, a boy named Mickey Hoffner, some advice having to do with the wind, which neither of them heard and both were too daunted by him to ask him to repeat.

Senn High School was roughly sixty percent Jewish, forty percent working-class Irish, Germans and Swedes, with six or seven black kids and no Hispanics at all. Mandel didn't think of Danny Montoya as particularly ethnic—the word was not then in use—but chiefly as an amazing athlete. But that morning, even as Maj Singleton introduced them—"Jerome Mandel, Danny Montoya. Jerome here's going to show you around"—Mandel sensed that Danny wasn't going to be happy at Senn.

Danny was wearing rust-colored pants, with outer stitching and severely pegged at the ankles, a shocking-pink shirt with a Mr. B. collar (Mr. B. being the singer Billy Eckstine, "That Old Black Magic" man), and square-toed blue-suede loafers. His hair was heavily pomaded and swooped into a duck's ass at the back. The clothes had been bought at Smokey Joe's, a zoot-suitery on Halsted off Maxwell Street. If Maj Singleton bothered to notice Danny's clothes, he gave no sign. This get-up may have worked among the black kids at Crane Tech, but for Senn every item was wrong.

Mandel used to eat lunch outside, at Harry's, where the more with-it Jewish kids hung out. He didn't fancy taking Danny out there with him, at least not in these duds. He walked him to his first class, and told him that he'd meet him for lunch fifth period at the entrance to the school's cafeteria. In the cafeteria, Mandel asked Danny how things were going.

"OK," he said. "Not bad."

"Anything I can do to smooth the way, let me know. I'm glad you're here."

"Thanks," Danny said. "But do you think I can get something better to eat than this gunk?" He pointed down to his lunch tray, which had the sandwich called a Sloppy Joe on it and some very gloppy macaroni and cheese.

"Tomorrow I'll take you to a better place," Mandel said. "Don't be offended, but maybe you aren't wearing exactly the right clothes. We dress a lot more casual here."

"Yeah," Danny said, smiling. "I noticed. I feel as if I'm dressed for maybe the wrong play."

"Where did you get your backhand?" Mandel asked, changing the subject. "I'd kill a guy for your backhand."

"Everything I know about tennis, I know from my father," Danny said. "He worked as a locker-room valet at a ritzy tennis club in Manila—that's in the Philippines—and picked up the game on his own. He spent a lot of time teaching me, beginning when I was three or four. I've got a brother Bobby, he's only five now, you should see him. He figures to be a lot better than me."

The next afternoon, Maj Singleton called a practice at Indian Boundary to introduce the team to Danny. Everyone paired up afterward to hit some balls, and Danny and Mandel hit together. Rallying balls back and forth, Mandel felt himself getting into Danny's rhythm, and how satisfying that rhythm felt! "Whap" went the balls Mandel hit, "pock" came Danny's returns, all right at Mandel, so he scarcely had to move to return the ball to him. *Whap, pock, whap, pock,* Mandel could have stood out there on that court through the night, so fine did he feel rallying with Danny.

When Mandel came up to the net, Danny provided him precisely placed lobs, so that he could hit practice overheads. He fed him volleys to his forehand and backhand sides. Mandel felt the level of his own game rising, just by being on the court with Danny. They played a set, which Danny won 6–2. Mandel wasn't quite sure how he got the two games, but was very pleased he did. At the end, meeting at the net, Mandel was breathing like someone who had just completed a marathon, Danny was cool and smiling.

On another afternoon, Mandel and Danny played doubles together against two other boys on the team, Tim Ritholz and Dicky Simpson. Danny was a perfect partner, unselfish, backing up Mandel whenever necessary, cheerfully congratulatory whenever he made a winner at the net. He made difficult half-volleys look easy. His sense of the angles of the doubles court—and doubles, he taught Mandel without having to say a word about it, was essentially a game of angles, geometry in motion—was perfect. Like all really good athletes, Danny had mastered form, and yet was ready to abandon good form when winning the point required it. In the few autumn practices the team had, Mandel, warming up with Danny, playing doubles with him as his partner, felt he was playing well over his head; and it occurred to him that exactly there, over his head, was the best of all places to play.

Mandel and Danny had no classes together, but they met every day for lunch. Mandel never took him to Harry's but instead to other places a little farther from school. Sometimes, when he had the use of his mother's car—a 1953 Chevy Bel Air, cream-colored with green trim—Mandel would drive off to Morse Avenue and they would have lunch at Ashkenaz Delicatessen. Danny had long since changed his Smokey Joe wardrobe, and now came to school, like everyone else, wearing Levis and a V-neck sweater over a white T-shirt. If Danny made any other friends at Senn, he never mentioned them to Mandel; whenever he saw Danny in the halls between classes, he walked alone. The darkness of his skin, made even darker by his long summers on the tennis courts, made him a fairly exotic figure. Mandel once asked him if he wanted to meet any girls, and Danny told him thanks but he already had a steady girlfriend in his neighborhood.

Danny's happiness at Senn wasn't a question Mandel felt he ought to ask. He wasn't sure he was all that happy at Crane Tech, either, at least he never spoke fondly about missing it. With a Filipino father and a white mother, Danny would always, Mandel supposed, be without any definable group into which he could easily slip. What went on in the classrooms was of less than minimal interest to him. At their lunches together, Danny and Mandel talked chiefly about sports, girls, offbeat places in the great city in which they had both grown up. He never rationed his marvelous smile; his walk had a natural spring to it; he had enormous cordiality. If Danny was unhappy, he kept it to himself.

When the tennis team held one of its autumn practices, Mandel usually drove Danny over to the Loyola El Station afterwards. One night, Danny had dinner at the Mandels' apartment, and that night he drove him home. Dropping him in front of his building on south Hoyne, he was reminded of the toughness of the neighborhood in which Danny

and his family lived. Mandel in those days had begun reading the popular novels of that day, many of them set in slums, *The Amboy Dukes, A
Stone for Danny Fisher, The Hoods, Knock on Any Door,* books that, as he
would later understand, eroticized the lives of the poor.

One Saturday afternoon in November, Mandel picked up Danny
at his apartment. In the hallway, two mailboxes, sprung from their
hinges, hung open. Unappetizing food smells—cabbage, maybe—clung
to the air. When he rang the bell, Danny came down, wearing a dark
brown leather jacket, in which he looked great. He told Mandel that
his parents were out back, and they walked around to the rear of the
building, where Danny introduced him to his mother and father.

Danny's mother was hanging wash on a line in the concrete backyard. She was shapeless and not wearing any makeup. Her hair was
stringy. She wore a gold cross over a housedress. She seemed worn-out,
though she was probably then not more than forty. She said only that
she was pleased to meet Mandel, and went back to hanging her laundry.

Mr. Montoya, who was handing his wife clothespins, stopped to
shake Mandel's hand with enthusiasm.

"Nice to meet," he said, in choppy English. "Danny tell all about
you. How kind you are to him. His mother and I grateful for this."

The neighborhood, which seemed so menacing at night, in daylight
turned out to be chiefly dilapidated. Windows on a number of buildings
were boarded up. A six-flat apartment building on Danny's block had had
a fire, and no attempt was apparently being made to repair the damage;
the charred ruin just stood there, like a blackened tooth in an already unattractive mouth. A few blocks to the west, across Western Avenue, Skid
Row began, with red-faced drunks wandering the streets.

Danny and Mandel drove two blocks over to Bell Avenue, where
Danny's girlfriend Claire was waiting for them outside the bungalow
that she and her five brothers and sisters lived in with their widowed
mother. Her father had been a Chicago cop, killed four years ago, as
Danny had earlier explained, in the line of duty, while chasing a drug
dealer down an alley off Wilson Avenue on the north side. Claire went
to Immaculata, was Irish, and Danny's age. She was small, dishwater
blonde, and was wearing jeans and a sweatshirt. Young as she was, there
was already something a little tired-looking about her around the eyes,
or so Mandel thought.

The three of them drove down to Maxwell Street. The day was crisp and sunny. Maxwell Street was humming. Older men grabbed their arms, telling them that terrific bargains were to be had within their dark clothing shops. Carts in the middle of the street were loaded with fake Zippo lighters, neckers-knobs for steering wheels, playing-cards with blurrily photographed naked women on them, eight-battery flashlights, condoms of the kind known in those days as French ticklers. A butcher sold live chickens. An ancient-looking black woman was seated on a kitchen chair hovering over a blanket on which she displayed dishes, some of them chipped, that she offered for sale. A Gypsy family sat before its doorway, hawking fortune-telling and suggesting that maybe more than mere fortunes could be obtained within. The smell of fried onions and Polish sausage on the open-air vendors' grills suffused everything.

Danny, as always, seemed completely at ease. He bopped along, with his jaunty walk, very much with the show, laughing at the young black guy who stopped him in the hope of selling him a gaudy-looking wristwatch. Claire, less confident, clung to Danny's arm. Mandel didn't say much to her after Danny introduced them. He felt she looked on him as a rich (by her standard, anyway) Jewish boy from the far north side, possibly slumming, which, though he preferred not to think so, he may well have been doing.

Danny bought Claire a necklace with a St. Christopher's medal. They walked over to Roosevelt Road, where Mandel showed Danny that he could get very slightly factory-damaged Florsheim plain-toed cordovan shoes for $10 at a place called Wolinsky and Levy. They stopped for hot dogs at the Vienna sausage outlet store on Halsted. They looked at the wild clothes on display in the windows at Smokey Joe's. On the drive home, the three of them sitting in the front seat—this was before the age of bucket seats—Claire fell asleep on Danny's shoulder, continuing to clutch his arm. "She's not been feeling so good lately," he told Mandel.

Danny Montoya never actually played for Senn. A week or so after the return to school from Christmas vacation, he didn't show up at his and Mandel's usual meeting-place for lunch. The next week Mandel asked Maj Singleton if he knew anything about Danny's absence. The Maj told him that Danny had decided not to return to Senn, but said nothing more. Mandel was disappointed but not completely surprised. Danny had no known social life at the school apart from him, which, for a naturally gregarious kid, must not have been easy. He got no real coaching from Maj Singleton; nor did he need any. Maybe he just became bored with the long bus and El rides up and back to school.

Mandel felt he ought at least to call Danny to ask what was going on. His father's name (Gustavo Montoya) was in the book. He left messages for him with Danny's mother twice, and only a week or so later did Danny call back.

"Yo, Jerry," he said. "Got your message. What's up?"

"Nothing much. What's up with you?"

"It's complicated," he said. "I'm getting married. Two weeks from next Saturday. Claire's pregnant."

Mandel didn't know what to say. Congratulations, maybe? God, how terrible, maybe? He felt a combination of pity for Danny's situation and also a touch of admiration for his entering adulthood so calmly. Mandel asked Danny if he were planning on going back to school anywhere else.

"Don't think so," Danny said. "Nothing much there for me. School's not my best game. Don't think I'll miss it much. I've got a job. I'm working at Claire's Uncle Matt's grocery right now, till something better turns up. Gotta run. Stay in touch, OK?"

They didn't stay in touch. Once married and working for a living, Danny, Mandel assumed, must have quit tennis, because his name wasn't any longer in the papers in connection with local tennis tournaments that spring and summer or any time thereafter. Danny slipped prematurely into an adult world and Mandel was allowed to remain a boy for another five or six years, still searching for the perfect backhand, which he never found. He never found out what became of Danny and, though he may have had a stray thought or two about him over the years, he otherwise disappeared from his mind, until twenty-five or so minutes ago when he saw him, a salesman, at Home Depot.

Mandel arrives at Target before Danny. Danny came over; under the orange Home Depot apron he'd shed, he had on a pair of khakis and a blue polo shirt. His hair, unlike Mandel's, is still dark but thin in front. Mandel searches for the face of the boy in the man, but has difficulty finding it. Danny, he notes, seems to be doing the same to him.

"Can I get you a coffee, a hot dog, or something?" Danny asks.

"A coffee will be great," Mandel says.

"Maybe I'll have just a coffee, too," Danny says, touching his paunch.

"It took me a minute or two to bring you back to mind," he says, when they return to the table with their coffees. "You went out of your way to be nice to me during the time I transferred to Senn. I don't think I ever thanked you for that."

"More like I was sucking up to you," Mandel says. "I admired the way you played tennis tremendously. I can still picture you, like Muhammad Ali, floating like a butterfly, stinging like a bee. You were amazing."

The man across from Mandel flashes that great smile and something of the boyish Danny Montoya returns. "I had a few good moments back then. Tennis was the only game our old man let my brother Bobby and me play. Baseball, football, basketball, everything else he put off-limits. Concentrate on one sport, he used to say, be really good at one thing. He wasn't someone you defied. Not in those days anyhow. You still play?"

"I stopped not long after high school. My ambition was a lot greater than my talent, and since I could never shake off the ambition, I just quit playing."

"What do you do? I mean for a living," Danny asks.

"I teach biology," Mandel said. "At Loyola University. I mainly teach future high-school biology teachers."

"Where did you get an interest in biology?"

"From not getting into medical school, to tell the brutal truth. After not being accepted to med school, I graduated from the University of Illinois with a degree in zoology. Having nothing better to do at the time, I went on to get a couple more degrees in the subject. But what about you? What've you done all these years?"

"I've mostly been a salesman. I was seventeen when my first daughter was born. Claire and I had three kids, all daughters. I nearly drowned in estrogen. Did you ever meet Claire, my wife? She died two years ago, lung cancer."

"I met her once," Mandel says, thinking it not worth reminding Danny of their day on Maxwell Street. "I'm sorry she's dead."

"Anyhow, after a bunch of odd jobs, I got into selling cars. Then I worked at selling home-improvements, which I did for more than thirty years for a firm called Royal Lumber. I did all right at it. I'm semi-retired. I'm working here at Home Depot part-time. I live with my second daughter, Jackie, in Buffalo Grove. She's divorced with four kids of her own. I help out a little, financially and with baby-sitting. I have a daughter fifty-two years old. Jesus! Tell me, please, how the hell that happened?"

Mandel fills Danny in on his own family life, his two sons and now his five grandchildren, his two marriages.

"Do you ever think about tennis?" Mandel asks Danny. "Do you ever play it? Do you watch it on television?"

"I don't think about it or play it or watch it."

"You were really good, you know, amazingly good."

"Nice to hear that, but if you think about it there wasn't any place for me to go with it. If I'd come along twenty or thirty years later, maybe my father would have sent me to one of those professional tennis camps, where they take over kids at seven or eight years old. Maybe then things would have been different. But I probably got about the most out of the game I could. I was never a hard hitter. I could never have been a big-time player."

"I recently read a book by an English mathematician," says Mandel, a little worried about sounding pretentious, academic, "who, attempting to justify his own career in mathematics, says that only a tiny minority of people can do anything really well. When you were out on the tennis court you qualified as one of those people."

"It wasn't a very important thing to do," Danny says. "It was tennis, only a game."

"That it was just a game doesn't matter. I've never come close to doing anything in my entire life as well as you played that game."

"Come on! You teach at a college. I'll bet you were a pretty good father, right? That's not nothing. I'm a lot prouder of my daughters than I am of my having won a few tennis trophies when I was a kid."

"There're lots of good fathers, good husbands, good teachers. But I never saw anyone fly over a tennis court as beautifully and happily in command of things as you."

"Forgive me for saying so, Jerry," Danny says, "but I wonder if maybe you're not laying it on a little thick. You're not planning to sell me life insurance before I get up from this table, are you? You wouldn't try to sell to an old salesman, would you?" He flashed the great smile.

"All I'm saying is that for a brief stretch of time, you belonged to a small but elite club of people who did something magnificently well. Maybe it didn't have world-shaking significance, but it was pretty damn rare."

"Sorry, but I don't quite see the point," Danny says, glancing at his watch. "Yo, I'd better get back to work." He stands up and drains off what is left in his coffee cup.

The two late-middle-aged men walk the sixty or so yards from Target back to Home Depot.

"Good to run into you again," Danny says.

"Same here," Mandel says. They shake hands. Neither says anything about getting together again.

Driving home, Mandel realizes that what he couldn't get across to Danny is that, though his life has been easier than Danny's, though most people might think the work he does more useful, he, Danny, for a few brief years, because of his magical talent was able to soar, while his, Mandel's, life, lucky though it has been in so many ways, has been spent entirely on the ground.

That night, Mandel's wife asleep beside him, he lies on his back and tries to put all his problems out of mind: small money worries, squabbles in the department at the university, the news that his grandson may be dropping out of Yale because of depression.

Mandel is back at Indian Boundary Park, where he is sixteen and playing doubles with Danny Montoya as his partner. The sun is high in the sky, the grass outside the courts is dark green and dewy after a light rain, the balls make a crisp sound coming off the strings of their wooden racquets. The partners work a complex switching maneuver at the net that sets Mandel up for an easy overhead smash. Out on that court, Danny Montoya's skill has, somehow, rubbed off on Mandel. His strokes are wonderfully smooth and his shots deadly accurate; he can make the lovely fuzzy white tennis balls do anything he wants with them. "Good serve, Jerry," Danny says, smiling as he looks back from his position at the net after Mandel has served an ace, *pow!*, straight down the center service-court line. Danny double-flips his racquet, walks over to the deuce court, crouching, a few feet behind the net. "Do it again, kid," Danny says, looking, briefly, over his shoulder. And Mandel does it again, and again and again, over and over, again and again.

Even in the midst of this dream, he realizes he is dreaming, and already feels a tinge of regret that he will have to wake.

OUT OF ACTION

It was a pretty good night at Gamblers Anonymous. Eddie Rothman had been coming to these meetings, held in the basement of
the Methodist Church on Lawrence Avenue every Tuesday night save
holidays, for more than three years now. Most of the meetings were excruciatingly boring, but Rothman kept coming to them for the simple
reason that his doing so seemed to work. He had been out of action, as
the gamblers say, for the full time, and so he had to conclude that GA
worked—at least for him, at least thus far.

Rothman had told his own story over the first month or so that
he had begun attending GA meetings. His problem was sports betting,
especially college football, but other sports, too.

After his father's death, Rothman had taken over the family business, the manufacture and importing of novelties: We're-Number-One
gloves, miniature cameras, dream catchers, fuzzy dice, cellphone cases,
junk jewelry. He was then thirty-seven with two kids. He'd been a
gambler what seemed like all his life, beginning with betting parley
cards in high school: Pick three teams on the point spread and win six
dollars on a dollar bet. He and his pals played lots of poker after school
and on weekends; also blackjack and games called in-between and pot-
luck and gin rummy, Hollywood Oklahoma, spades double, for half a
cent a point.

Rothman, who had good card sense, more than held his own in
these games. Once, though, at the age of sixteen, he lost $130 in an af-
ter-school potluck game, which took the edge off his appetite for dinner
that evening. His friend Bobby Lekachman's older brother Ted had a

211

bookie, and he could place a $25 bet on a ballgame through him. Eddie won more of these bets than he lost. After dropping out of Roosevelt College in his second year and going to work for his father, Rothman acquired a bookie of his own, a guy named Lou Rappaport, and began to up his bets on ballgames to $100 a shot. He came out ahead, though not by much.

He liked to have a bet going at all times. Life in action was better. The action made him feel, somehow, more alive. He probably gave more thought to the sports pages than to the novelty business. There were lots of what his father used to call "green deals" in Rothman's business, deals made for cash and off the books. When his father died and Rothman took over the business, he used a fair amount of this extra "green" to step up his bets, to $200 and sometimes $500 a game. He started betting basketball and baseball games; in baseball, he bet pitchers, of course, but also the streak system, betting on the teams that won the day before, against those who lost the day before. His craving for action grew stronger, and he was beginning to lose a lot more than he won. This was probably because he needed the action, couldn't lay off, no longer betting only on those games about which he felt confident.

Winston Churchill, Rothman read somewhere, claimed he got a lot more out of alcohol than it got out of him. Rothman used to think the same of his own gambling, but eventually he recognized this wasn't so. He knew he was in trouble the weekend he bet two grand on a Friday night PAC Ten game in Arizona, lost, doubled down on Saturday, taking Ohio State over Indiana giving 14 points, and lost again, and doubled down yet again on Sunday on the Bears–Lions game, where the point spread beat him, making for a twelve-grand trouncing for the weekend. He did the same thing the following weekend, only at twice the stakes. He lost $4,000 on Arizona versus Oregon State, lost $8,000 on Notre Dame over Pittsburgh on Saturday, and then $16,000 on the 49ers over the Rams, putting him down $28,000, which called for just about all the money from green deals that he had stowed away in his vault at Midcity Bank.

Rothman knew he had to slow things down. He went two weeks in the middle of football season without placing a bet. Naturally, every bet he would have made but didn't during this drying-out period turned out to have been a winner. The third week he went back into action and won on Michigan State over Purdue, but lost twice the sum he'd won on the Packers–Colts game, putting him five grand down.

Fortunately, Debbie, Rothman's wife, was not a woman at all interested in business, or in where Rothman's money came from. So at least he didn't have to worry about hiding his losses from her—not yet anyway. He tried not going cold turkey on gambling, but on tamping things down; betting hundreds instead of thousands. But the same thrill wasn't there for hundreds, and he felt especially foolish when a slew of hundred-dollar bets came in for him and he thought how much money it would have been if they had been bets in the thousands.

The weekend of the college bowl games Rothman lost $45,000, and he didn't have it to pay his bookie, a cheerful man in his late sixties named Ike Goldstein. When he told Ike he would need some time to get the money, Ike, over the phone, in a voice in which Rothman heard menace, said, "If I were you, I wouldn't take too long to get it."

Rothman had to tell Debbie as well as his older brother Mel, an orthodontist with a successful practice. A family meeting was called. Everyone agreed it was best to keep it from Rothman's mother, who was suffering from early signs of dementia. Mel's wife, Laurie, was also present. Rothman felt as if he had been called down to the principal's office for writing obscenities on the walls. His brother lent him the $45,000, and a schedule for repayment was set up. The loan was given on condition of Rothman's pledge to attend Gamblers Anonymous meetings, which Rothman promised to do.

He put himself on a strict mental diet. He stopped watching ball games on television, ceased reading the sports pages. Immediately he realized how large a part of his life had been taken up by these things. He often found himself with nothing to say when customers and other men brought up the Bears or the Cubs, or asked him how he enjoyed the Series or the Super Bowl. He had to find other interests, subjects for conversation, damn well nearly had to revise his personality.

Out of action, with no bets going, his life at first seemed flat, stale. The withdrawal, he assumed, wasn't near so rough as that from drugs or alcohol, because the addiction didn't have a physiological basis. But it was rough enough. Was gambling, he wondered, the alcoholism of Jews?

So every Tuesday night Rothman dragged himself off to Lawrence Avenue for the 7:00 p.m. meeting of Gamblers Anonymous. He worked until six on Tuesdays, stopped along the way at Wendy's for a spicy chicken sandwich and small order of fries and a large Coke, which he ate in his Audi. He took the Coke into the meetings with him.

Tonight's meeting had four new members. One, a guy in his late twenties, his hair in a ponytail, tattoos on his forearms, got up to announce that we were looking at the man who personally stopped the Miami Heat's twenty-seven-game winning streak. "I did it of course," he said, "by betting on them against the Bulls. That's all I want to say right now, but you'll hear more about my past adventures in future."

Another of the new members, a man in his middle fifties, dressed in a velour Fila running suit, said that he woke up a week ago after his wife had gone to work, and, while having his coffee in the living room, thought how shabby the furniture in their apartment had become. So he called in a used-furniture dealer, sold the living-room furniture and the dining-room set, and took the money—$1,200—to the track at Arlington. His thought was that when he returned home he would surprise his wife by telling her that the next day they would go off with his winnings and buy all new furniture. "Surprise, surprise," he said. "Didn't happen. I lost the twelve hundred. We've been eating in the kitchen ever since." After a pause, he added, "I'm here among other reasons to save my marriage."

The third new member announced that his name was Les Ehrlich. He had a layered haircut, hair combed over his ears, an expensive suit. He told how he had blown his family's roofing business and two marriages through gambling. He was now selling household improvements, and on his third marriage. Unless he was in action, he said, he failed to see the point of life. He had had a number of bad weeks in a row, and instead of explaining to his wife how he had really lost his money, he began putting bits of lipstick on his shirt collars, so that she would think he was having a love affair and spending the money on a woman rather than gambling it away. "Sick stuff, I realized," he said, "and that's why I'm here tonight."

The fourth new guy stood up to say that his name was Lenny Adler and that if it was all right he'd prefer not to speak this evening, or until he had the lay of the land on how things worked. He added that his gambling had put him on the edge of suicide and that he was grateful for the existence of a place like GA where he could meet and talk with people who knew something about what he had been through.

This Lenny Adler was short, on the pudgy side, with thin sandy-colored hair, much receded, with a touch of mousse added, giving it a wet look. He wore a gray suit, a light blue shirt, no necktie. He had an almost too clean look about him, as if he just stepped out of the shower. He appeared to be in his early forties, around Rothman's age. He had a manicure and a blue sapphire ring on the little finger of his right hand. He looked prosperous, or at least as if he might once have had some serious money.

At coffee after the meeting, Adler approached Rothman. "Did you by any chance go to Von Steuben High School?" he asked.

"I did," Rothman replied.

"I thought so. You looked familiar."

They discovered that they had been there at the same time, though Adler was two years older. Would he, Adler wanted to know, be interested in ducking out for a drink to talk about old times? Maybe Rothman could fill him in on how things worked at GA.

Driving in Adler's white Porsche, a Boxster, they found an Irish pub on Ashland Avenue called Burke's. The place wasn't crowded, though seven or eight thin-screen television sets around the room were all silently playing ball games. They took a booth.

Adler told Rothman that he was a salesman at Loeber Porsche in Lincolnwood. He was currently separated from his second wife, who lived with his fifteen-year-old daughter, Jennifer, in Morton Grove. He was living in a furnished apartment in the Somerset Hotel, on Sheridan at Argyle.

"A beautiful girl, my daughter, but a handful," Adler said. "Someday she'll make some unlucky man completely miserable, I'm sure."

"What's your weakness, your gambling jones?" Rothman asked. "Mine was sports betting."

"Casinos," said Adler. "Craps and blackjack. Fifteen or so years ago, I had to travel out to Vegas or Atlantic City to get into action. Now the goddamn things are everywhere. What's that line about the lottery? It's the tax the state charges people who don't understand basic arithmetic. There ought to be something similar said about casinos. It's the tax the state charges guys dumb enough to think they can beat the house."

"What makes you think GA is going to do you any good?"

"I'm counting—I guess I better not say betting —on it, though who knows? At least the stories are better than I imagine those at Alcoholics Anonymous must be."

"Some are pretty wild," Rothman said.

"The guy who got up tonight and talked about putting lipstick on his shirt collars? I think I can top that one, though I'm only going to tell it to you. Toward the end of my second marriage, I used to put a dab of lipstick on the fly of my boxer shorts to try to establish the same thing. Who knows, I figured it might even encourage my wife to outdo her rival."

"Did it work?"

"No. But I figured it was worth a try. No matter, though. One of the nice things about gambling is that it takes your mind off sex, as you may have noticed."

"Sex and everything else," Rothman said.

"It can be a problem, that everything else, no doubt about it," Adler said. "But when it's going well, gambling gives a high like no other I've known."

"No argument."

"How long you been out of action?" Adler asked.

"It'll be three years, four months in May," said Rothman, "but who's counting."

"Impressive. You ever feel the ache?"

"Less and less," Rothman said. "But it can still creep up on me."

"Is that why you keep going to these GA meetings?"

"I go," said Rothman, "because I'm nervous about not going. Besides, I used to be a streak-system bettor, and I don't want to break my own streak. Might change my luck."

"Luck," Adler said. "I remember using that word a lot before it had the adjective *shitty* before it."

They stayed at Burke's until nearly midnight. Rothman called Debbie at ten to let her know he would be home late, lest she think he had fallen off the wagon and was in a poker game. They talked about their boyhoods in Albany Park, which Adler referred to as the

Old Country. They talked about their similar boredom with school, about there being nothing in the classroom—any classroom—for either of them. They talked about marriage and how gambling didn't go with marriage. Rothman said he once heard someone say that a married philosopher was a joke, but a married gambler was even more ridiculous.

But mostly they talked about their adventures in the life: the big scores each had made gambling, and the even bigger losses they had taken. They discovered that they were a lot alike. The major difference between them, at least for now, was that Rothman had money, was "holding," in the term they used at the track, and Adler was tapped out, and with his alimony and child-support payments figured to be for the foreseeable future.

The following Tuesday, attendance at Gamblers Anonymous was skimpy (it had been raining all day). Rothman counted nine people at the meeting, where usually there were twenty or so. Two of the four new guys of the previous week failed to show up, and never would again. Soon after the meeting opened, Lenny Adler, who sat across the large conference table from Rothman, stood up to speak.

"I'm pleased to be here among people who know all the pleasures and horrors of the gambling life," Adler began. "Yet for all we have in common, each of us has his own story, I'm sure. Mine is fear of being a loser, which is, of course what, thanks to gambling, I've become. A big-time loser.

"But to start at the beginning, I was, or at least felt myself, a loser right out of the gate. My father came out of Korea and drove a cab. Veteran's Cab was the name of the company. He planned for it to be a temporary thing, but he did it for the rest of his life. He played the ponies, my old man, nothing serious, a two-buck bettor. Gambling didn't bring him down. The ambition gene, I guess, was missing from his make-up. My mother, who was a kind and good-hearted lady, was early afflicted with macular degeneration, which made her practically blind by the time she was thirty. I had two sisters, both older than me, each full of temperament and unhappiness. We lived above a drugstore on Wilson near St. Louis Avenue. I grew up in a home that, from the time I was maybe seven or eight years old, I knew I wanted to get the hell away from, pronto.

"And I did, even as a little kid. I found my refuge on the streets. I hung out in the schoolyard at Peterson Grammar School. My first gambling took place there—marbles, mibs, we called them. I practiced very hard at mibs, because for me they were more than a game. I needed to win. I needed to think about myself as a winner because I knew that, in my family, I had drawn a loser's hand.

"My next gambling was lagging pennies, then nickels, and quarters, the kid's game of trying to pitch coins as close as possible to a line in the sidewalk. I worked hard to be good at this, too. As I grew older, I used to sucker guys into games of Horse on the half-court basket set up in the schoolyard. I wasn't a great basketball player, but I trained myself to shoot left-handed, which was usually all I needed to win at Horse. Other kids may have found fun at the playground, but for me a lot more than fun was involved. It was where I went to work.

"In high school I hung around with a bunch that modeled themselves on Syndicate guys. From the age of fourteen we smoked, shot craps, played nickel-dime-and-quarter poker, went to the harness races at night at Maywood, drove out to the cathouses in Braidwood and Kankakee. Gambling was at the center of everything.

"I sat in classrooms bored out of my gourd. The only way I could have been a good student would have been if someone bet me I couldn't get A's. I graduated somewhere in the lower quarter of my class and then lasted a single semester at Wright Junior College.

"I began selling cars at the age of nineteen. I had an Uncle Earle, my mother's brother, who had a used-car lot. Lots of down time on a car lot. I used mine to study the sports pages and call in bets. By now the need to stay in action was second among my priorities only behind the need to breathe. Baseball, football, college and pro basketball, I had a bet going every day.

"Las Vegas killed me. I went out there when I was twenty-three with two other guys I was working with at the time at Z. Frank Chevrolet. I thought I'd died and gone to heaven. The glitz, the glamour, the show biz, it all blew me away. I went away from that first trip an eight-grand-and-change winner, most of it from the blackjack tables. A bad omen, my good luck my first time in Vegas. I was hooked.

"I started making trips every eight weeks or so. The time when I wasn't there I didn't quite feel alive. Soon I was down as a high-roller, which meant they comped my room at the Mirage.

"Was I a sucker, a chump, a loser? Of course I was, but I scarcely noticed. The question I would ask myself during those days was not how much did I lose but when would I have enough to go back. This was action to the highest power, around the clock, every day. I loved it.

"Of course when the local casinos started up, I was done for. I used to stop off at them the way another guy might have stopped at a 7-Eleven to pick up a quart of milk. It didn't take me long to rack up debts of more than two hundred grand. They just built a casino in Desplaines, the Rivers it's called, a fifteen-minute drive from where I lived with my ex-wife.

"I neglected to mention that I was married and have a teenage daughter. You want to talk about rotten luck, my wife's first husband was an alcoholic, then she marries me, a guy hooked on gambling. The night she discovered that I had put a second mortgage on our house and had loans out on both our cars, she said, in a voice so calm that it spooked me, she said, 'You know, Lenny, the nice thing about alcoholics is that at least they pass out.'

"I've probably already gone on too long to say 'to make a long story short,' but the fact is that I'm up that famous creek without a paddle, and the bottom of the boat is starting to leak pretty badly. I've got to find a way to get out of action and stay out. The last thing I wanted to be in life was a loser, and I realize that this is what I've become, in spades. That's why I've come here for help. I'll shut up now. Apologies for going on so long."

Rothman couldn't recall a better talk in his three years of coming to GA meetings. He sensed everyone else at the table was impressed. Rothman got up to say that if Adler ever needed any help, ever felt himself slipping, he hoped he'd call him. Lenny Adler smiled and said he appreciated the offer, and would no doubt one day take him up on it. The meeting was a fairly brief one. After it was over, Rothman came up to Lenny Adler to tell him that he meant his offer in all seriousness. He gave him his cell and business and home phone numbers.

"The first few months are the toughest," he said.

"I'll hang in there," Adler said.

At next Tuesday's meeting a new member named Arnie Berman got up to say that he thought he might be unusual in this company for he thought of himself as an unusual breed, a conservative, a cautious gambler.

"I've been cautious all my life," he said. "I suppose I got this from my parents. My father was in his middle fifties when I was born, and he'd lived through the Depression. He was full of advice about saving and being careful generally about money. Maybe it was in reaction to him that I took up gambling.

"But the odd part is that I took it up, as I say, conservatively. I bet only favorites. I like the ponies, and I found myself betting favorites to place and sometimes even to show. A friend of mine, guy named Art Rosen, also big for the ponies, used to joke that instead of going to the track I should have bought Israel Bonds—the return was about the same.

"Of course, it wasn't the same. You can bet conservatively and still lose your ass. Which over the years I have done. I might get down big on a heavy favorite—the Patriots against the Jaguars, say—and when I lost, usually owing to the spread, I felt the need to make it back quick. I found myself doubling down a lot. Not so conservative anymore. Anyhow I figure that over the past decade I'm down maybe a quarter of a million dollars. I'm single. I'm not out on the street. But I'd like to learn how to quit, which is why I'm here tonight."

After the meeting, Lenny came up to Rothman. "Takes all kinds, I guess," he said, nodding his head in the direction of Arnie Berman. "But this guy ain't my idea of a good time. Betting on a horse to show! I'd as soon bet on the Hancock Building to be still standing tomorrow morning. I'm more of a long-shot man myself. In fact, Eddie, I think of my entire life as a long shot."

Lenny Adler missed the next GA meeting, but in the middle of the following week, at 6:30 p.m., in his car on his way home to Northbrook, Rothman got a call from him on his cell.

"Eddie," he said. "I'm in my car and on the way to the Rivers Casino. Please tell me I'm a schmuck and to turn back."

"Easy to do," Rothman said. "You're a schmuck, now turn back. Where are you anyhow?"

"I'm just about to get on the Kennedy at Foster."

"Get off it," Rothman said, "and meet me twenty minutes from now for dinner at a Chinese restaurant called Kow-Kow on Cicero and Pratt. Got that?"

"Got it," Adler said. "And thanks. You're a friend."

Kow-Kow was an old Cantonese restaurant, from a time when Cantonese was all that was known of Chinese food in Chicago. Rothman remembered it when it was on Devon Avenue. The patrons in the place tonight, most in their eighties, seemed to date from that time. He took a table in the center of the room and ordered a Tsingtao beer. He studied the menu, which still had Chop Suey and Chow Mein on it. Half an hour later, Adler hadn't yet arrived.

Nor would he. Rothman waited a full hour for him, then called his wife to say he would be home for dinner after all. He thought about calling Adler back. On second thought, he said to himself, screw him.

Lenny Adler did show up for the next GA meeting. He came in ten or so minutes late, and did not greet Rothman. When his turn came to speak, he got to his feet and said:

"I missed the last meeting, for the disgraceful reason that I fell off the wagon. Last week I lost twelve hundred bucks, mostly at blackjack, at Rivers Casino. On my way out there I called my new friend Eddie Rothman, who is here with us tonight. Eddie told me to turn back and meet him for dinner at a Chinese restaurant. I was going to do so, then the thought hit me that the problem with Chinese food is that an hour later, you're hungry to be back in action again. A bad joke, O.K. But what I do want to say is that after my Rivers Casino adventure I not only felt like a loser, but a guilty loser. Is this progress? I'm not sure. What I am sure about is that it's a mistake for me to miss GA meetings, and I'll try my best not to miss another."

Listening to this, Rothman had his doubts. Lenny Adler was maybe a little too glib. When he suggested a drink to Rothman after the meeting, Rothman took a pass, saying that he had to be up early the next day.

"Another time?" Adler said.

"Right," Rothman said. "Take care."

Driving home, Rothman thought about Lenny Adler's sincerity. Was he serious about coming to Gamblers Anonymous. Or was he just killing time. During his three plus years there, lots of guys, after telling their stories of defeat and heartache, never returned. Maybe the GA arrangement just wasn't for them; they weren't comfortable in it, with its confessional mode. Maybe they were able to straighten themselves out on their own. But most, Rothman thought, went back into action, with predictably disastrous results.

He recalled a young lawyer, guy named Jerry Feingold, a big guy, handsome, played basketball for New Trier, afterwards for Michigan. Went to law school, had a practice in the Loop. He broke down in tears his first night at GA. His father had twice bailed him out of heavy gambling debts, the second time for forty-odd grand. He never came back. A month or so later, Rothman read about his jumping from the window of his seventeenth-floor LaSalle Street office. He'd heard from Marty Handler, the man who ran the Lawrence Avenue GA chapter, that Jerry Feingold had got into the Mob for more than fifty grand, and felt he couldn't return to his father to ask for more help. He left a wife and two little kids, ten and eight.

When Rothman got home, Debbie told him he had a call from a man named Leonard Adler. She had written down the number.

"Are you ticked off at me for any reason, Eddie?" Adler wanted to know when Rothman called him back. "Did I do something to piss you off?"

"Don't know why you'd think that. You call me for help, I offer it, and you don't show up. Keep me waiting in a Chinese restaurant for an hour. Not so good."

"I owe you an apology. I thought I already made it in public earlier tonight at the meeting."

"What I wonder is whether you're really serious about breaking your gambling fix. Fell off the wagon kinda early, I'd say. I mean, you'll do what you want. But if you aren't serious about this, then I would ask you not to come to me for help you don't really want."

"I am serious, Eddie, never been more serious about anything in my goddamn life. Give me another chance, another shot."

"Sure," said Rothman. He thought his voice sounded unconvincing. "Of course. Why not?"

"Thanks, pal. You won't be sorry, I promise."

"I hope not," Rothman said, hoping that in his voice he had buried the doubt he strongly felt.

Lenny Adler showed up for the next four GA meetings. At each of them he sat next to Rothman. At each he spoke briefly, announcing that he had gone without action the week before and felt terrific about it but knew he still had a long ways to go.

After the last of these meetings, he invited Rothman for a drink. Rothman wasn't eager to go, but felt it would be unkind to say no, so they agreed to meet at Burke's. The bar was more crowded tonight than on their previous meeting there. The soundless television sets showed tennis matches, soccer games, night baseball. To Rothman, even after all this time, these games were little more than porno by other means, and he kept himself from looking at the screens.

They found a booth, ordered drinks—a martini for Adler, a vodka and tonic for Rothman.

"Any interest in going to the Bears season's opener on Sunday," Adler asked. "I've got seats on the forty."

"None whatsoever." Rothman said. "Watching a ballgame, any ballgame, without having a bet on it would be torture. It would be like a big-game hunter going on safari with a water pistol. I do better to stay away."

"You really are a disciplinarian, Eddie."

"I may not have many strengths," Rothman said, "but at least I know my weaknesses."

"You're a philosopher."

"Sure," Rothman said, "right. Someone said the unexamined life isn't worth living. The problem is that the examined life isn't much fun."

"Maybe you need a vice," Adler said.

"What'd you have in mind? Drugs? Adultery? Child molestation?"

"I'll need time to come up with the right vice for you. I'm sure it's out there."

"How about you? Was another week out of action tough on you?"

"Truth is, it was. They all are. I'm not as good at admitting to my weaknesses as you are."

"Nothing to do but tough it out."

"Sometimes I think a booze or drug problem might be easier."

"More likely it would only be sloppier."

"When did you know you had the gambling jones beat?"

"I don't think of having beat it. I think of holding it off. I'm playing for a tie, a draw."

"Not very glorious," Adler said.

"It is if you consider the other possibility. My goal is to avoid humiliation, because, given my style as a gambler, that's the only place gambling can end up for me. Probably a good idea to have a goal here yourself."

"I'll have to think about that," Adler said. "Just now my only goal is not to give away all my money to strangers."

"Not good enough, is my guess," said Rothman. "Something a little more specific is needed."

"I'll think about it. Maybe you'll help me on this one."

"Anything you need," said Rothman, "say the word."

Adler came in late for the following week's GA meeting, toward its close, looking harried. He barely greeted Rothman, then took off right after the meeting ended. The following week he didn't show up at all; nor the two weeks after. Rothman assumed that he fell off the wagon, and was back in action, with the usual disastrous results.

Then, on a Saturday night, at 2:13 a.m., according to the digital clock beside Rothman's bed, the phone rang and it was Lenny Adler.

"Eddie," he said. "Lenny Adler. This is an outrageous time to call, I know, but I'm in deepest of deep shit, and need your help."

"I'm in my bedroom," Rothman said. "Let me take this downstairs."

Rothman picked up the kitchen phone. He opened and stared into the refrigerator as Lenny Adler continued.

"Here's the thing, Eddie. I'm into the Baretta family for sixty grand. You know about the Barettas?"

"No," said Rothman, taking a pint of Häagen-Dazs peach sorbet out of the freezer. "Who are the Barettas?"

"They're the Mob in Oak Forest, and they're real brutes, killers."

"So," said Rothman, taking a spoon out of the silverware drawer.

"So they showed me a photograph of another guy who owed them roughly the same amount I do. Actually, they showed me a photograph of his hands. They'd cut off his thumbs."

"Why are you telling me this?" Rothman asked, though he already knew the answer.

"Because if I don't have twenty grand, a third of what I owe them, by Tuesday, I'm going to be in the same condition, fuckin' thumbless.

I need to borrow the twenty from you, Eddie. There's no one else I can turn to."

"Any guarantee I would get it back?" Rothman asked. "You haven't exactly proved yourself the most reliable guy in the world." Rothman tried to penetrate the peach sorbet holding the spoon without using his thumbs. It couldn't be done.

"If I wasn't scared shitless, Eddie, I'd never have made this call. I've never been so terrified in my life."

"Look, Lenny, it's past two in the morning. I'll call you when I get into work tomorrow."

"Thanks, Eddie, thanks. I'll wait to hear from you."

When Rothman arrived at his place on Washington, a block west of Halsted, he saw Lenny Adler's Porsche out front. He had already decided to lend him the twenty grand. Not because he thought he would get it back; he doubted he would. He was stuck, Rothman was, with a conscience. He couldn't allow another human being to be brutalized if he could help it. Rothman recalled the threat in his old bookie Ike Goldstein's voice, and the fear it had put into him. Besides, in the more than three years out of action, he had accumulated more than eighty grand in green deals that sat doing nothing in his Midcity Bank vault.

Lenny Adler emerged from his car when Rothman appeared. They walked up the flight of stairs to the door marked Rothman Enterprises. Rothman changed nothing in his father's simple office after his father died; there was still the metal desk, the small chair on wheels, the four metal file cabinets, the plastic chaise longue in which his father, in his last years, used to take twenty-minute naps.

"All right, Lenny, I've decided to loan you the money. How about your car as collateral?

"The car isn't mine," Adler said. "It belongs to the dealership. But I'm not going to let you down, Eddie. How could I? You're saving my life. I'm never going to forget it."

"I'm going to make out an IOU for you to sign. I'd also like to know how you plan to schedule your repayments on the twenty grand."

"First I'll have to repay the Barettas back the other forty I owe them. Then I'll pay you, how about at the rate of two grand a month, beginning six months from now? Does that sound reasonable?"

"It does if it's also realistic."

Adler signed the IOU. Rothman wrote out a personal check for the twenty grand, walked around his desk, and handed it to Adler, who glimpsed it, folded it, and put it in his shirt pocket. Rothman held out his hand. Adler took it, but drew Rothman to him and hugged him.

"You're the real thing," Adler said, "a true *mensch*. I'm more grateful than I can say."

When Lenny Adler didn't show up for the next night's Gamblers Anonymous meeting, Rothman was disappointed but not shocked. Adler also missed the next two GA meetings. Rothman began checking the papers and watching local television news for any word about a man having been the victim of a Mob murder, but there was nothing. He tried calling Adler on his cellphone, but the number was out of service.

After Adler missed the next, his fourth, GA meeting, Rothman called him at Loeber Porsche. He was told that there was no Lenny Adler working as a salesman there, nor had there ever been. They never heard of Leonard Adler at the Somerset Hotel either. He asked his friend Stan Margolis, who fancied himself an amateur expert in local mafia matters, what he knew about the Baretta family. Stan said he never heard of them. When his canceled check was returned from the bank, it was signed Leonard Adler and then signed below that with the name Ira Lerner.

Rothman realized that he had been conned, and took not the smallest pleasure in the fact that it had been done by a real artist. He had unconsciously slipped back into action. He had backed a long shot, and lost. This was not a story, he decided, that he would ever stand up to tell at Gamblers Anonymous.

SHORT TAKES

HATS OFF

I hope it isn't too early to begin predictions for the new millennium, because I have a small, modest, even parochial one to make, and here it is: Before the first decade of our third millennium, a Jewish high holiday service will be led by a rabbi—I do not say an Orthodox rabbi—wearing a baseball cap. Whether that cap will be worn backwards, I cannot predict. It will, though, be one-size-fits-all.

This vision came to me roughly a month ago when I saw a man—in his middle sixties, I would guess—come out of a nearby synagogue in a dark suit. In his hand was the small velvet bag in which Jews keep their prayer shawl, prayer book, and sometimes phylacteries, and atop his head sat the black cap with white lettering of the Chicago White Sox. In his look I noted not the least glint of humor, playfulness, irony. It was evidently his standard headgear, part of his regular get-up.

I own a few baseball caps myself—one a replica of the old Gas House Gang St. Louis Cardinals of the 1930s, another with Stanford written across the top, a third with the name of the town of Stonington, Connecticut—but I tend not to wear them on religious holidays, at funerals, to circumcisions, or while lecturing at the Johns Hopkins University School of Medicine. I wear them, in fact, infrequently and mostly to keep off the sun, for I find that they do not increase my natural beauty.

I do not know exactly when baseball caps went ubiquitous, as they now are, but I do recall my first memory of one being worn indoors. I was teaching a course in a seminar room in the library at Northwestern University when a student entered wearing the black cap with the

229

orange logo of the San Francisco Giants. "Mr. O'Brien," I said, "that hat, are you perchance wearing it for religious reasons?" When he allowed that he wasn't, I gently suggested he remove it, which he did, without argument or obvious resentment. Not long after, when I suggested another student remove his baseball cap, he did so, displaying a fierce bramble of hair, and told me that he was wearing it because he hadn't a chance to shampoo that morning and was having what we should now call, in our nicely nuanced psychological age, "a bad hair day."

I continued to ask male students to remove their baseball caps in my classrooms. But when female students began wearing them, with their ponytails sticking out the back, I knew the game was up. All that is left for me now is occasional sniping. When recently teaching a class on irony, I said that the ironic method entails saying one thing and meaning another, and offered as an example that "I find nothing so invigorating as teaching about the meaning of evil in the novels of Joseph Conrad to a group of students wearing their baseball caps backwards." No baseball caps showed up in that class for another three weeks.

A salesman at Brooks Brothers once told me, with great chagrin, that he had a twenty-six-year-old grandson who didn't know how to tie a necktie. Many more people, much older than twenty-six, apparently are unaware that men aren't supposed to wear hats indoors, let alone that they used to be doffed or at least tipped outdoors in the presence of women. Anyone who does remember such things can only have exulted at that scene in *The Sopranos*, the HBO soap opera, when Tony Soprano, dining in a respectable Italian restaurant, goes up to a youngish man wearing a baseball cap and quietly suggests that, if he doesn't remove it, he will at the very least maim him. I could, as we say, "identify."

The spread of the baseball cap is part of the large trend toward the informalization of American clothing. A friend who has a men's shop tells me that nowadays his only customers for suits are lawyers. I myself buy fewer suits. I still teach in a necktie, for I like the distance it puts between the students and me. I also prefer to fly wearing a necktie, perhaps because, should the plane go down, I wouldn't want to meet my Maker underdressed. Yet, great stiffo that I am, I nonetheless find myself more and more lapsing into the informal. Not long ago I proposed to a friend, quite as formal as I in these matters, that, at dinner that evening with our wives, we forgo wearing neckties. A longish pause ensued. "Audacious," he said.

Joe DiMaggio was perhaps the only man of intrinsic elegance whose looks were not diminished by a baseball cap. Impossible to imagine Cary Grant, Fred Astaire, or Noel Coward in one. Coward it was who once discovered himself, in a business suit, at a party in which every other man in the room was in white tie and tails. "Please," he said, "I don't want anyone to apologize for overdressing." I don't believe he could have quite brought that off had he been wearing the cap of the Arizona Diamondbacks.

A SARTORIAL DOUBLE FAULT

I never saw Tommy Haas, the German tennis player third seeded in this year's U.S. Open, in the sleeveless shirt that the U.S. Tennis Association's marketing director banned him from wearing. But, sight unseen, I approved of the ban straightaway. Television commentators, remarking on Mr. Haas's not being allowed to wear his shirt, said they thought what players chose to wear was really a matter of taste. I couldn't agree more: good taste and bad.

I write as a sixty-odd-year fan of tennis and a former boy player. Back then, along with a kid named Bob Swenson, now an epidemiologist in Philadelphia, I won the Chicago City High School Doubles Championship. To put this accomplishment in proper perspective, in those days the best tennis players went to suburban schools and the team we defeated in the finals, from Fenger High School, wore gym shorts (with just a touch of boxer undershorts peeping out above the knee) and brown U.S. Ked gym shoes.

If I were to analyze my tennis game in those days, I would have to say that I had stylish strokes, was not all that effective, but very well dressed. From the beginning, I was swept away by what I took to be the intrinsic elegance of the game. Although it would be years before I had read her, so was Edith Wharton, who wrote that "It seems to me such a beautiful game—without violence, noise, brutality—quick, graceful, rhythmic, with a setting of turf and sky." Just so.

Good that Edith Wharton isn't alive today to hear Maria Sharapova grunting away, making each long rally sound like something occurring behind doors at a Masters and Johnson laboratory. Nor do I know what she would have made of Serena Williams's black lycra catsuit—described in the *New York Times* as "curve clutching"—worn for the U.S. Open. I'm certain that Lleyton Hewitt's baseball hats worn backward are something of which she would not approve.

Perhaps this is because neither do I. I can't cheer for any player wearing a baseball cap backward, and I only root for Mr. Hewitt, a courageous and powerful (even though small) player, when he is hatless. I'm not too crazy, either, about the oversized shirts, always won outside one's inevitably baggy shorts, that most men players have taken to wearing, so that before both serving and return of service they have to bunch up the excess of material on the shoulder of their shirts in an almost tic-like way.

At least Andre Agassi's denim shorts never caught on, worn in the days when, also weighed down with heavy-duty stubble, long hair, earrings, hat, and over-large shirt Mr. Agassi looked like nothing so much as a gypsy on the way out of town with two stolen chickens in his bag.

I grew up under another notion of tennis elegance. The best job I have ever had in a very fortunate life was, at thirteen, that of ball boy for the lessons given by the pro and coach at Northwestern University, a heavyset, gruff, and extremely nice man named Paul Bennett. I was allowed to play all day for nothing on Northwestern's then perfectly rolled sand-colored clay courts. Most of the $6 or $7 a day I earned shagging balls and demonstrating the three kinds of serve—twist, flat cannonball, and slice—Mr. Bennett taught but had become too fat to demonstrate himself, I spent on El fare, soft drinks, and tennis togs.

I dressed in strict imitation of the top players of the day—the early 1950s. This meant Jack Purcell shoes, white with a blue line across the toes. I bought Fred Perry shorts, in a rich safari tan. I owned two white Lacoste chemises, and wore a sweatlet on the wrist of my racket hand. Ah, if only I played as well as I looked, you might have seen me at Wimbledon.

E. Digby Baltzell, the man who invented the acronym WASP, said that the beginning of the end of white, Anglo-Saxon, Protestant culture came with the advent of referees in tennis. He meant by this that, such was the honor system built into the old version of the game, no gentleman would ever cheat on a line call, let alone attempt to one-up his opponent. Fast forward now to John McEnroe, even today in seniors' tournaments, in his stately mid-fifties, in full-throttle fulmination, foul-mouthed and scowling, all in the name of being highly competitive.

My obviously Jewish name might suggest that I am not in the best position to defend WASP culture. In tennis, as elsewhere, this culture was exclusive and could be cruelly excluding. In the late 1940s and early '50s, Pancho Gonzales, one of tennis's greatest players, was made to feel his public-courts origins. Well-born or wealthy Jews—Vic Sexias, Dick Savitt—were occasionally allowed a place. Althea Gibson, the first important black player in the game, showed herself at least as refined as any woman who ever played tennis.

When tennis has been at its best, it seems to me, is when the old WASP standard of deportment has combined with a deeply democratic spirit. Perhaps nowhere was this in better evidence then during the reign of the remarkable generation of Australian players, among them Rod Laver, Lew Hoad, Ken Rosewall, Neal Fraser, Roy Emerson, and John Newcomb. These were all young men from less than wealthy homes who, while playing brilliantly, always acted gentlemanly. They were intensely competitive without being, a la John McEnroe and Jimmy Connors, pigs of competition. And they all wore white.

The more colorful clothes that contemporary players now wear are in part a pure capitalist plot—the more various the tennis clothes, the larger the number of items to put on sale in sporting goods and other shops—and in part a plan to democratize the game itself, make it seem less a country club and hence less a rich person's sport. Of course, all these garish duds are very expensive.

The ugly new tennis clothes don't make anyone play worse. They chiefly make the game seem less elegant and slightly more clownish. Hats on backward, shirts out of shorts, colored socks make the guys banging the ball around Louis Armstrong and Arthur Ashe Stadiums nowadays, despite their 130-mph serves and multi-million-dollar annual incomes, look to me as if they might be playing for Fenger High.

THE RUNNING OF THE BULLS

A few years ago I had a call from Gene Siskel, who lives in Chicago, as I do. Siskel is a man others envy, possibly hate, for having
what looks like one of the world's best and easiest jobs: sitting before a
television camera, chatting about movies, for maybe—who knows?—a
couple million a year. He had heard that I thought the depiction of a
character in the movie *Quiz Show* was anti-Semitic, and Siskel, who
prides himself on his radar for anti-Semitism in the movies, thought I
was wrong. He called to argue, which we did, rather civilly, neither
side winning.

Toward the close of our conversation, he asked if I happened to be
a sports fan. I allowed as I was. He said he had some really wonderful
tickets to the Bulls games, and perhaps we could go sometime. "Sure,"
I said, "sounds swell to me."

In fact, I had been a Bulls fan from the basketball team's beginning in the city. I saw the team play in the middle 1960s in the old
Amphitheatre, near the stockyards. I courted my second (and final) wife
with half-season's tickets in the early '70s. Late in the fourth quarter of
a close game, after Chet Walker had been fouled, she turned to me,
clutched my hand, and announced, "We're in the bonus." Ah, thought
I, a woman who knows about being in the bonus—here is a woman I
must marry.

At one point in the '70s, I had a press pass to the Bulls games because I had arranged to write a piece for the *Chicago Tribune* on Bob
Love, who had perhaps the most delicately elegant jump shot I have
ever seen.

237

A few years later, I would knock off from my scribbling and drive down to the Angel Garden Orphanage gym on Ridge Avenue near Devon and drop in on Bulls practice sessions. I was born too late to travel to Pamplona to see the running of the bulls, but, I'm pleased to say, early enough to watch the Chicago Bulls practice before the great hype and hoopla of celebrity sports, with all its security and secrecy, had set in.

A few days after our conversation, Siskel called back to ask if I were free to join him in a week's time when the Bulls played the New Jersey Nets. We arranged to meet at his apartment. On the way to pick up the other two guys who were to go with us, Siskel explained that, when the Bulls moved from the old Chicago Stadium to the new United Center, he was offered these tickets, which, even though they were very expensive, he felt he couldn't refuse.

The seats were in the first row, on the floor, directly across from the Bulls bench. There were four of them, they cost $325 a shot, or $1,300 a game, and since the team plays forty-odd games at home . . . well, you do the math. Siskel decided to call up three wealthy friends to ask if they were interested in taking eleven games' worth of seats from him. All answered yes, if play-offs were included. Did I neglect to mention that with these tickets, parking was free?

The actual seats are well-padded bridge chairs behind a vinyl counter with places for food and drink and a television set (so that you can simultaneously watch the real thing and the televised thing). A waitress took our orders. Nothing easier to get used to, I have always found, than prosperity.

Siskel had learned a thing or two from these seats. "When Scottie [Pippen] breathes through the mouth," he alerted me, "it means he's going for the hole." And, lo, Pippen did, every time. The Bulls lost the game, blowing an 18-point lead to a lackluster Nets team. When the game was over, I told Siskel that I assumed that, at these prices, one got to take home one's chair. It proved not to be so.

So for one night in my life, I sat in the Jack Nicholson seats, albeit without the hair plugs, the four-day growth of beard, or the malicious grin, but up close and nicely distanced from my detestable fellow fans. I shall never have a better seat, and consequently feel it pointless ever to return to the United Center. I cannot abide downward mobility.

Driving home, I couldn't quite get the price of those seats out of my mind. It wasn't my money, but even so I felt letting someone else pay so much so that I could watch a mere game was, somehow, immoral. Very well, I asked myself, what would I pay $325 to see? Nobody currently alive, I quickly concluded. The best I could come up with was that I would pay $325 to watch Enrico Caruso making love to Mae West, but only if he were singing while doing so and she, while all this was going on, emitted a continuous stream of brilliant off-color wisecracks. Well, maybe not $325. Two-fifty tops.

BEST SEAT IN THE HOUSE

I was watching the Chicago Blackhawks play the Los Angeles Kings in the western Stanley Cup final round when, in the second period, the television camera panned to Tom Cruise, sitting alone in a rink-side seat. "Tom Cruise is a big Kings fan," the announcer said.

Celebrities at sporting events is by now a tradition of fairly long standing. Johnny Carson used to turn up in the stands at Wimbledon. Jack Nicholson has been in a front-row seat at Lakers basketball games for as long as I can remember. Dyan Cannon is another regular at Lakers games. Spike Lee and Woody Allen seem to attend most Knicks home games, Lee usually in Knicks hats and shirts. Billy Crystal, I note, is often in the stands at the L. A. Clippers' games. I recently saw Justin Bieber—why does a man my age even have to know that name?—sitting, bedizened in golden necklace, bracelet, three-pound wristwatch, and baseball cap worn deliberately askew, at a Miami Heat game.

Chicago, the city of my birth, upbringing, and planned burial, has no such celebrities attending any of its sports games regularly. The reason is that Chicago has no thunderingly big-name show-biz celebrities living in the city. Just now, with the city's exorbitant murder rate and busted public-school system, this is a less-than-serious problem. Apparently, though, the Chicago Bulls public relations team have felt the want of having a celebrity of some kind, any kind, in the stands for its home games. Or so I concluded when, nearly a decade ago, Gene Siskel, then part of the television movie-reviewing team of Siskel and Ebert, invited me to attend a Chicago Bulls game with him.

241

As celebrities go, Gene Siskel was small beer, but he was on television regularly, and the only road to serious celebrity in our day, apart from a successful movie career or a scandalous political one, is to be on television with some frequency.

As for Gene Siskel, I had never met him, and I rarely read him. I did, a time or two, watch *Siskel & Ebert & the Movies* on our local PBS station, though without the exhilaration brought on by eureka-like enlightenment. Our connection was through a friend named Maury Rosenfield, who did know Siskel and had gotten into a discussion with him about Robert Redford's 1994 movie *Quiz Show.* Maury had mentioned that I thought there were anti-Semitic touches in the movie—chiefly in John Turturro's part as Herbie Stempel, the crude Jewish character whom Ralph Fiennes's Charles Van Doren defeats and replaces as the main attraction on the television quiz show *Twenty One.* Siskel claimed that he had a powerful radar when it came to spotting anti-Semitism in the movies, and he saw none in Redford's movie. He was sufficiently worked up about this to ask Maury Rosenfield for my phone number so that he could argue the point with me directly.

When Siskel called, we had a polite disagreement on the subject, with no winner emerging. Toward the end of our conversation, Siskel asked me if I were a sports fan. When I said that I was, he told me he had excellent tickets to the Chicago Bulls games, and if I were interested, he would like to take me to a game.

"Sure," I said, "that would be great."

The night I met Siskel in front of his impressive apartment building across from Lincoln Park, he told me that we would be joined for the game by the journalist Alex Kotlowitz and a man named Jeff Jacobs, who was Oprah Winfrey's business manager. We were to meet both of them at Harpo Studios, Oprah's headquarters in the West Loop.

We weren't in Siskel's car ten minutes when he told me how lucky he was to have his job, and all the money that television syndication brought in. His first connection with the movies came through the novelist John Hersey, who was his housemaster at Yale and who lined him up with a job at the *Chicago Tribune.* At the *Trib*, he was asked what he wanted to do, and he said he wanted to write about movies. This was before movies became the great subject of the college-educated middle class and movie critics became mini-stars, their opinions on everyone's tongue. (Soon enough, the passionate interest in movies waned, to be followed and eclipsed by earnest discussions about restaurants.)

Siskel's good luck, he told me, had made him wary. Both his parents had died in their early fifties, and he would soon be turning fifty himself. He had young children. He feared the imminence of his own death. And die he did, five years later, of a brain tumor, at fifty-three.

"I've got great seats," he said. He told me that the Chicago Bulls management wanted him to have front-row seats for their games. He had to pay for the tickets, though, and at $325 a seat, with four tickets for every home game, the tab for the season was $53,300—not an easy check to write, he allowed. He was, however, able to sell off many of the tickets to well-to-do friends.

At Harpo, we were met by Kotlowitz, Jacobs, and Oprah. Without makeup, Oprah Winfrey looked as any fortyish black woman at the end of a hard day at the office might look. Instead of catching a bus for an apartment in South Shore, however, she would be stepping into a limo headed for a swank Michigan Avenue duplex. She joked cordially about our boys' night out, and about basketball itself being, she guessed, "a guy thing."

We drove up Madison Avenue to the United Center arena. Siskel's seats were in the front row, across the floor from the players' benches. Waitresses took our drink orders. This was the 1993–94 season, a dreary time for the Bulls, the year that Michael Jordan retired from basketball in the hope of starting a baseball career. That night the Bulls were playing a characterless New Jersey Nets team, to which they lost by eighteen points. Was I on television, photographed along with Chicago's not-very-impressive celebrity, a middle-brow if nationally recognized movie critic? I have no notion, and a little less interest.

Afterward, in the parking lot, Siskel picked up his car phone—cell phones were not yet in regular use—to make a restaurant reservation: "Hello," he said into the phone, "this is Gene Siskel, and I'm calling to reserve a table for four, roughly twenty minutes from now."

(His opening comment—"This is Gene Siskel"—reminded me of a story about Ira Gershwin and his wife and another couple who, early on a Saturday night, were contemplating dinner at Sardi's. "I don't think we can get a table there on such short notice," Gershwin said, "but let me try," and off he went to make the call. He came back to report that it was no-go, no tables were available. The husband of the other couple said he would like to try his luck at it, and went into the other room to make the call. "Yes," he said, "it's fine. Sardi's, at eight p.m., table for four, center of the room. No trouble whatsoever." How did he manage to do that, everyone wanted to know. "Simple," the man said, "I just told them I was Ira Gershwin.")

At the restaurant, as I paused over an enticing dish of linguine and clam sauce, Gene Siskel said, "Now that I have all of us together, I'd like to talk a little about where black–Jewish relations are heading." I inwardly groaned: In a world where tact did not matter, I would have lifted my plate and glass of wine and moved to another table. Instead, I sat through a conversation that seemed to put lead on my fork.

Siskel drove Alex Kotlowitz and Jeff Jacobs back to Harpo, where their cars were parked, and then drove me back to his apartment, where my car was. I thanked him for dinner and for the ticket to the game. We shook hands, and agreed that we hoped to meet again, but never did. On the way home, I decided I preferred seats much higher off the floor.

A SUPER (YAWN) SUNDAY

This is going to be Super Bowl XXXI, and it is with no pride whatsoever that I have to report having watched the preceding XXX. Only two have left memories in my mind. The first, when Joe Namath and the Jets shocked the greatly favored Baltimore Colts. The second, when my own team, the Chicago Bears, crushed the New England Patriots. For the rest, all those Sundays now constitute a blur, in which I can barely make out the lined faces of the tyrannical Vince Lombardi, the merciless Don Shula, the phlegmatic Tom Landry, and the anxious Marv Levy.

According to a recent piece in the *New York Times Magazine*, interest in professional football has greatly lessened in recent years. I suspect this is true, even though it was printed in the *New York Times*. It has lessened greatly for me, with more than fifty years in the supine business of being a sports fan. The athletes no longer seem admirable or even interesting, and are exceeded in unattractiveness only by the small but dreary pack of owners; the money has screwed things up hugely; and the hype is no longer even close to believable. I should like it much better, in fact, if they began to call it, instead of the Super Bowl, the Nice Bowl, and, while at it, dropped the Roman numerals.

So fatigued am I by the spectacle of it all that I have come to feel a strong personal dislike even for the announcers. Dick Enberg's endless agreeableness makes me want to challenge him to a fight. John Madden's enthusiasm for the crudity and brutishness of the game no longer seems quite credible; and it would be wonderful if some clever investigative reporter were able to uncover that Madden was working on a

245

translation of the poetry of St. John Perse during the long commercial breaks. Monday Night Football is one of the few sports-watching habits I have been able to break, and it is pleasing no longer to have to worry about Frank Gifford's and Al Michaels's hairlines.

Yet if pro football seems to be losing ground, it has a lot of ground to lose. For a time it looked as if the game were to become as much a part of the culture as baseball once was. Seven or eight years ago at lunch, Erich Heller, the great critic of Central European literature, whose illness had forced him to move into a retirement home, in his case an all-male retirement home, said to me, in his strongly Teutonic accent: "Joe, I haf a qvestion to esk of you."

"Of course, Erich," I said. "What is it?"

"Who," he asked, "is dis Ditka?"

Good God, I thought, poor Erich, up in his rooms reading Goethe and Rilke, even he has had his life invaded by Mike Ditka. "Erich," I replied, "believe me, you don't need to know."

For all my grumbling, I think you should know that I shall once again be at my post—that is, on my duff on a couch before the television set—for this year's Super Bowl. The reason is that for the past fifteen years, my wife and I have been the hosts of a Super Bowl dinner for her congenial family. (My own family, whose theme is ingratitude, has too few members left who still speak to one another to make such a dinner tenable.)

We eat a swell dinner, various cousins contributing side dishes. We organize a small betting pool, with the person who comes closest to guessing the total points scored winning. Bonhomie fills the room. Only the quality of the game itself has been wanting. In recent years, the true excitement has been over the commercials, which are more amusing than the football and which by now must cost up to a quarter million dollars a nanosecond.

As the game drones on, people drift in and out, and the chief interest is in who will win the pool. Although sentiment and pro football go together like oil and water, I have decided to like the Green Bay Packers this year, partly because the team represents a small town, and even more because it does not have a single owner or small syndicate of owners, but is owned, in effect, by the town itself. Having no Jerry Jones, no Jack Kent Cooke, no Mike McCaskey, no beautiful and talented Al Davis, no egomaniacal, publicity-seeking zillionaire, gives the Packers a fine negative allure.

As the family cynic, I shall doubtless once again hold forth on the state of the sport. The subject of this year's sermon will be that sports, and especially pro football, is a metaphor for absolutely nothing. Three-hundred-and-fifty-pound interior linemen are not gladiators, soldiers in the trenches, but only extremely well-paid brutes in shoulder pads and helmets. Third-down conversions are just that—a chance for another four downs. You may punt in football, but never in life. Nothing in the entire game, truth to tell, applies to life. Professional football is merely a game, an increasingly specialized and brutish one that you probably don't want your sons to play, and anyone who attempts to make more of it is fooling himself or trying to con the rest of us.

Have a Super Sunday.

A SECRET VICE

In the early-twentieth-century medical encyclopedias, the article "The Secret Vice" was about onanism. Inevitably accompanying the article was a photograph of a practitioner, a young man, poor fellow, who looked to be in the moral equivalent of advanced leprosy.

I have a secret vice of my own to report, and this is listening to talk-radio shows devoted to sports. I practice this vice only in my car, when alone, and until now nobody knew about it. Why, I have often asked myself, do I degrade myself in this way? For my own intellectual health, I've got to stop, and stop soon.

In the console of my car are CDs of Dvorak string quartets, Mitsuko Uchida's sublime rendition of Schubert piano music, Sarah Vaughan singing old standards, and Joel Grey doing the subtler show tunes. This ought to be sufficient to keep me from the tedium of city traffic. Not so, it turns out.

Instead I prefer to hear argumentative men gas away on the exploits of other large and sometimes bulky men hitting, kicking, and stuffing balls of various shapes and sizes over differently shaped fields and courts. I, who during the evening might be reading a biography of Dante (Alighieri, not Culpepper), in my car listen to the thin iconoclasm and even thinner commonsense observations of ex-jocks and newspaper sportswriters.

Chicago has two stations devoted to sports talk. Some of the men employed by these stations come on as very moral and perpetually ticked off; others are worldly and calmly cynical; everyone is terribly knowing.

Part of the attraction is what I believe the feminists would call "masculinist." One of the shows I listen to advertises itself as America's last corner bar. It has three so-called hosts: a pugnacious Irishman, a not especially brainy Jewish guy, and a retired Green Bay Packers defensive lineman. All are happily overweight. They eat unhealthily and are pleased about it; for them women are purely sexual objects, except wives, who are figures of mild terror that exist to raise one's children and be outfoxed.

For your sports-talk show man, host or audience, life is largely lived in front of the television set, watching two, three games a night, and uncounted ones on lost weekends. No war on terror is going on, the state of the economy is a matter of little concern, gay marriage is a subject good chiefly for raw jokes. The only questions worth pondering are how corrupt are college sports, was Notre Dame right to fire its football coach, and was Sammy Sosa on steroids the years he hit more than 60 homers.

Much of the content of sports-talk radio is about old, obviously unsettleable arguments: Who are the five all-time best quarterbacks in the NFL? How does Barry Bonds's record stack up against Babe Ruth's? Are all basketball games really won on defense? Gruff opinionation usually wins the day: "Whaddya mean you'd rather have Peyton Manning than Brett Favre in the red zone late in the fourth quarter in a playoff game? Look at the numbers, for God's sake." Ephemeral scandals and trades, potential and real, fill the day's chitchat. The same few bones are gnawed continuously.

Occasionally I learn a little something. When the White Sox traded a power-hitting outfielder named Carlos Lee, I wondered why. On one of these shows I learned that, though Lee hit more than 30 home runs and batted around .300, and had an error-free year in left field, he also hit 50 points lower with men in scoring position, and more than 100 points lower with two outs with men in scoring position, and the reason he fielded as well as he did is that he played a short left field and the balls that sailed over his head did not count as errors.

These shows are all the radio equivalent of interactive—they allow the audience to put in its rusty two cents through call-ins, emails, faxes. I've never called in or sent an email myself. Even though I've wasted a vast portion of my life watching games, I find I have no strikingly original insight into any of them. I could, I suppose, call in politely to point out that the word "fortuitous" doesn't mean fortunate or that "differential" has more properly to do with equations and with engines than the differences in scores. Somehow, though, I feel my pedantry would not be well received.

My mind would be so much better engaged listening to serious music. Shoot the Schubert to me, Hubert, should be my byword, or Hit me with more Dvorak, Jack. Yet I listen to the trivia-meisters of sports-talk radio instead. All I can do is admit to the vice, and, in the manner of Alcoholics Anonymous, hope, now that my vice isn't secret any more, that I've taken a first step toward recovery.

SPORT MAGAZINE

I haven't read the sports pages with any care for decades. I began to ignore them when I first started reading the *New York Times*, lo, many moons ago. That once-august paper's sports pages were never quite first class; its writers found a way to drain the joy out of the contemplation of what was supposed to be a jolly pastime. I used to enjoy Red Smith and Jimmy Cannon on sports, and for a time I looked forward to Roger Angell's pieces on baseball in *The New Yorker*. In Herbert Warren Wind, that magazine had a superior writer on golf and tennis; Wind was so good that I could read him on golf, even though I hadn't the least interest in the sport.

As a reader about sports, my intensity peaked sometime around my fourteenth year. About three years before that, I started reading *Sport*, a monthly whose first issue was published in 1946, only a few years before I had begun reading it. I was a boy who had no stamp collection, electric trains, or an interest in science, and I read no books but comic books. Sports were the only thing that interested me—playing them, listening to people talk about them, and with the advent of *Sport* magazine, reading about them.

Sport used a lot of color photography, and was the only show in town in sports magazines, having preceded by eight years *Sports Illustrated*, a magazine I always thought too middle-class and country club in its general outlook. I believe in its early years it carried a column on bridge. *The Sporting News*, a weekly published out of St. Louis in tabloid

253

format, tended to emphasize the statistical, and in its coverage of minor-league baseball and other sports arcana conveyed rather more than one needed—or at least that I wanted—to know.

Television radically changed the way sports could be written about. Before television, most sports fans did not have an eyewitness experience of games and hence of the more spectacular plays that had taken place during them. We learned about these things second-hand, from sportswriters and radio sportscasters. Sports writing in those days was almost exclusively about descriptions of catches, homers, touchdown runs, tackles, baskets, and the rest. Since the advent of television, when most of us got to see these things from our couches, sportswriters have had to fall back on writing about personalities, financial negotiations, and, with the ugly intrusion of steroids, pharmacology.

Sport covered the four major sports of the day—baseball, football, basketball, and boxing (which has since dropped away as a major sport)—but also tennis, hockey, golf, and track & field. I wasn't conscious of bylines as a boy, but I have since learned that among its contributors were Grantland Rice, John Lardner, Roger Kahn, and Dick Schaap. I do recall that the editors all used diminutive versions of their first names; two of the editors were Al (not Allen or Albert) Silverman and Ed (not Edward or Edgar) Fitzgerald.

Sport went in for profiles of contemporary athletes. The era was aglitter with what were not yet called superstars. In baseball, these included Joe DiMaggio, Ted Williams, and Bob Feller; in football, Sammy Baugh, Charlie Trippi, and Charlie "Choo-choo" Justice; in basketball, the great Kentucky teams coached by Adolph Rupp, Easy Ed Macaulay, and Bob Cousy; in hockey, Maurice "the Rocket" Richard, his younger and smaller brother Henri "the Pocket Rocket" Richard, Walter "Turk" Broda, Gordie Howe, and others. These articles were not especially deep; from a profile of Yogi Berra I remember a sentence that read, "Yogi likes plenty of pizza in the off-season, where he can usually be found at his pal Phil Rizzuto's bowling alley." I read everything in *Sport*, and felt sadness when I was done with an issue, for I would have to wait another month for more.

Near the front of the magazine was the "Sport Quiz," which, in a series of multiple-choice questions, tested the reader's knowledge of sports, contemporary and historical. A poor student then and ever after, this was the only quiz on which I ever wished to do well. I don't believe I ever had the satisfaction of scoring 100 percent on the "Sport Quiz," but doing so would have brought more satisfaction than winning a spelling bee or having gone to Choate.

The feature of *Sport* I most admired were the articles, one in each issue, called the "Sport Classic." These were about historical figures in sports, some of them alive and no longer competing, others long gone. They appeared not with photographs, but with full-page painted illustrations. (I had friends who cut these out of the magazine and tacked them up to their bedroom walls.) More than sixty years later, I can still see the illustration for Man o' War, the great thoroughbred who dominated racing in the years after World War I. Other *Sport* Classics were on Jim Thorpe, Ty Cobb, and "Big Bill" Tilden. I gobbled them up, all of them. They provided the first bits of history that truly interested me.

I'm not sure when I dropped away from reading *Sport*. I continued to read it through high school, though with diminished ardor. By the time I went off to college, I was still hooked on sports, and would be throughout my life, but I was now hooked on other games, games with such names as literature, philosophy, history, visual art, and serious music.

Sports Illustrated, propelled by Time, Inc. money, ultimately knocked *Sport* out of the box. Over the years, the magazine passed through the hands of ten different owners. Attempts were made to shift its emphasis and approach to the subject of athletic competition that had itself changed radically, owing to television, free-agency, scandal, and big money. *Sport* magazine finally folded in 2000. I'm not sure many people noticed.

In my early thirties, in 1970, in response to an essay I published in *Harper's*, I received a pleasing letter of praise, on *Sport* magazine stationery, from Al Silverman, the magazine's chief editor. I wrote back to thank him and tell him how important his magazine was to me when I was growing up. I also mentioned that if he ever had a subject he thought I might write about for his magazine, I should be delighted to do so. He wrote back suggesting I do an article for *Sport* on an All-American running back then at Ohio State, later to play briefly for Green Bay, named John Brockington. The fee was $500. I thought about it and thought about it, and in the end decided that, though

I loved to watch superior athletes perform, and enjoy reading about them, interviewing them and writing about them was not for me.

I gave the invitation a pass, and with it surrendered any chance I might have to become a contributor to the magazine that I, an obsessive magazine reader all my life, enjoyed above all others. I have a lingering regret about this. Had I written that article, I could have noted on a resume that, along with *The New Yorker*, the *Times Literary Supplement*, the French *Commentaire*, the German *Merkur*, I was also a proud contributor to *Sport*.

THE AGONY OF DA FEET

The Stanley Cup finals, in which the New York Rangers play the Los Angeles Kings, has begun, and I shall not be at my post—or more precisely, in my chair, footstool at the ready, a glass of ice water on the lamp table to my right. I suffered too greatly watching my home team, the Chicago Blackhawks, lose to the Kings, 5–4 in overtime of the seventh and deciding game for the western conference title. The Blackhawks jumped out to a 2–0 lead in the first period, and the Kings kept tying things up, and never led until that deadly overtime, on a slightly flukey goals that left the ice and flew over the shoulder of the Hawks splendid goalie Corey Crawford.

The time was around 10:30 p.m. (CST), and I turned off the television set and hobbled, dejected, into the bathroom for my bedtime ablutions. "Don't let yourself take this seriously," I told myself, "the Blackhawks had a good season, and you, as a camp follower, were given a good ride. Perspective, old boy. It's only a game, and one that doesn't really touch your life." From this conversation with myself you can see what a sensible fellow I am.

I am not a sore loser, not in the least, only a mildly depressed one. This seventh game could have gone either way, and it didn't go the Blackhawks (and my) way. I shall of course live with this loss. What choice have I? Yet I cannot help reflect that it is an insignificant yet real setback. Because of it I shall not get to watch the Blackhawks play for the Stanley Cup, which, to my great pleasure, they won last year. I shall be deprived, at a maximum, of seven hours of excitement watching heavily padded Canadians and Eastern Europeans race up and back over the ice, banging one another into the boards, in the hope of winning a large silver cup, which each member of the victorious team gets to hoist over his head.

I should add that my watching hockey is less than subtle. I never played the game as a boy, and I don't even now know all its fundamental rules. I went to a few games at the old Chicago Stadium as a kid, but only last year did I learn the meaning of icing and the role the blue line plays in the game. I understand penalties, but rarely do I notice the actual infractions that bring them about. I'm not sure I grasp what "offsides" means. The only players I know are those on my home team. I would fail a quick quiz in which you asked me what cities the Sharks, Sabres, or Predators represent. Since I watch most Blackhawk games, as I watch most sporting events on television, with the sound off, I am not likely soon to improve my knowledge.

What I do know is that watching hockey, even at my crude level, is immensely stimulating. So much so that during close games late in the third period I sometimes find my fists clenched; at the last two minutes or so, with the Blackhawks a goal up or behind, I have been known to leave my chair and watch the ending of a game on my feet. I do not pump my fists when the Blackhawks win such close games, but, somehow, the world seems an infinitesimally but genuinely brighter place when they do.

The mostly young men who play hockey strike me as physically tougher than most other athletes. I don't believe there is a DL, or Disabled List, in hockey. Stories of players finishing games with serious injuries abound. I remember many years ago hearing about a Blackhawks player—I cannot call up his name—requiring no fewer than thirty-three stitches in his face from having been slashed by a hockey stick in the first period, and returning to play in the third period. In interviews at least hockey players seem more modest than do athletes in other professional sports. The import of their utterances is no weightier than that of other athletes, nor are they asked more penetrating questions by the Medes, as I have come to call television newscasters and sports announcers, but they appear less willing to rattle on about themselves in what any sensible person would realize is an egregiously vain way.

Such is the speed of hockey that it makes all other sports look as if they are played in slow motion. I don't say that this makes hockey superior to other sports—it is nowhere near as subtle as baseball, or as elegant as basketball, or as strategy-based as tennis. But the intensity of hockey is such that it calls for a spectator's full attention. So fast is it that I only occasionally actually see goals scored, and only really witness them, from various angles, on television replay. I watch other sporting events with a *Times Literary Supplement* or a biography on my lap. Hockey allows no space for reading, except at commercials or intervals between periods. What I mildly resent about this sport is that it doesn't allow me to get much reading done.

Dreary to support a seasons-long losing team—as a Cubs fan I can attest to this—but there is something dispiriting to support a winning team that does not go all the way to a triumphant conclusion to its season. In conversations with my fellow couch-potatoes—among old friends, young men and women where I bank, men at my local supermarket—I sensed a dampening of spirits at the Blackhawks defeat. "Spanning the globe to bring you the constant variety of sports . . . the thrill of victory, the agony of defeat," Jim McKay used dramatically to announce, to the accompaniment of trumpets, at the opening of the old *Wide World of Sports* show, though when first I heard it I thought he was saying the agony of da feet.

Television sports is nicely rigged to keep the couch potato in a nearly permanent state of distraction. Now that the hockey season is (for me, at least) over, the National Basketball Association Finals begin, the baseball season is well under way, the French Open tennis tournament is into its second week, and at the end of the month Wimbledon will have begun. A faithful television soldier, I shall be at my post for all of it.

Yet I should like to have it known that I have taken to sleeping in a black, short-sleeved shirt with the Blackhawks logo on its front, the number 19 and the name Toews (the team's captain is Jonathan Toews) on the back. Which I guess means that I have now officially become a hockey fan.

A number of years ago I requested my son, to whom I did not pass on the sports-watching disease—scientists aver that it is not hereditary—to shoot out both my kneecaps and commit me to a sanatorium if ever he caught me watching NASCAR, and I almost included hockey in the request. Whew! That, in retrospect, was a close call.

OPINIONATIONS

THE SPORTS LENINIST

When it was reported to Vladimir Ilyich Lenin, the head of the new Soviet Union and the leading advocate for the world communist revolution, that the workers were being killed in Germany, or made to suffer excruciatingly in China, Lenin, showing no emotion, would exclaim: "Good. Worse is better." By worse is better he meant that the worse the conditions for the workers, the sooner the revolution would come about, the better for communism. Not a generous emotion, but, in its own perverse way, a logical one.

Worse is better is generally my own reaction when I hear about strikes, scandals, and acts of ugliness or unmitigated selfishness in one or another big-money American sport. A pro basketball player attempts to strangle his coach? Excellent. A University of Nebraska football player is accused of rape? Jolly good. A baseball player, a pitcher, after having been given multiple chances, has slid back into his old drug habits? Delightful. It couldn't be worse, and worse is better.

The revolution this sports Leninist yearns for is the nostalgic utopian sports scene of his boyhood. It was a time when sports were not completely besotted by money—and, let me add here, I happen to be a pro-capitalist Leninist—the sports pages did not yet read like the financial pages, and there was a nice unwillingness to delve too deeply into the psyches of admired athletes who probably don't possess any.

As a sports Leninist, I have to confess being saddened to learn about the settlement of the lockout of the National Basketball Association players. This year's labor problems caused the NBA to cancel games for the first time in its history, and I was rather hoping that the entire season would go, whoosh, right down the tubes. (Few things would have been worse for the sport, and how much better worse would have been!) In this dispute between players and owners, as in almost all such conflicts in professional sports in recent years, I found my antipathies nicely riven. A plague, I felt, on both their condominiums. Owners, players, agents, league officials, no one, as they say in Hollywood about film scripts with dubious commercial potential, to root for.

Now, alas, the strike will not take place, and an abbreviated NBA season of 50 games will commence—sometime in early February—and I regret to have to report that I shall probably be watching more than my share of them. The reason I shall be doing so is that I live in Chicago, where Michael Jordan plays, and, as a man who has wasted so much of his life watching games, I feel it would be a mistake, in the direction of incompleteness, not to witness Michael (no last name needed) finish out his career.

A few years ago, Bobby Knight, the impressively unattractive coach of the Indiana University basketball team, said that we would never see another basketball player as good as Michael, nor would our children, nor would our children's children. He may have been right. This past year Mr. Knight claimed that Michael was the best player of all time, a term I took to include all games—that is, he claimed that Michael Jordan plays basketball better than Ruth played baseball, Fischer played chess, Einstein played physics. He may have been right again.

Because Michael makes all other players seem rather drab, I felt I would retire from watching pro basketball at the exact time that he retired from playing it. A strike would have been the perfect time for Michael to announce his retirement and, unbeknownst to him, mine. I believe I would have quit watching pro basketball without too great strain; the insane salaries, the illogical ticket prices helping support them, the general characterlessness of the athletes, I could have said goodbye to all that, and left it in the charmless hands of those inveterate basketball fans, Woody Allen, Spike Lee, and Jack Nicholson.

My hope now is that Michael will retire at the end of this truncated season. My interest in pro football is almost gone: the 300-pound-plus linemen and the 250-pound-plus running backs have made the game uncomfortably close to a freak show. I continue to watch baseball, even listen to a certain amount of it on the radio; but then, as George Will has said, baseball may be less a sport than a habit. But the larger problem is that I have begun to feel foolish being a fan. I feel foolish giving allegiance to any team made up of players—and this includes all professional teams and players now extant—whose loyalty to the team is patently a good deal less than my own.

Moments arise when one is permitted to put the sordor of contemporary sports out of mind, but they do not last for long. We're talking about money, here, kid, the long green, as they used to say at the race track, it's all that makes the world of sports go around. Go around it does, true enough, but in the most juddering and irritating way.

The NBA had the makings of a beautiful strike. My sense is that scarcely anyone has thus far missed watching what is in any case an overlong and rather artificial schedule of games. Another few months without this particular circus and people might have noticed that life was quite as good, perhaps a touch better, without it. Better distractions might have been found. What a pity! How much better worse might have been.

AREN'T WE GRAND?

Straightaway after the Chicago Bears defeated the New Orleans Saints and then the Indianapolis Colts defeated the New England Patriots the type was set, the story locked in. Lovie Smith, the Bears coach, and Tony Dungy, the Colts coach, are both African-Americans, and this will mark the first time that an African-American coach has brought his team to a Super Bowl. That there would be two African-American coaches with teams playing against each other was too big a journalistic bonanza to ignore. Far from ignoring it, the fact has been endlessly emphasized. Great vulgar minds think alike.

Yet every time I hear mention of Lovie Smith and Tony Dungy as African-Americans, I wonder if this emphasis on ethnicity is a good thing. The more it goes on the more I feel that on game day Jesse Jackson will be called in to kick extra points, with Al Sharpton holding. Lovie Smith and Tony Dungy are superior men, smart, dignified, cool under fire, and high above the average of ex-jocks who have gone on to coach National Football League teams. Why make such a journalistic meal out of their being African-American? Nothing nearly similar would be taking place if the two coaches were Italian, Jewish, Irish, Ukrainian, or Texan.

History provides, I suppose, a partial excuse. For many years black football players were thought insufficiently intelligent to play quarterback in the NFL. Professional football itself wasn't integrated until 1946, and it awaited the year 1974 before James Harris, out of all-black Grambling College, started a playoff game as quarterback for the Los Angeles

Rams. Lots of brilliant African-American quarterbacks—Doug Williams, Warren Moon, Randall Cunningham, Steve McNair, Donovan McNabb, Michael Vick—followed, so that today black quarterbacks seem as common a phenomenon as white ones.

Both Messrs. Dungy and Smith happen to coach teams with white quarterbacks. And Lovie Smith has been exemplary in standing by his young quarterback, Rex Grossman, through a season in which Mr. Grossman has performed unevenly and consequently has been lashed by press criticism.

As someone who lives in Chicago, I have watched Lovie Smith over the past three years that he has been the Bears head coach and find myself much taken by his quiet authority. Being a coach in the NFL entails being able to command an often out-of-control bunch of too-young multimillionaire jocks, the executive gifts to handle several sub-coaches (offense, defense, special teams and more) and orchestrate their combined efforts on the field at game day, and to deal with a low-grade sports press always on the *qui vive* for stirring up troublesome controversy.

Mr. Smith has handled all this with calm mastery, never losing his cool, never compromising his dignity. He came to the Bears following a coach who, standing on the sidelines, showed such stress that it seemed advisable to have him strapped to an EKG machine throughout the game; and a coach before that who specialized in humiliating his players by screaming at them on the sidelines when they made mistakes. Lovie Smith, the emotional antithesis of both these predecessors, is a gent.

Tony Dungy, a longtime friend of Mr. Smith, is no less gracious under fire. Alert, intense, but never neurotically wired on the sidelines, he is a man in charge. Last year, during the football season, he underwent a family tragedy, the suicide of his eighteen-year-old son, which he handled with dignified reticence, religious humility, and manly stoicism.

Tom Brokaw wrote a bestseller about the men in World War II whom he called "The Greatest Generation." My own nominee for the greatest generation would be that of those African-American jazz musicians—Louis Armstrong, Duke Ellington, Count Basie, and others—who practiced their subtle art through decades of ugly racial prejudice while maintaining a high artistic standard and an unruffled elegance of demeanor. Lovie Smith and Tony Dungy strike me as the equivalent, in sports, of those men.

Why, then, emphasize the African-Americanness of these two excellent coaches? Doesn't doing so suggest a patronizing sense of amazement at their accomplishments—as if to say, who'd have thunk not one but two black men could be at the top of their line of work? Doesn't doing so also suggest a note of self-congratulations for Americans—as if to say, look how far we've come in giving these men a chance? Aren't we grand in our virtue?

African-Americans will naturally enough take their own quiet pride in the achievements of Lovie Smith and Tony Dungy as every other ethnic group does when its members produce extraordinary achievements. (There must, somewhere in America, be an Armenian Athletes Hall of Fame.) But won't America more truly have come of age as a tolerant and mature society when men and women of genuine accomplishment can stand apart, on their own, without being weighed down by the heavy freight of their race, religion, or ethnicity? Hold the public relations; forget the ethnic pride. Let the game begin!

BORED WITH BASEBALL?

Baseball, the national pastime, may be past its time. Evidence suggests that the game's popularity is slipping. *Sunday Night Football* remains the highest-rated television sports program, while the ratings for "Fox Saturday Baseball" continue to drop. Over the past few decades, the number of kids playing Little League baseball has steadily declined. Last year's World Series attracted a television audience of only 12 percent of U.S. viewers, well down from the 50 percent who watched it 25 years ago.

In the age of the Internet, computer games, cable, and on-demand television, my guess is that many now consider baseball to be too slow, and hence boring. A baseball game takes roughly two-and-a-half to three hours to watch, during which time the ball is probably in play for no more than 10 minutes. True, a chess match between grandmasters doubtless doesn't include more than three minutes of action; the rest is forethought. But let that pass.

In every baseball game, vast stretches of time are taken up by batters stepping in and out of the box adjusting gloves, helmets, and genitals; pitchers on the mound going through their strange, twitchy rituals; pitching changes; holding runners on base; arguments with umpires; time between innings; and so much—for some viewers so excruciatingly much—more.

As for other sports, as I grow older I find the tension of hockey not easily borne. With pro basketball, the not-so-dirty little secret is that in most games everything comes down to the last five or six minutes of play. I continue to find football—college and pro—watchable, though

I do so with a slightly guilty conscience, as I like to think I might have done as a Roman watching gladiators go at each other in the Coliseum. I subscribe to the Tennis Channel, but only a limited number of matches truly hold my attention each year.

But baseball is something else again. Far from being bored by baseball, I grow more and more enamored of it. I usually watch it with a book or magazine on my lap. I appreciate its calm stretches—I luxuriate, even, in its dullness. The catcher takes a trip to the mound to settle down a pitcher losing control—fine by me. A relief pitcher trots in from the bullpen—take your time, kid, I want to tell him. A manager comes out to argue an ump's call—I like a good argument, even if I can't actually hear it. I use these breaks to read a few paragraphs of my book or magazine.

Baseball is the only sport that I can bear to listen to on the radio. I used to joke that in my (non-existent) prenup with my wife, I am permitted to listen in bed to the broadcasts from the Cubs' West Coast games. (Recommendation to insomniacs: no more efficient soporific exists than listening to baseball in bed in the dark.) I also enjoy listening to Cubs and White Sox radio broadcasts in my car. Radio calls for imagination, and the action of a baseball game is more easily seen in the mind's eye than any other American sport.

I feel fortunate for having grown up before Little League came into being, before play for children became intensely organized. My friends and I used to meet every day in the summer at the Boone School playground to choose sides for a game. We also used to play a game called line-ball, which required only two or three boys on each side.

I stopped playing what in Chicago we called "hardball" once out of grammar school. In my grammar-school days I was a shortstop, a position I played on a gravel field with a trapper's mitt purchased at Montgomery-Ward. I was good but far from great. In high school, it never occurred to me to try out for the baseball team, because the glamor sports—that is, the sports where girls attended the games—were football and basketball. I played on the frosh-soph basketball team, though mostly I rode the bench. I also became interested in tennis, a warm-weather sport that took me further away from baseball.

But in later years I came back to baseball, and now like it more than I ever did as a kid. Through the long and gloomy Chicago winters

I await the magic words "pitchers and catchers report" announcing the beginning of spring training. In the off-season, I read about trades and the acquisitions of free agents. The length of baseball's season is also part of its charm; it's a sport where, in a three-game series, last-place teams can sweep first-place ones. Each season has its own rhythm, its ups and downs, with the drama of individual players on display.

Three years ago, the White Sox acquired Cincinnati Reds slugger Adam Dunn. He replaced Jim Thome, a much-beloved player, and had one of the most dismal seasons possible, hitting a measly 11 homers and driving in a pathetic (for a slugger) 42 runs, ending the season with a .159 batting average. Dunn rode out this disaster of a season without tantrum or complaint—I came simultaneously to feel sorry for and admire him—but came back the next year to hit 41 home runs and drive in 96 runs and, because of lots of walks, he had an impressive on-base percentage.

For the six months from April through September, one gets to enjoy what I think of as the everydayness of baseball. Most weeks, teams play six days out of seven, and some weeks they play every day. I have the good fortune to live in a city with two major-league teams. I begin my day checking to see whom the Cubs and White Sox are playing, at what time, and on what channel. The day feels a bit fuller for having a game in it, even if I am not always able to watch it.

Baseball is slower than other games because it is brainier, and more subtle and mysterious. The transaction between pitcher and batter, each with the other's recent performance history in his head, each trying to outguess the other, can be more intricate than transactions on the commodities market. No one can explain why even excellent hitters go into slumps, or superior pitchers go off the rails and lose their effectiveness. Great speed, a strong arm, power at the plate—all gifts from the gods—are an immense advantage in baseball, but none will avail a player who does not also possess a high baseball intelligence. On and off the field, baseball remains the thinking man's game, par excellence. Those who think it boring need to think again.

MARCH SANITY

Are you ready for March Madness, the Big Dance, the Final Four, the feast of college basketball that will dominate the next two weeks of the lives of all respectable couch potatoes hooked on sports? I, somehow, find I'm not, and I'm trying to figure out why. Might it be that I'm already surfeited with college basketball, and that the upcoming NCAA tournament presents itself rather like an enormous pudding after an already too heavy meal of altogether too many previous courses?

The problem, alas, is not that simple. All the college basketball I've watched this season seems to have deliquesced into a single game, with the concluding score being 64 to 57, in favor of the team I have decided to root against. The players, mostly black kids with heavily tattooed arms and strange first names, seemed to be, if not all from the same team, oddly interchangeable. One afternoon I was watching Wisconsin play Purdue and noted eight white players on the floor. Amazing! Despite its having caught on in Europe and Asia, basketball has long been a dominantly black sport.

One game I did see that stood out this past season was Notre Dame, at home, defeating Louisville at the end of a fifth overtime. I wasn't so much cheering for Notre Dame as I was against Rick Pitino, a coach I've watched regularly trade in loyalty for dollars—nothing, let it be noted, singular about him in this—but also yell at his players in public in an unattractive way. Like a number of other coaches, Pitino is averse to sitting down during a game, and attempts to direct play standing up at the sideline, a distraction to everyone.

College basketball and football coaches—a small number of exceptions allowed—may be among the most unpleasant human beings in American public life. What has made them unpleasant is not just the competition that has put them under intense pressure, but also the money that rains down on those who come out of that competition as winners. Immense television revenues fall into the coffers of colleges with winning football and basketball teams—or, as they are sometimes euphemistically called, "successful programs." The salaries for college coaches at the highest levels are up there in the millions, and these salaries are not given for character building or instruction in elegant manners. Watching them on the sidelines, red-faced, screaming at referees and umpires, calling out their own players, the phrase that comes to mind to describe most college coaches is "ugly customers." There have always been such coaches—Jerry Tarkanian at the University of Nevada, Las Vegas, Bobby Knight at Indiana, Woody Hayes at Ohio State—but nowadays they seem to preponderate.

One of the things I shall be cheering for during the NCAA basketball tournament is that certain coaches don't make it to the final four. That John Calipari and his Kentucky team aren't even in the tournament this year is cause, in my view, for hiring a small marimba band in celebration. Because of their coaches, I'd like to see Kansas ousted early—so, too, Louisville and Ohio State, and a few years ago I would have added Duke.

I've decided I was wrong about Duke and Coach Mike Krzyzewski. I tended to root against Duke not only because they were such consistent winners, but because it had (and, so far as I know, still has) one of the most wretched English departments in the country, filled with Marxists, deconstructionists, and other assorted goofies. (Nobody said couch potatoes were logical: football fans cheered against the Baltimore Ravens because they hated its stalwart linebacker Ray Lewis, or, long before, baseball fans against the Cincinnati Reds because they loathed Pete Rose.) I also thought of Duke as a school for spoiled children, which is what, on the West Coast, they call USC (University of Spoiled Children). But I've changed my mind about Duke because it has supplied so many professional players—Carlos Boozer, Elton Brand, Mike Dunleavy, Luol Deng, Grant Hill, and others—who have shown impressive discipline on the court and don't do egregious things off it.

Coach K. must be teaching something worthwhile besides the imperative of beating North Carolina.

Part of my problem with contemporary college basketball is that for a long while now we are not seeing it at its best. The reason for this is that the best college-age basketball players depart the game as soon as possible to play for the big money in the National Basketball Association. The result is that the best college-age ballplayers aren't playing college ball. Nor are they around long enough for solid teams to form—teams that have been playing together for three or four years, and know one another's moves and grooves. The money to go pro is just too tempting, especially when the education offered isn't, for the most part, in the least serious.

Some of the very best players now in the NBA, in fact, have never bothered to drop into a college classroom: Kobe Bryant, Kevin Garnett, and LeBron James most notable among them, have shown no ill-effects for missing out on college. Lots of other excellent pros—such as Derrick Rose, Carmelo Anthony, Anthony Davis—have spent only a single year playing college ball.

On the subject of a sound, or even an unsound, education, is there anything more depressing than when, during a timeout in a college basketball game, the camera hones in on 10 or 20 kids in the stands, half of them with their faces painted red or green or blue, screaming that their team is number one? Higher education indeed. Another twist of the inanity rag is the new cheering sections that some schools have devised for home-court games in which everyone, dressed in school colors, hops up and down for what seems to be the full course of the game. The idiocy of this makes banging thunder-sticks together from behind the basket to distract visiting team free-throw shooters seem positively court of Versailles in its refinement.

I note that I've done lots of grumbling here, none of which will keep me from watching a goodly share of NCAA tournament games. I'll be at my post, television on, sound turned off, happy that I shall not have won (because I shan't be entering) a Wendy's restaurant contest that includes lunch with the former college basketball coach and current maniacal announcer Dick Vitale. Surely one of the great negative pleasures is never to be in the same room with Dick Vitale. "Awesome, baby," as Vitale himself might say, "with a capital A."

THE JOY OF NOT BEING THERE

"Nothing Beats Being Here" reads an ad for the forthcoming U.S. Tennis Open that I noticed the other day on the Tennis Channel. My first response, which is also my second and third response, is that the one thing that *beats* being *there*, and beats it indubitably, is *not* being *there*. I don't know what tickets to the U.S. Open cost, but if they are in the range of other major sporting events, they are probably around the same price as opera tickets. Then there are the streaming, steaming, sweating crowds. Toss in the likelihood of not being able to get seats with a good view of the proceedings, the costly food, and being at the mercy of the weather, and there is no doubt about it: nothing beats being there except not being there.

Thirty or so years ago, I had a notion for writing a book about attending all the major sports events in a given year. I would go to the Kentucky Derby, the Indianapolis 500, Wimbledon, the Masters at Augusta, Georgia, the World Series, the Super Bowl, the finals of the Stanley Cup and the NBA. In the book, I would recount the feeling, the atmosphere of being at these events as well as the events themselves. I imagined traveling in first class, people-watching on Bourbon Street, enjoying strawberries and cream in England, sipping mint juleps in Louisville, and falling into king-size beds in four-star hotels at the end of excitingly exhausting days.

What was I thinking? I seem to have forgotten how joyless some of these events can be, even under the best of circumstances. Here, for example, is the masterly sports writer Red Smith commenting in 1948 on the Indy 500: "The flying start was a burst of colors. Since then, it has been an unceasing grind, hour after hour, making the eyeballs ache, the temples throb. Every car has a different voice, none soothing."

I never wrote up a proposal for the book, but whatever sum my agent might have asked for as an advance for my doing it, I would now be willing to pay for not writing such a book. Hellish, nightmarish, sheer torture are among the words that come to mind today when I think about attending all those events; doing them all in a single year feels suicidal.

When the U.S. Open begins, I shall be at my post, not in Arthur Ashe or Louis Armstrong Stadiums in Flushing Meadows but ensconced in my chair, a cup of coffee or tea or a glass of Riesling on the lamp table at my side. I shall probably record on my DVR what look to be the most promising matches, and thus be able to watch them at my convenience. While watching, I plan to take two or three breaks to grab a nectarine from the refrigerator, check my computer for e-mail in the next room, or maybe walk out on an errand, all while the match in question is left on hold. In fact, if the match itself doesn't live up to expectations, I might well fast-forward it toward its final set. Ah, the simple pleasures of not being there.

As it happens, I shall be going to a Chicago Cubs–Washington Nationals game this week. My ticket cost $75; it will cost another $35 to park my car; and a beer, a hot dog, maybe some peanuts will add another $20—a quick 130 bucks for an afternoon at the old ball park. I'm going because a friend from high-school days suggested it. I'm also going because by this time next year or the year after Wrigley Field will likely have added a Jumbotron, one of those monstrous scoreboards that resemble a Brobdingnagian smart phone, though one that never shuts off. Under the tyranny of the Jumbotron, while sitting at once tranquil Wrigley Field, conversations about the game, old friends, the state of the world will have to give way to the race of the M&Ms, Fan Cam, players statistics, advertisements, and rock music.

Pro basketball games, I note, no longer allow any time for repose. Once a time-out is called, out come the dancing girls, miniature blimps, acrobats, jugglers, magicians—everything but human sacrifices. Sports promoters seem to believe that, as on radio, there should be no dead time during a game: something must be happening every second. Silence is prohibited. The eye must have something to engage it at all times.

No bag is more mixed for the couch potato than technology and sports. Technology can make viewing sports events on the scene at ball parks, stadiums, and tennis courts more irritating, as in the instance of the Jumbotron, while making viewing them at home more pleasing. Owing to DVRs, replays, slow-motion cameras, and the rest, watching sports on television makes the couch potato feel in better control of the game experience. I haven't been to more than five or six hockey games in my life, but at none of them have I ever actually seen a goal get scored; I only saw people around me jump to their feet and begin to scream. Only through television replay, usually entailing a slow-motioning of the action, have I seen goals scored. Reliance on replays applies to so many other fast-action moments in sports.

Readers of this column will doubtless contend that despite all I've said, nothing beats being on the scene, among the hordes otherwise known as fellow fans.

Depends. . . . A friend told me not long ago that he had the misfortune of taking his young daughter to a Chicago White Sox game and found himself seated in front of a beer-an-inning man whose diction by the sixth inning was limited almost entirely to loud, slurred four-letter words.

The last time I can remember enjoying being in a crowd at a sports event was at a Chicago Bulls–Milwaukee Bucks game more than forty years ago. It was played in the dead of winter at the old Chicago Stadium. The underdog Bulls won in the game's final seconds, with their far from graceful center, Tom Boerwinkle, taking more than thirty rebounds playing against Kareem Abdul-Jabbar. As the crowd left the stadium, snow was falling; everyone seemed to be high in the best sense of the word. It was a time of racial tension, but you would not have known it from the common feeling of exultation in that post-game crowd. People made and threw snowballs. Lots of laughter was in the air. Nowhere else in the world I should rather have been at that moment.

At *this* moment I am rather content to watch games alone on television. Am I, in this regard, little more than another member of the lonely crowd made possible by digital technology, preferring to take my solitary pleasure, seated before my television set, remote in hand? ("Remote" is a perfect name for an instrument that helps keep one remote from the outside world.)

Judging by falling attendance at baseball and basketball games, many people are doing the same thing, staying away and watching sports from their living rooms or dens—voting, you might say, not with their feet but with their rear ends. How better, come to think about it, for a couch potato to vote?

LEAVE THE KIDS ALONE

A recent article in the *Wall Street Journal* was headlined "Youth Participation Weakens in Basketball, Football, Baseball, and Soccer." In solid journalistic fashion, the article went on to document the decrease in sales in sports equipment, the many new interests competing for the time and attention of the young, and the opinions of various experts in health and physical education. A girl from an athletic family gives her reason for abandoning the track team in her high school in Ohio—too time-consuming—and high-school athletic directors blame video games for the decreasing participation in sports. "The causes of declines in youth sports aren't clear," runs a characteristic paragraph. "Experts cite everything from increasing costs to excessive pressure on kids in youth sports to cuts in school physical-education programs."

Kierkegaard, who isn't quoted in the article, spoke of being "drowned in the sea of possibility," and it is true that kids today are faced with a great many more possibilities for their leisure time than they were 30 or more years ago. Many of these possibilities come bearing screens: computers, smart phones, PlayStations, iPads, and other toys from what is now nonchalantly referred to collectively as digital culture. In an odd way, life was richer without these gadgets, for then, kids could fall back on a toy that was much less expensive and vastly more educational. The toy was called the out-of-doors.

The *Wall Street Journal* makes no mention of what I suspect may be a chief cause for the slackening of participation in athletics among the young: the organization of play by adults. My boyhood took place during the middle 1940s and early 1950s, and I have only recently come to realize what a lucky generation mine has been. We have lived through 60 years of unprecedented prosperity. The males among us were too young for the Korean War and too old for the Vietnam War. Having been born toward the end of the Depression, ours was a low population cohort, and consequently we went through none of the torture of getting into good colleges that generations after us continue to have to endure; on the contrary, these schools pursued us.

My generation was also born before play was organized, which was no small break. By organized I mean broken into leagues, conferences, and divisions, with adult coaches and parents sitting or standing around watching. This year Little League baseball will celebrate its 75th anniversary, but I'm pleased to report that it hadn't arrived in our neighborhood when I was a kid. Nor did parents come to watch us play. Fathers were at work; mothers, though not so many of them worked at 40-hour-a-week jobs as do now, nonetheless had better things to do with their time than watch their children at play. To use a term that, in another context, got Daniel Patrick Moynihan in trouble, we grew up under the reign of Benign Neglect, and it was swell.

Insofar as the sports of my boyhood were organized, we organized them ourselves. After school and during the summer, we met on the school playground. We chose up sides for softball or hardball games. If we hadn't a full contingent of 18 players, we played something called Pitcher's Hands Out, which meant that we eliminated the right side of the infield and the right fielder.

Things sorted themselves out so that each of us gravitated to his natural positions. We had no umpires, but managed to settle arguments on our own. The same seat-of-the-pants organization applied in the autumn with football. Basketball was played at nearby Green Briar Park. Games were arranged with kids from other schools, public and Catholic, through boys—never through grown-ups. A kid on our football team even went to our local alderman, a man named Alban Weber, who sprang for football jerseys. Somehow it all worked out smoothly.

We didn't need adults. Moreover, we didn't want them. Having parents watch would only have brought a new and not very useful pressure. Bad enough to make an error in a game among one's friends; to have one's mother and father witness it could only make it worse. Even more embarrassing would have been to have had one's father get into an argument with an umpire or yell at kids on the other team.

With a single exception, I do not recall any parent ever watching us at play. My own parents couldn't have been less interested in my minor athletic achievements. They never asked and I never mentioned anything about them. The one exception to a parent being on the scene came in high school with a man named Lester Goodman, who seemed to attend all his son Michael's softball games. A Latinist among us dubbed him Omnipresent. Why the hell wasn't he working, like the rest of our fathers, we wondered?

I'm pleased to discover that a psychologist at Boston College named Peter Gray, who specializes in children's natural ways of learning and the value of play, seems to agree with me. In his view, adults who attend the games of their children are "reducing [their] children's freedom to play on their own. . . . Adult-directed sports for children began to replace 'pickup' games; adult-directed classes out of school began to replace hobbies; and parents' fears led them, ever more, to forbid children from going out to play with other kids, away from home, unsupervised. There are lots of reasons for these changes but the effect, over the decades, has been a continuous and ultimately dramatic decline in children's opportunities to play and explore in their own chosen ways." Amen, brother.

The study I am awaiting is one that will convincingly demonstrate that the greater the amount of attention a parent gives to a child, the greater the child's chance of failure as an adult. I myself, without any proof whatsoever, in the unsubstantiated manner of the pure essayist, am coming to believe it. "The battle of Waterloo," the English of Empire days used to say, "was won on the playing fields of Eton." Owing to the hovering, clinging, needless interference of parents in their children's games, I wonder if we might someday say, "American adulthood was lost on the playing fields of suburbia."

DON'T HIDE
YOUR EYES, UNIONIZE

The great American fraud that dare not speak its name, though anyone who owns a television set is aware of it, is college athletics. Amateur though they are supposed to be, the only thing truly amateur about them is that they do not pay the (supposed) students who play them, at least not directly.

The two great money-making college sports, of course, are football and basketball—money-making, that is, if the school has a successful program. I love that word "program," a euphemism behind which lies a vast network of recruiting, excessive practice time, heavy travel during the school year, and coaches paid millions of dollars in the hope that they will, through the "program," bring in many millions more.

The least-noted award in all of sports must be the Academic All-Americans. Some rare kids playing big-time college football or basketball are no doubt able to get some studying done, but only the greatest naïf would believe that for any major college athlete the classroom is remotely where the action is.

A joke *chez* Epstein suggests how much better LeBron James would be had he had a solid liberal-arts education. Some of the best players in the National Basketball Association cut out the middleman, so to say, and went straight from high school to the pros. Many other pro basketball players have been what is called "one and done," meaning they left college for the pros after a single year of college competition. That year was only there to demonstrate to the professional franchises how talented they are, and thus jack up their salary demands.

A number of years ago I gave a lecture at Clemson University, a school with major football and basketball programs. A man from the physical education and recreation department was assigned to escort me around the campus. I asked him if he had ever had any contact with William ("The Fridge") Perry, the first famous 300-pound lineman in the National Football League, then playing for the Chicago Bears, who had earlier gone to Clemson.

"I did," he said. "William wrote a paper for me on the use of public parks, and when I told him that the paper didn't really sound like him, he left quietly. The next day two of his academic advisers showed up in my office to tell me that I had hurt William's feelings. When I asked them if William had in fact written the paper, they allowed that he hadn't actually written it, but he did do some of the research." As I say, they have a strong program at Clemson.

No one talks about it, and I have never seen any statistics on the subject, but surely a preponderance of major college football and basketball players are African American. Watching the University of Wisconsin in the Final Four NCAA tournament, I mentioned to my wife that Wisconsin started four white players. "Is that," she asked, "legal?"

In exchange for playing on a Division One school team, young African Americans get free schooling and room and board and sometimes small living allowances. (Every so often there is a far from shocking scandal when it is revealed that an alumnus has slipped a few grand into the pockets of a star athlete, or bought a convertible for him.) Most of these athletes hope that their college years will serve as entrée into the NFL or the NBA, where million-dollar contracts await. Only a small number will, of course, succeed in this hope, but, what the hell, it's worth a shot. A few among the basketball players will play in Europe. Others will drop out, drift off, for the most part not in the least touched, intellectually anyway, by their few years in college.

Before last year's NFL draft, watching ESPN, I saw pictures of the players likely to go highest in the draft. Some had their shirts off; a few posed showing their biceps. I felt as if I were watching a Roman slave market, with gladiators up for sale. Multi-millionaire gladiators, to be sure, but gladiators all the same. They risk their bodies for our pleasure. The feeling wasn't a pleasant one.

The money in big-time college sports isn't all cash on the barrel head from fan tickets and whopping television receipts. Successful college basketball and sports programs pay off in other ways. In 1996, the year that Northwestern University's football team went to the Rose Bowl, both student admission applications and alumni donations went up substantially. And so it must be at other schools.

At Northwestern, Kain Colter, the school's graduating quarterback, came out on behalf of college athletes' unionizing. Colter's notion was that college athletes are employees, and as such deserve the rights of employees, health insurance notable among them, since college football is a dangerous sport. Northwestern University's vice president for athletics, a man named Jim Phillips, responded with a predictable barrage of clichés, congratulating Colter and those of his fellow team members who signed a petition to unionize. "We love and are proud of our students," his press release read. "Northwestern teaches them to be leaders and independent thinkers who will make a positive impact on their communities, the nation, and the world. Today's action demonstrates that they are doing so." Phillips went on to say that "Northwestern believes that our student-athletes are not employees, and collective bargaining is therefore not the appropriate method to address these concerns. However, we agree that the health and academic issues being raised by our student-athletes and others are important ones that deserve further consideration." Note, please, "student-athletes," a phrase with a truth-quotient somewhere near zero.

The response of the NCAA officials also leaned heavily on student-athletes. "This union-backed attempt to turn student-athletes into employees undermines the purpose of college: *an education*. [My italics, flashing neon not being available.] Student-athletes are not employees, and their participation in college sports is voluntary. We stand for all student-athletes, not just those the unions want to professionalize. Student-athletes are not employees within any definition of the National Labor Relations Act or the Fair Labor Standards Act. We are confident the National Labor Relations Board will find in our favor, as there is no right to organize student-athletes."

The NCAA's confidence was misplaced, and the NLRB found that the college athletes do have the right to organize. The decision appears to have been based in good part on the obvious fact that they, the athletes, are in school strictly because of their athletic ability. As Peter Sung Ohr, a regional director of the NLRB, put it: "The record makes clear that the employer's scholarship players are identified and recruited in the first instance because of their football prowess and not because of their academic achievement in high school. . . . No examples were provided of scholarship players being permitted to miss entire practices and/or games to attend to their studies."

Neither Northwestern nor the Big Ten nor the NCAA accepted the decision, and have appealed it. To what college athlete unionization, if finally cleared of all legal hurdles, is likely to lead is unclear. Medical protection is high on the list of the athletes' demands. Being allowed to receive money for endorsements is another agenda item. Practice hours is further matter of concern. Will college athletes be allowed to strike, just before, say, bowl games or the NCAA basketball tournament? Anything could happen.

As someone who invests no strong belief in the goodness of labor unions, or in the union movement, whose great period of idealism has been over for more than half a century, I find myself welcoming the attempt of college athletes to unionize. Doing so at least injects a note of reality into the deep fraudulence that has been college athletics. Employees college athletes are, and to pretend that they are otherwise— that they are student-athletes or, as I used occasionally to hear Northwestern's football team described, scholar-athletes—is a lame joke. My best guess is that the outlook for the future is for unionized halfbacks to be crashing into the secondary and power forwards with the union label to be slam dunking during the Final Four. Dink Stover of Yale, I daresay, will be spinning in his grave.

SUMMING UP

TRIVIAL PURSUITS

If I had a press agent, I would ask him to call a press conference at which I would announce my retirement as a sports fan. "Today, I consider myself the luckiest man on the face of the earth," said Lou Gehrig when he announced his retirement from baseball. My opening line would run only a little differently: "Today, I consider myself the stupidest man on the face of the earth." I would then go on to explain that for more than half a century I have watched boys and men and a lesser number of women throw, chase, and hit various balls in various parks in various cities and countries, that doing so has not made me one whit smarter about the world or my own life, and that if I had it to do all over again I would spend the time learning to play the harpsichord.

Why this heavy note of regret? Why this confession of a misspent youth and middle age? Because I feel foolish for having spent so much time on what now seems an empty enterprise: sports—and I mean just about all sports. The only game that I continue to admire, the game of golf, I have never even played and rarely watch. For the rest, I have just been part of the crowd of suckers, of whom surely more than one is born every minute. And I would like to get out now, before I wind up dying in front of a televised ball game, the last words I hear those of some multi-millionaire athlete, in a flurry of "you know"s claiming that he always tries to give 110 percent.

Dying in front of a television set during a game reminds me of what I now think of as a minor literary embarrassment. Roughly forty-years ago I published an essay titled "Obsessed with Sport" in *Harper's Magazine*. It may be the essay of mine that has been reprinted more than any other; it appears chiefly in high school and college readers, for the reason, I suppose, that the subject of sports has some intrinsic interest for young male students. I shall get to what I said in the essay presently, but I regret to have to report that at the essay's end I wrote about an older neighbor who quietly expired while listening to a ball game. The final sentence in that essay reads: "I cannot imagine a better way." Now, twenty years later, I can think of lots of better ways.

My chief point in" Obsessed with Sport" was that sports, at least sports down on the field, are free of fraudulence and fakery. Athletes, I argued, either come through or they don't; in their world, performance is all and public relations nothing. "Much has been done in recent years in the attempt to ruin sports—the ruthlessness of owners, the greed of players, the general exploitation of fans," I wrote. "But even all this cannot destroy it." I was wrong. They have destroyed it. I continue to watch an enormous amount of sports, mostly on television, but increasingly I have begun to get up from a game the way I often do from a movie, saying to myself, "Well, that was clearly a bloody waste of time."

Sports have crossed a line of a kind that a once charming neurotic might cross into harmful psychosis. It's neither amusing nor refreshing anymore. Has it always been this bad, and have I allowed myself not to notice? "Fifty years in the business," says Zero Mostel in *The Producers* in a line I have always loved, "and I'm still wearing a cardboard belt." Fifty years of watching sports, I say to myself, and I only now discover how mean and dreary it all is.

"Serious sport," wrote Orwell, in a brief essay called "The Sporting Spirit," "has nothing to do with fair play. It is bound up with hatred, jealousy, boastfulness, and disregard of all rules." Orwell felt that the rise of sports since the end of the nineteenth century was tied in with nationalism—"that is, with the lunatic modern habit of identifying oneself with large power units and seeing everything in terms of competitive prestige." Orwell was, of course, especially good at making things seem as grim as possible. "One of the most horrible sights in the world is a fight between white and coloured boxers before a mixed audience," he wrote. He believed that sports do little more than mimic warfare, and he noted: "If you wanted to add to the vast fund of ill will existing in the world at this moment, you could hardly do it better than by a series of football matches between Jews and Arabs, Germans and Czechs, Indians and British, Russians and Poles, and Italians and Jugoslavs."

Ten, even five years ago, I would have attempted to dispute Orwell on every one of his points. Today I don't feel all that confident in challenging him on any one of them. One of the things that made sports seem worthwhile was the notion of sportsmanship, and this, it strikes me, is all but dead. Except in the game of golf, the spirit of fair play—of doing the right thing, of putting aside the question of winning or losing in order to play the game as it is meant to be played—has now disappeared.

First, fans gave up on sportsmanship. Nearly every crowd for a sports event—from boxing to tennis, from football to baseball—is now a key element in deciding the contest itself. The ugliest sports crowds are probably those for boxing who clearly want to see blood ("In hell," the sportswriter Thomas Boswell has written, "boxing would be the national pastime"). But fans seated under the baskets at professional and college basketball games are today given balloons and placards to distract visiting-team players shooting free throws. Large football crowds maintain a level of screaming that doesn't allow visiting teams to hear their quarterbacks' signals. The crowd at a sporting event is often called the twelfth, or tenth, or sixth man, and a damned unpleasant man he mostly turns out to be.

Whether the crowds are following the athletes or the athletes the crowds in this unsportsmanlike conduct remains an open question. Athletes and, even more, their coaches have come to specialize in strategies that years ago would have been considered little more than cheating. I'm thinking here of such things as running out the clock in football games, basketball coaches screaming at referees in order to gain an edge on close calls, tennis players disputing every decision that goes against them as a form of terrorizing linesmen.

When I was a boy tennis player, playing without an umpire or linesmen, we boys called our own games. One of the working principles, or so I was taught, was for me to give all close calls on my side of the court to my opponent, and for my opponent to give all close calls on his side of the court to me. A crucial moment in the decline of sportsmanship came with the rise to the top stratum of tennis of Jimmy

Connors and John McEnroe. Before these players, there was nothing contradictory about being fiercely competitive and at the same time absolutely honorable. After them the nature of competition itself changed: because one was competitive, it was understood, one didn't wish to lose any edge at all. One was permitted to complain about every close call and to behave badly, to use profanity with officials and to act like a perfect creep on the court. I regularly found myself rooting for Connors's and McEnroe's opponents, and to this day, now that they have become rather revered senior players, I find myself still rooting against them.

Not that I enjoyed sports chiefly as a branch of ethics, but I did feel that—perhaps naïvely, I now begin to think—it contributed to discipline of the sort that could lead to good character. I am not sure why I felt that, since, come to think of it, the list of gentleman athletes is extremely small. The great golfer Bobby Jones is indubitably on it, a man who not only may have been the best ever to play the game but was also successful in other areas of his life: Jones finished the four-year engineering course at Georgia Tech in three years, passed the Georgia bar halfway through his second year at Emory University School of Law, wrote (very well) every word of his own books. ("I was misquoted," said Charles Barkley, of the Phoenix Suns, when someone mentioned something from his autobiography.) From all accounts, Walter Johnson also qualifies; a friend tells me that Johnson was scrupulously careful about pitching inside to opponents lest he injure them with one of his blistering fastballs. Rod Carew seems to me a gent, as did Arthur Ashe. I have the impression that the same can be said of Al Rosen, third baseman of the Cleveland Indians, Mike Schmidt, third baseman of the Philadelphia Phillies, and Andre Dawson. Julius Erving, the elegant Dr. J., qualifies, as does Cal Ripken Jr., who seems a nice man in the mold of Stan Musial. Bob Gibson, the great St. Louis Cards' pitcher, may not have been a gent, but he has always seemed to me an entirely serious person. I'm not sure any football players, amateur or professional, qualify.

If sports has not produced a long roster of gentlemen, it has produced a good number of characters, oddballs, nuts. Casey Stengel, he whose syntax was surpassed only by his semantics—on his seventieth birthday he said, "Most people my age are dead at the present time"— easily makes the cut here. So does Whitey Bimstein, the fight trainer, who, when training a fighter in the Catskills, was asked what he thought about the country and answered, "It's a pretty nice place." Lawrence Peter Berra, who could float a full famous-quotations volume on his own, clearly makes it: "In baseball," Yogi once pithily said, "you don't know nothing." The light heavyweight Archie Moore, who fought nearly into old age, earns a starting position on the interesting-character team. This list could be greatly expanded.

Why are there today so few athletes who seem worth meeting for a cup of coffee? Where once there were a fair number of gents or amusing characters among athletes, today there are a great number of what can only be called sad cases: guys with drug and booze problems, women athletes with serious eating disorders—let us not even speak of paternity suits. "Drug-taking and dealing, alcoholism, drunk driving, spousal abuse, manslaughter, tax evasion—the sports page reads like a police blotter," wrote Bill Brashler, a Chicago journalist. "Culminating, of course, with O.J."

Any even moderately successful athlete today is of course a multi-millionaire. Instead of causing them to hide under the bedsheets at night, trembling and thanking God for this lovely piece of good luck, the money seems only to have made athletes unpleasantly arrogant. So many contemporary athletes are clearly in business only for themselves. Oddly, some of the biggest moneymakers, not only in salaries but in endorsements, have been some of the most unpleasant human beings: the football players Brian Bosworth and Deion Sanders, the tennis players Andre Agassi and Jimmy Connors, the baseball players Barry Bonds, Alex Rodriguez, and Jack McDowell, the basketball players Derrick Coleman and Christian Laettner are all prominent names on this roster.

In pointing out the unattractiveness of contemporary athletes—and let us not forget the equally odious supporting cast of team owners and agents—I am scarcely making an original point. The sportswriter Mike Lupica, in *Esquire*, gives out what he now calls the "Annual Deion Awards" (after Deion Sanders; they were formerly called the Andres, after Andre Agassi), and he never seems pressed for endless examples of egregious behavior, from taking drugs to selling out fans to impressive greed.

Much of this is owing to the huge quantity of money that is thrown at them. Even on those occasions when people in sports forgo more money for what seems to be loyalty, there is something slightly dubious about it. Rick Pitino, then the basketball coach at Kentucky, and Gary Barnett, the football coach at Northwestern, decided not to take more lucrative jobs in order to remain with their schools, teams, and fans. Yet, one cannot help noting, these guys have not exactly chosen to join the Salvation Army. Both men, after endorsements, will probably make several million a year anyway, and Pitino has since fled to the NBA, and returned to college basketball at Louisville. I remember the days, in the early 1960s, when the University of Arkansas paid its winning football coach, Frank Broyles, $25,000, which forced the university to raise the salary of the president to $26,000, for appearance's sake.

Today even appearance is gone. So has the guise of modesty on the part of athletes. "Once modesty was the norm," Thomas Boswell has remarked. Even if some athletes were terrible creeps in private, they felt the need to come off as honorably self-effacing in public. This is less and less true today. The bow is part of the performance, yet the spectacle of the touchdown dance, the shattered backboard, the showoff home-run trot round the bases—all this is something new and dreary in sports. Boswell thinks the change came about in the 1960s—Muhammad Ali and Joe Namath were central figures in the breakdown of modesty—and was reinforced by the worship of money that came out in the open in the 1980s. "They don't pay nobody to be humble," Deion Sanders says, and he may, regrettably, be correct about this.

But even when athletes don't act badly, they seem to me to have become strangely self-absorbed and immensely uninteresting. One of the criticisms of NBC's coverage of the 1996 Olympics was too great a concentration on the personal lives of the athletes. What I found most striking was how little in the way of personal lives they had. Almost every man and woman jack among them was a fanatic, an obsessive, a deep-dish dullard and drip who, apart from his or her ability to run or swim or jump, was of very little human interest. Such mad concentration on bodies isn't what sports ought to be about. In the lives of these athletes things have gotten badly out of proportion. Even the heroics of the Olympic gymnast Kerri Strug, who achieved an impressive vault with a badly sprained ankle, made her seem somehow quite as sad as gallant. Whatever the payoff—cash, glory, personal satisfaction—all the training, pain, contorting of body and personality don't seem really worth it.

Perspective on sports has pretty clearly gone more than a little askew. Red Smith, the best American sportswriter, once wrote: "I tried not to exaggerate the glory of athletes. I'd rather if I could preserve a sense of proportion, to write about them as excellent ballplayers, first-rate players." Yet Smith worried that he had nonetheless "contributed to false values—as Stanley Woodward said, 'Godding up those ballplayers. . . .' These are just little games that little boys can play, and it isn't important to the future of civilization whether the Athletics or the Browns win. If you accept it as entertainment, then that's what spectator sports are meant to be."

During a recent summer in Amsterdam, taking a breather in my hotel room after a long afternoon with seventeenth-century Dutch painting, fighting alongside my detested fellow pilgrims for a closer look at various Rembrandt self-portraits, I turned on a BBC television broadcast of a golf tournament in England to hear an announcer say about an English golfer that he was "usually the most wonderful of chippers," and I thought what a nice thing to be, the most wonderful of chippers. This same announcer said of another figure from English golf who had just died, "He made many a beautiful persimmon-headed club for me. He'll be sorely missed." I have left instructions that I be shot in both kneecaps if ever I even mention buying a set of golf clubs, but I found all this talk enchanting in its right perspective, its proper proportion. In another BBC broadcast, this one of a women's doubles championship, an announcer remarked: "The audience applauds in appreciation of some lovely skills on display." Just so, just right—and just about impossible nowadays in American sports.

John Dos Passos, who was himself myopic and poor at games, once observed that the average American is not a failed artist but a failed athlete. I fear that it is true of me. Not long ago I gave a half-hour talk in Los Angeles that went unusually well. I was playing at the top of my not-all-that-powerful game. Diction, rhythm, timing, everything seemed to be in excellent order. The crowd responded to each of my small witticisms and seemed to grasp my larger points; I could feel them absolutely on my side, enjoying themselves as I was soon enough enjoying myself—the perfect ham, elegantly sliced and handsomely served. Afterward coffee was provided. Thirty or so people must have come up to tell me how splendid they thought my talk, which I clutched, twelve pages in a manila folder, to my chest, rather as I might a tennis racquet.

It occurred to me that I wished it was a tennis racquet. And I felt about this sweet praise the brief but elevating adulation I had always hoped to win from sports when I was a boy but never quite did. I wanted to be a brilliant athlete and never was, but for less than half an hour I was a brilliant talker—and so I was able to win through intellectual talent what had been denied me by physical talent. Small though my triumph was—perhaps there were two hundred people in the audience—it felt very good, yet I needed the analogy with sports to make the pleasure fully comprehensible to myself. Something very strange about all this.

I have friends who compete in triathlons, others who play in senior men's tennis tournaments, and still others who play golf for sums of money that would cause me to change my shirt every few holes. But I am myself fresh—and I suspect permanently—out of personal sports fantasies. I picture myself on no dream teams, even in my dreams. I don't imagine ever playing any game in an earnestly competitive way again. Competition has almost no interest for me, and the only sport it can be said that I participate in is a constant wrestling match with the English language, from which, most days, I settle for a draw.

And yet, in ways I don't quite understand, I remain hooked on sports. I note from my journal of a few years ago that I went to the Cubs–Phillies game at Wrigley Field, took a not-quite-four-hour break—a break for bread between circuses—then watched the Chicago Bulls play the Seattle Supersonics in a playoff game, and that both teams, Cubs and Bulls, won. Sammy Sosa, the Cubs right fielder, hit three home runs, Michael Jordan scored twenty-eight points in a game the Bulls won by a restful seventeen points. I guess it was a fine day.

I read somewhere that a man who has watched sixteen straight quarters of professional or college football can be declared legally brain-dead, so that his living will ought to go into effect. Been there, as we currently say, done that: I have watched four bowl games on New Year's Day, and maybe more than four if you count a fair amount of channel surfing. My brain might have been a bit mushy at the conclusion of the day, my bottom put to the *Sitzfleisch* test, but I was otherwise unimpaired.

My life is measured less by nature's seasons than it is by the sports seasons. And the sports calendar, along with being fuller than the regular calendar, is more seamless as one sports season slides into another. This past year the NBA season ended in early June as the U.S. Open in golf ended, so that one could turn to baseball, only to be distracted for a few weeks by Wimbledon, then by the Olympics, then by the opening of the pro football pre-season, the U.S. Open in tennis, and then turn back to follow baseball as it rolled into playoffs and the World Series, at which time the NBA season had begun again.

I don't know if there is a twelve-step recovery program for withdrawal from sports spectatorship, but if there is, I should be interested in joining it. The athletes, in their guise as human beings, are helping my withdrawal a good bit, and so are the games themselves. I find myself, for example, watching less and less professional football. So brutish have professional football players become—we are now well into the age of the three-hundred-pound-plus lineman—that it is rather difficult in any way to imagine oneself one of them. When I was a boy of ten or eleven, I used to imagine myself a fleet-footed, splendidly elusive halfback for the Chicago Bears exquisitely loping through the broken field of tacklers from the Washington Redskins or New York Giants. If I were ten or eleven today, I don't think I could quite bring off such an imaginative feat.

Today I should not be shocked if, on the sidelines, one of the Chicago players removed his helmet to reveal he was not an uppercase but a lowercase, real bear. Maybe this is the tack that professional football will take in the future: no more human beings, but actual bears pitted against actual rams, or actual lions against actual Bengal tigers. This would doubtless infuriate the animal-rights people and cause the National Football League to be accused by a certain kind of speciesism, but it would have the compensation of making contract negotiations easier. How it would affect the free-agency rule I do not pretend to know.

If I am now watching a good deal less pro football, regaining my autumn and winter Sundays, I am also easing off on watching tennis. Along with the enjoyment in the game I had as a young player, what really captivated me about tennis was its intrinsic elegance. The white clothes, the simple geometry of the court, the handsome wooden racquets, the sweet terse chatter exchanged by players—"take two," "too good," "ad out"—all of it delighted me. Almost all of it has now changed. The Davis Cup, once a highlight of the tennis year, seems to have lost its meaning and is being played out perfunctorily each year, like a dull marriage. Although the players of today may be better than those I admired when young—Pete Sampras might have swept Pancho Gonzales; Andre Agassi, Rod Laver (though I doubt it)—the game gives nowhere near the pleasure it once did, at least not to this spectator. Watching Monica Seles play Arantxa Sanchez Vicario, two players who grunt with every stroke, I feel that I am inside a hernia testing center. Watching the finalists at Wimbledon or at the U.S. Open, I find that one of my biggest problems is figuring out whom to pull for; and often I am unable to make a decision before the match is concluded.

I hope soon to cut out all televised figure skating and gymnastics competitions. Tonya Harding's 1994 attack on the knee of her rival Nancy Kerrigan before the U.S. championship seemed an almost logical extension of the intense competition, with its great pool of money awaiting the ultimate winner, that is bred by the sport. But Nancy Kerrigan's own nearly blind mother's protestations about her daughter's being cheated out of an Olympic gold medal a year or so later, when she finished second to Oksana Baiul, was not itself exactly a thing of beauty either. The pressure on the kids from every quarter—parents, coaches, sponsors—seems too great; it seems, in fact, inhuman. And the sport itself, which seems to come down to whether one can make a series of six or seven triple jumps of various kinds without misstep, in the end isn't all that interesting.

Scarcely anything remains to be said about the allied sport of gymnastics, especially women's gymnastics, which has come to seem almost a division of S & M, with the coaches in the role of sadists and the poor emaciated girls in that of masochists. "I can't bear to watch any more of that sad dwarf throwing," a friend of mine remarked apropos of a recent Olympic gymnastics competition. The sport is just too cruel, allowing no tolerance for the least imprecision. The tales of the training that these kids go through come uncomfortably close to child abuse. Apart from the sheer physical horrors of their training, girl gymnasts are put to listening to Norman Vincent Peale tapes and reading sports inspiration books about thinking tough. I don't believe this is quite what Plato had in mind when he advocated gymnastics as an essential part of the training of future philosopher kings.

Whenever I hear about the many hours of practice, the sessions in the weight rooms, the playing through pain, and the rest of the regimen of obsession and torture that contemporary athletes put themselves through, I become more and more convinced that the only kind of athlete to be is a natural athlete, someone to whom sports comes naturally and remains easy, someone gifted by the gods. I grew up around a few such athletes, and now more than ever they are my ideal.

At the age of thirteen, I worked shagging balls and occasionally demonstrating strokes for a tennis pro named Paul Bennett, Sr. At the day courts where he taught, a boy of seventeen named Al Kuhn was far and away the best player around. So good was he, in fact, that one year he was—if memory serves—ranked second in the country for boys eighteen and under; first ranked was a kid named Barry McKay, who went on to play for the University of Michigan and had a reasonably successful professional career. But what impressed me about Al Kuhn was that he seemed never to practice. Sometimes he would show up at the courts at eight in the morning, smudges of lipstick on his face supplying the evidence that he was just returning from a date. He would proceed to play a dazzling, nearly flawless set and then return home, either to sleep off his long night out or to arrange for a date for the next night. I don't know what became of Al Kuhn, but I hope that he is a very rich man living in some pleasant clime and that his avoidance of hard work has paid off handsomely.

To return to my retreat from sports, I watched scarcely any college basketball last year, and then, when the time came for the NCAA tournament—"the Big Dance," as the television hype calls it—I watched it only sporadically and with disengaged interest. The Monday night of the final game, I went, with no hesitation, to a concert. The problem with college basketball, to my mind, is that it is becoming almost impossible to imagine it as anything less than a training ground, a minor league, for the National Basketball Association. And this has come to seem all the more so when kids drop out after their junior or sophomore or now sometimes freshman year to enter the NBA draft. What's more, they are probably correct to take the money and run. It's not as if their college degrees, almost inevitably in hopelessly soft subjects, are worth much anyhow. The coaches themselves seem as far as possible from amateur. These coaches are all just guys out there hustling a living—and, with shoe contracts and other endorsements, a jolly lucrative one.

I was close to achieving a similar freedom from college football, but in recent years Northwestern University, where I teach, fielded not only winning but very attractive teams. The year the Wildcats went to the Rose Bowl, they beat the dreaded Notre Dame early in the season, which got my attention. After blowing a game to their weakest opponent, Miami of Ohio, they, as we clichémeisters have it, never looked back. This was a team that didn't stage little stag parties in the end zone after scoring a touchdown; its players didn't do the obscene sack dance after mauling a quarterback. Its blocking and tackling seemed clean and crisp. Whenever any of its players was interviewed, he seemed both modest and well spoken. Although the Wildcats lost in the Rose Bowl, they acquitted themselves honorably against the University of Southern California, another of the standard football factories.

And yet, somehow, I do not wish them to do it again. I can wait—in my grave, surely—another forty-eight years for Northwestern to return to yet another Rose Bowl. Even though the school apparently did everything very much on the up-and-up, there is something about sports in our age that makes even this magical season, at least to me, mildly depressing. For one thing, the coach imbued his players with heavy dosages of positive thinking. A place-kicker on the team, a young man then seeking a master's degree in journalism, said that if his coach told him that he could go through a wall, he would believe it. I myself don't think he should believe it. For another, in the aftermath of the victorious season, both admission applications and alumni contributions to the school greatly increased. Owing to football, a spirit of boosterism prevails. Sales of hats, T-shirts, sweatshirts are way up. People seem to have, you should pardon the expression, Wildcat fever. I have a touch of it myself, though in me it comes with an ample serving of dubiety. Still, I fear I am now hooked into another season. Go . . . so to speak . . . Wildcats.

Not watching baseball games is a more complicated matter. I ceased playing baseball, or what we used to call hardball, after grade school, and I was not all that good at it to begin with, so I find it odd that this game means more to me than any other. "Professional football and basketball are spectacles," George Will has written, "baseball is a habit." Baseball denotes the arrival of spring. I like the sound of a game humming away on the car radio. It can be an excellent soporific and one I sometimes use to assist a Saturday afternoon nap. Radio broadcasts of night games from the West Coast are the surest cure I know for insomnia. Geometrical and simple though the game appears, it is a game about which, after all these years, I continue to learn new things. People complain about the dullness of baseball, but I side here with Red Smith, who once described it as "only dull to dull minds."

When Ken Burns's documentary on baseball was shown on our local PBS channel, I received a call from one of the station's producers asking if I would agree to come down to talk briefly about my happiest baseball memories. "Sorry," I answered, "but I haven't any." This is chiefly owing to my being, through the accidents of geography and birth, a Chicago Cubs fan. Everyone has heard all the Cubs jokes, which mostly have to do with long suffering. People theorize at great length about why the Cubs' record has been so dismal: the team hasn't appeared in a World Series in more than half a century. And now some mad physiologist has concluded that defeat in sports results, both in athletes and fans, in lower testosterone levels. A journalist in Chicago named Richard Babcock, noting this, remarked that, if it were so, Cubs fans would long ago have become extinct.

So, of course, would all Cubs, except that they are frequently traded or, when free-agency time rolls around, they sell off their services to a higher and more winning bidder. We have reached the extraordinary condition in sports in which fans are more loyal to their teams than players. Most of the latter do not live in the city from which they haul away their obscenely large salaries. Fewer and fewer have any genuine interest in baseball history and traditions. Fans seem to be of no interest to them. Owners, for their part, could perhaps care less about fans, but it is difficult to see how. There was much talk about fans' being put off by the 1994 baseball strike, but I wasn't. I didn't need a strike to remind me of how selfish both players and owners have become.

Yet I cannot quite bear the notion of giving up this game. I go out to Wrigley Field two or three times a year and enjoy the entire ritual. I leave home roughly an hour before the game to get a free parking space. I buy a three-dollar bag of peanuts outside the park from the same good-natured man; he looks to be about my age, and we usually chat for five minutes or so. Through the courtesy of a friend, I have good seats eight rows off the field, on the first-base side near the visiting team's on-deck circle. I generally go to the game with someone, but I have also gone alone and been perfectly content. The greenness of the park lulls me; the people around me seem splendidly normal, neither corporation men nor women with the least pretense to belonging to the *chicoisie*. I much prefer it when the Cubs win, but even when they don't, it still feels like it has been a good outing.

I only feel this way about Wrigley Field. I no longer care about going to Wimbledon, or the Rose Bowl, or a Super Bowl, or a big heavyweight fight, or the Kentucky Derby, or a World Series game (unless, fat chance, the hapless Cubs happen to be in it). I wish vaguely only to *have gone* to such events—not actually to go. I have sat in a $325 front-row seat at a Chicago Bulls game and been a little disappointed that at this price one didn't get to keep the chair; it was amusing to have done this once, but I do not long to do it again.

First one gives up one's athletic fantasies, then one gives up one's fantasies even as a fan. I believe that this leaves, in the matter of sports, only reality. And reality here seems vulgarly to insist that, since I am no longer a child, perhaps it is time to put away childish things—and, sadder, that, past a certain age, being a fan is perilously close to being a chump.

A sports-free, like a smoke-free, environment ought to be my goal, but I fear I have too great an investment, in time and in habit, in all these games to hope to achieve it. No, I probably haven't the character to cease watching sports entirely. I am a hopeless old addict, never to be completely cured, who can only pass along this advice—with thanks to the verse scheme of Philip Larkin—to the generations not yet born:

> Games are the trivial invention of man.
> Better to pull a book or CD from the shelf.
> Leave off watching when you can,
> And never play any games yourself.

STILL HOOKED

I cannot allow this book to end on the somewhat dark note of "Trivial Pursuits," an essay published in the 1990s. Not, to be sure, that much has improved in the off-field aspects of sports in our time. Few interesting personalities among athletes have emerged. The fraudulent pretense that college football and basketball are amateur sports continues. Sportsmanship has long been a lost concept. The steroid era lingers in baseball, and possibly in professional football. Those dopers who blotted and blurred baseball records forever—Bonds, Sosa, McGwire, Clemens, et alia—have not been brought to book. Talk of danger from concussions threatens to put a crossbody block on football at all levels, from high school to professional. From salary caps to the installation of Jumbotrons to continually rising ticket prices, sports are more and more dominated by money. The greed of team owners and players is too obvious to require analysis. So often do sports feel corrupted that one sometimes feels a touch corrupt oneself even watching them.

Yet watch them I continue to do, less and less frequently in person, which is to say on site, more and more from my comfortable chair in our living room. I watch them chiefly with the sound turned off. I do so because I feel that the amount of useful information or amusing comment supplied by sports broadcasters is pitifully small next to the barrage of clichés and inanities they emit. But for a big game or sporting event I am usually at my post, the very type of the couch potato, the hopeless if no longer altogether ardent fan.

My relation to sports is rather like that of a man who long ago bought a stock and has long awaited it to show growth or split or

307

declare dividends, none of which it has done, nor is it likely to do so, but he cannot unload it because he has been too long invested in it. So has my time been invested in sports. I'm in too deep to get out now. I'd look and feel foolish if I did.

Sometimes I wonder what I might have done with the time I have put in watching other men and women play games. Might I have used the time to learn ancient Greek, or to play flute, or to understand quantum mechanics, or any number of more worthwhile things? Seems unlikely. I have never had a hobby, nor felt the want of one. Much of the time I spend watching sports on television is what is known as down-time: in the evenings, or weekend afternoons, when I am not in any case good for much else, when you may as well, as they say of pitchers who lost their stuff, put a fork in me, I'm done.

I had lunch recently with a man, a contemporary, who told me that he regretted not having taken an interest in sports. He said that he sometimes thought he ought to acquire such an interest, read the sports pages, tune in to an occasional game. I told him it was too late. Unlike boozing or drugging, the sports addiction is acquired in childhood or not at all.

I don't truly regret the time I have put in first as a boy playing at sports and that much longer time as an adult (I dare not say grown-up) watching them. Mine has for the most part been a lucky life, in which for much the better part of it—as a writer and for thirty years as a college teacher—I didn't have to work at a regular job or punch a clock or keep regular office hours. My solitary work has, however, kept me out of the regular stream of life. How easy it might have been, living alone with books and my own scribblings, to become over-refined, if not rarified. Not that I am such a charmingly regular guy, but sports have helped a little to keep me in the game of normal life. Being moderately knowledgeable about baseball, football, basketball, and the rest has given me a chance to cross educational and social class lines. I am not all that enamored of the players in my own educational-social class, that of fellow intellectuals and literary artists, and would scarcely want to spend most of my free time in their company. My interest in sports has given me a passport into cheerier company, and for this I am grateful.

When I witness something spectacular happen on a baseball or football field, or basketball or tennis court, even now I still feel the old exhilaration. When a touch of elegance under pressure on the part of a perfectly fit young male or female athlete arises, I am no less impressed today than I was more than sixty years ago as a kid. When the outcome of a ballgame—any ball you choose to name—is close I continue to find myself swept up in the drama of it. When one of the teams I follow wins the night before, I wake the next day feeling a touch more optimistic about life. When it comes to sports, in other words, I'm still hooked.

I imagine myself returning from my annual physical, where I learn that, both shoes having fallen, I have three months to live before retreating into a hospice and thence to certain death. How to spend those three months? I wouldn't spend them on a trip around the world. I wouldn't devote all of each day listening to Beethoven late quartets or reading Dante or gazing upon the perfect paintings of Raphael or Vermeer. I might well do some of these things, but that would still leave me lots of time—depending on the season—to catch a White Sox night game or watch the Bulls or the Bears of a Sunday afternoon. And I prefer to think I would still look forward to doing these things.

A man roughly my age named Pritikin who lives in Chicago regularly shows up in the Wrigley Field bleachers in cut-off jeans, often carrying large, homemade signs of encouragement to the Cubs. I heard him interviewed one day, when he was asked how he had become such an intense Cubs fan. "You think I'm a big fan?" he said. You should have known my father. My father's deathbed words to me were, 'Trade Kingman.'"

Dave Kingman, as every baseball fan of a certain age knows, was a long-ball hitting, poor-outfielding, frequently striking-out major-league ballplayer during the 1970s and early '80s. Pritikin's father's advice was sound, even if his son was not in a position to do anything about it. Still, all sports fans will understand Pritikin, Sr.'s impulse, and have had similar ones about other ballplayers, even if they do not express them on their deathbeds. They will understand because they are a little crazy, which may well be, come to think of it, the first requisite for being a serious sports fan.